CULTIVATING JUSTICE

EMPOWERING YOUTH
CULTIVATING JUSTICE

COLLETTE HILLIER

Copyright © 2024 by Collette.Store
All rights reserved.

No portion of this book may be reproduced in any form without written permissions from the publisher or author, except as permitted by U.S. copyright law. For permissions, quantity sales, special orders or course outlines contact: Collette@Collette.Store.

This publication is designed to provide accurate and authoritative information regarding the subject matter covered; however, it is sold with the understanding that neither the author nor the publisher is herein engaged in rendering legal or other professional services. While the publisher and author have used their best efforts in preparing this book, they make no representations or warranties with respect to the accuracy or completeness of the contents of this book and specifically disclaim any implied warranties of merchantability or fitness for a particular purpose. No warranty may be created or extended by sales representatives or written sales materials. The advice and strategies contained herein may not be suitable for your situation. You should consult with a professional when appropriate. Any information provided in this book referring to third-party sources or websites is strictly for the convenience of the reader. The author does not endorse, nor oppose, the contents of the third-party sources contained herein.

First edition 2024
Book cover illustration by Leryanne S.

ISBN (paperback): 979-8-9913803-0-0
ISBN (ebook): 979-8-9913803-1-7

Dedicated to the youth of yesterday, today, and tomorrow

Dear Advocate,

This book is written in the hopes that you will care enough about your world and the people in it to make a difference. The stories that follow are taken from real life. Most of the young people in these stories didn't know how much their stories would matter. They didn't know that we would look to them as pioneers for our personal freedoms. They probably didn't know that their struggles would become their greatest assets, or that their stories would end up in the United States Supreme Court. These are the stories they lived that change how we all live.

Although I always saw myself as someone who could make a difference, I took a slow approach to advocacy in my youth. I let others worry about it. And I went to law school the hard way. I was already a mother of two, worked full-time, and was a student at night. As an older student, I thought I knew it all already. What a mistake. Now, I know that learning never stops. The world keeps spinning. People are evolving and society keeps moving along. As society changes and evolves, so should our values. Our Constitutional understanding evolves, as well; so much so that the cases in this book may be overturned and new precedents may replace the cases described here before this gets into your hands. I hope so. The law should be anything but stagnant and old. It should be exciting and new and fresh. It needs to be as we move forward. We don't study the law to know what happened in the past. We study it to know what we can do now in order to change the future, cultivating justice in a society that supports us all.

I decided to write this book to interest students in Constitutional law when I was an adjunct professor of legal writing at a small law school in California. So many of our Constitutional freedoms have been defined by youths who had the fortitude to stand up for themselves. Yet I realized that, while this information is widely available, civics education in public schools is lacking in some instances and non-existent in others. The National Education Association (NEA) recently published an opinion that civics education is in crisis nationwide. It reports that only 25 percent of students tested at a "proficient" standard in the National Assessment of Educational Progress Civics Assessment. This is surprising, since youths have done so much to shape our freedoms.

It seems that those who might use this information most are the least informed about their Constitutional rights and freedoms. The NEA reported that, "White, wealthy students are four to six times as likely as Black and Hispanic students from low-income households to exceed that [proficient] level." But it isn't by design; rather, it is lack of opportunity. The NEA cited mere rote memorization, rather than active involvement, as the reason for the inequity. Wealthier communities have the resources for experience-based learning opportunities like community service, guided debates, critical discussion of current events, and simulations of democratic processes, including the legislative process and mock trials. To be active participants in our system of self-government, the best civics education comes from getting involved in our democracy more than just casting a vote once every four years. We are all a part of our government every day.

But youths today aren't lazy or apathetic; they just feel like no one is listening. Like X Gonzales, for example, and the organizations Never Again MSD (#NeverAgain), and March for Our Lives, who criticized the National Rifle Association and its supporters after witnessing seventeen of their classmates killed in the mass shooting by a nineteen-year-old at Marjory Stoneman Douglas High School in Parkland, Florida. Their story is told under the debate over the meaning of the Second Amendment. And then there are the many young people who filed lawsuits against their states for failure to address climate change. Or Rosie Couture, who is one of the youths who founded the organization The Young Feminist Party (formerly Generation Ratify), which is an organization hoping to advance the Equal Rights Amendment (the missing Amendment to the Constitution). Couture said that sometimes youth get left out of the discussions that are most important to them, but it is important to have their voices heard. These students and others will prevail if they are vigilant. The following stories prove that change can take place and youth can make a difference.

But it is not only youth who are uninformed. Most adults in America do not realize the power of our Constitution or how it is utilized to make a better and more cohesive society. If you are in the majority of persons in America who cannot name the freedoms assured to us in the Constitution, or name the three branches of our government, you are not alone and this book is for you, too. According to an annual national survey by the Annenberg Public Policy Center of the University of Pennsylvania (APPC)[1], the understanding of Americans' constitutional rights fluctuates from year to year depending on the general unrest of the country. In times of turmoil, there appears to be a more accurate understanding of our rights and our relationship with the government. In times of tranquility, the interest in, and therefore the knowledge of, basic Constitutional principles goes down. Nevertheless, even in times of turmoil, at least half of the country cannot name the three branches of government or their basic freedoms.

According to the most recent annual survey of APPC[2], more than a third of those surveyed (37 percent) could not name any of the rights guaranteed under the First Amendment. More than half of Americans (53 percent) incorrectly think it is accurate to say that immigrants who are here illegally do not have any rights under the US Constitution. Only a quarter of Americans (26 percent) could name all three branches of government.

The Director of the APPC, Kathleen Hall Jamieson, noted that there is an assumption that we know what our rights are under the Constitution, but that the fact that many don't is troublesome. If you are in the minority of persons who *can* name our First Amendment Constitutional protections and all three branches of government, congratulations. You know more than most Americans, and these statistics may alarm you. But how many know how those Constitutional protections have evolved and how they affect the daily lives of everyone living in the US? This book is not meant to sound an alarm, but to wake up the power of the will to be free.

This book contains the stories of court decisions so that you may better understand your own freedoms and values, as well as the values and freedoms of others. I have not purposefully included or excluded some of the most famous US Supreme Court cases. Although I admit that I have some personal biases, I have tried to review in these few pages some of the cases that reflect the attitudes of Americans at the time that they were decided and that are still relevant, even contentious, today. I have also included some historical cases to explain or provide context. Its impossible to describe all sides of some rather heated issues. I've done my best, but I cannot be perfect. I think if we are all honest with ourselves, we will see that while "fair" is the ideal, real life is a little less than ideal. By all means, as you read these stories, formulate your own ideas and opinions. That is precisely what our Constitutional protections set out to do—create a means where individual ideas are protected.

Students of Constitutional law often ask why so many US Supreme Court cases deal with public schools and involve students under the age of eighteen. Remember that the Bill of Rights and following Constitutional amendments allow us to be free from *government* intrusion. Most of us attend public schools for the greatest number of hours in our days for approximately twelve to fifteen years. And public schools are, in and of themselves, government entities. Its employees, teachers, and administrators are all public servants. Public schools are located on government-owned properties. Difficulties and differences are bound to arise concerning public schools. In fact, there are probably no more heated debates than those that involve America's youth. Just research the number of bills introduced every year in your own state related to education, child welfare and safety, tuition, foster care, school facilities, and athletics.[3]

If you have an interest in becoming an advocate, I encourage you to do so. But even if you don't, this book is meant to open your eyes and realize that by contributing and being a part of our legal system, you can bring about change. Your struggles may not be different than the struggles of others. And your everyday struggles may very well make you an advocate without intent. But if you are lucky enough not to face any pressures against your freedoms, perhaps after reading this book you may feel more empathy for those who do. In order to understand another's struggles, we need to hear the details of their stories.

We have a responsibility to live peacefully and understand one another. As you read this book, I ask you to release your foregone conclusions. Unlearn what you think you already know. Learn about your past, your neighbors, your brothers, sisters, and your future selves. Open your minds and hearts as you read these stories. Only you have the power to change the future and the course of our freedoms. You must know. You must care. These are *your* rights!

With love and hope for our future,

Collette Hillier

Contents

Historical Notes	*xvii*
Chapter 1: First Amendment Right to Free Speech	*1*
What Did you Say?	
Mahanoy Area School District v. B.L.	*3*
(Brandi Levy, a minor) (2021)	
Tinker v. Des Moines (1969)	*6*
Chapter 2: Defining Freedom of the Press, and What Speech Is Free Speech?	*13*
New York Times v. United States, (1971)	*14*
("the Pentagon Papers case")	
Knight Institute v. Donald Trump (2d Cir. 2019)	*15*
What defines "words that incite imminent lawless activity"?	*18*
Brandenburg v. Ohio (1969)	*18*
Hess v. Indiana (1973)	*20*
What Is "Indecent" Student Speech?	*23*
Bethel School District v. Fraser (1986)	*24*
What Constitutes Fraud?	*25*
New York Times v. Sullivan (1964)	*26*
Chapter 3: Defining Freedom of the Student Press	*31*
What's news at school besides sports and the prom?	
Hazelwood School District v. Kuhlmeier, (1988)	*31*
Dean v. Utica Community Schools (E.D. 2004)	*40*
Chapter 4: Book Burning: The Right to Read	*49*
More on Free Speech and Freedom of the Press	
The Right to Read Defense Committee v.	*50*
School Committee, City of Chelsea (D. Mass. 1978)	
Island Trees School District v. Steven Pico (1982)	*52*

Chapter 5: The Establishment Clause and Freedom of Religion   64
Religious Teachings and Prayer in Public Schools
Understanding The Separation Between Church and State (PART I)

    Scopes trial (1925)   66
    Epperson v. Arkansas (1968)   67
    Barnette v. School Board of West Virginia (1943)   71
    McCollum v. Board of Education (1948)   74
    Engel v. Vitale (1962)   76
    Santa Fe School District v. Doe (2000)   78
    Kennedy v. Bremerton School District (2022)   86

Chapter 6: The Establishment Clause and Freedom of Religion   96
Public Funding of Private Schools and the Establishment Clause
Understanding The Separation Between Church and State (PART II)

    Everson v. Board of Education of Ewing (1947)   97
    Lemon v. Kurtzman (1971)   98
    Zelman v. Simmons-Harris (2002)   100
    Espinoza v. Montana Department of Revenue (2020)   105
    Carson v. Makin (2022)   107

Chapter 7: The First Amendment: The Right to Assemble Peacefully   110

    DeJong v. Oregon (1937)   110
    Edwards v. South Carolina (1963)   111
    Henry v. City of Rock Hill (1964)   114
    Cox v. Louisiana (1965)   114
    Shuttlesworth v. City of Birmingham (1965)   114
    Gregory v. City of Chicago (1969)   114
    NAACP v. Clairborne Hardware Co. (1982)   114

Chapter 8: The First Amendment: The Right to Petition   116

Chapter 9: The Second Amendment: Guns—Our Right, or Our risk?   122

    US v. Cruikshank (1876)   124
    Presser v. Illinois (1886)   125
    United States v. Miller (1939)   125
    Lewis v. United States (1980)   125

CONTENTS xv

District of Columbia v. Heller (2008)	*126*
United States v. Hayes (2009)	*126*
McDonald v. City of Chicago (2010)	*126*
Caetano v. Massachusetts (2016)	*127*
New York State Rifle and Pistol Association, Inc. v. Bruen (2022)	*127*
US v. Rahimi (pending 2023-2024)	*130*
Cargill v. Garland, Attorney General (pending 2023-2024)	*132*
National Rifle Association (NRA) v. Vullo (pending 2023-2024)	*136*

Chapter 10: The Third and Fourth Amendments: Rights to Privacy — 142

New Jersey v. T.L.O. (1985) — *143*
Stafford Unified School District #1 v. Redding (2009) — *147*
Ronisha Ferguson v. City of New York (2022) — *149*

Chapter 11: Fifth Amendment: Criminal Trials and Investigations — 156

J.D.B. v. North Carolina (2011) — *157*
In Re Tateana R. (2009 New York) — *160*

Chapter 12: Due process under the Fifth Amendment. — 164

Goss v. Lopez (1975) — *165*
Chapter 12—The Right to Due Process — *168*

Chapter 13: The Sixth, Seventh, and Eighth Amendments: A Right to Be Heard — 169

Coy v. Iowa (1988) — *170*
Maryland v. Craig (1990) — *171*
Ingraham v. Wright (1977) — *174*

Chapter 14: The Ninth and Tenth Amendments: The Vague "Liberty" Rights — 179

Griswold v. Connecticut (1965) — *179*
Cooper v. Aaron (1958) — *182*

Chapter 15: The Thirteenth and Fourteenth Amendments;   *196*
Equality for All

    Plessy v. Ferguson (1896)   *198*
    Brown v. Board of Education of Topeka (1954)   *201*
    Plyler v. Doe (1982)   *204*

Chapter 16: The Right to Vote!   *209*

    United States v. Reese (1876)   *209*
    Shelby County v. Holder (2013)   *213*
    Allen v. Milligan (2023)   *213*
    Elk v. Wilkins (1884)   *217*
    Leser v. Garnett (1922)   *220*
    Oregon v. Mitchell (1970)   *224*

Chapter 17: The Non-Existent Amendment—   *228*
The Equal Rights Amendment

    Roe v. Wade (1973)   *233*
    Planned Parenthood of Southeastern Pa. v. Casey (1992)   *252*
    Dobbs v. Jackson Women's Health Organization (2022)   *253*

Chapter 18: An Additional Amendment to the US Constitution?   *265*
The Future Looks Brighter

    Held v. State of Montana (2023)   *265*
    Juliana v. United States (2023)   *270*

Epilogue   *271*

Acknowledgments   *279*

Permissions and Licenses   *280*

References   *284*

Historical Notes

To briefly review, our federal government is made up of: the Legislative, the Executive, and the Judicial branches, each created to hold specific powers. The division of these powers prohibits one person, or one ideal, from retaining all of the power of the government. The primary responsibility of each of these powers is set forth in our Constitution. When all three systems are working cooperatively, the Constitution accomplishes its goals to "establish justice, insure domestic tranquility, provide for the common defense, promote the general welfare and secure the blessings of liberty . . ."

After the US Constitution was written and power was given to the three branches of federal government, people still wanted certain unalienable rights, meaning rights that could not be taken away by the federal government. Those rights are spelled out in the Bill of Rights, which is also known as the first ten Amendments to the Constitution.

The Bill of Rights was written to protect individuals against the government. Initially, people came to America to escape religious constraints and governmental interference. So it makes sense that the first thing that the people were concerned about was that the very government that they created would have too much power over individuals and their lives. The people wanted to follow their faiths, or no faith if they so chose, without government interference. They wanted to be able to speak out about the government if they felt that they were being treated unfairly. They wanted fair trials, and fair investigations, and what has come to be known as "reasonable searches and seizures" of property. In short, they wanted to be *free*.

While the Bill of Rights and following Amendments protect the people *from* the government, the federal government's three branches were devised to provide checks and balances of one another. The Legislative Branch, or Congress (made up of the Senate and the House of Representatives), are men and women elected by the people to write the laws that we, the people, lobby for as "bills." The Executive Branch is made up of the President and Vice President of the United States and their appointed advisors. They are responsible for conducting the business of and enforcing the laws that we, the people, want. The Judicial Branch is made up of the men and women who are the judges and justices of the US Supreme Court and other federal courts. The US Supreme Court's job is to interpret the meaning of the laws that we, the people, have passed by applying those laws to individual cases that have been brought by none other than We the People! So, can you see who is really in charge of our government? That's right. We are!

"Our Constitution is a remarkable, beautiful gift; but it's really just a piece of parchment. It has no power on its own. We the people give it power." BARACK OBAMA

Each of the fifty states has similar but individual systems to the federal government. States have their own constitutions; a legislative body that writes the laws for that state; elected officials, including a governor and other officers, who are responsible for enforcing the laws; and a judicial branch, which applies the laws to real people in their real life situations. Since public schools are run by the states, state laws rather than federal laws generally govern public schools. But any state law that exceeds an individual's Constitutional rights, as set forth in the Amendments, is a violation of the United States Constitution. This is why the US Supreme Court holds many of the state laws up to the light of the US Constitution, including those concerning public schools.

Lawmaking in the US is an enormous topic and beyond the scope of this book, but in an attempt to summarize so the reader can understand the significance of the information, stories, and references that follow, in America we have a hybrid system. Our legal system has both "code" laws (meaning written laws, also called "statutes") and "common law" (also called "precedent").

Code laws are the laws written by "bills" and passed by Congress. The United States Code contains the general and permanent written laws of the United States, arranged into fifty-four broad titles according to subject matter.[4] (Chapter 8 of this book includes more references and information on how a bill becomes law.)

The first section of the US Code is titled "Front Matter" and subtitled "Organic Law." It contains the Declaration of Independence, the Articles of Confederation, and the Constitution of the United States. These "Organic Laws" are the original laws of the land. They are the authoritative code laws of the United States. Early on in our country's youth, the Constitution created our federal government. The body of the Constitution provides the rules for the conduct of the federal government, while the Amendments[5] provide the people with individual rights.

The most notable "code laws" for the freedoms of the people in America are found in the Amendments to the Constitution, including the first ten that make up the Bill of Rights. The Bill of Rights, enacted in 1791, and the following Amendments, protect individuals *from* the *government*. When we talk about the subject of "Constitutional Law" we generally mean both the text of the body of the Constitution and the Amendments combined. When an individual has a claim against the government for a "violation of a Constitutional right," we generally mean the individual's rights under one of the Amendments has been violated.

Common law comes from the judicial branch of government, meaning our court system. Common Law is the body of law based on court decisions in lawsuits involving individuals like you and me. Courts decide two types of cases: criminal and civil cases. There are state courts and federal courts. To begin a lawsuit, an individual files a written "complaint" in court with the wrongdoings, or "allegations," explained. The individual suing, and the entity sued, each becomes a "party" to the lawsuit. The parties to a lawsuit are at times called either the "plaintiff" (the party suing) or the "defendant" (the party being sued); or "appellant" (the party appealing a decision of the court) or "appellee" (the respondent of an appeal).

The federal judiciary has jurisdiction over Constitutional questions and violations of Constitutional rights. Any individual can sue the government for a violation of their Constitutional rights. In a case against the government, the violated party must show that there was some "state action," which just means that the party violating the Constitutional rights was some member or form of government. The aggrieved party must also have "standing," meaning a showing that they were somehow directly injured by the acts of the government. The party must also show that the case is "justiciable." This means the case is "ripe for redress," meaning the injury has already occurred or will occur if the court does not interject, and that a court finding can provide some sort of remedy. If the injury has been resolved without court determination, it is said to be "moot" and the court will dismiss the case.

Our judicial court system is a tiered system. In our federal judiciary, the US District Courts are the entry-level courts, or trial courts of general jurisdiction, also referred to as a "lower court." If either party to the lawsuit does not agree with a decision from a lower court, that party can "appeal" the decision. A US Court of Appeal (also known as an "appellate court") is on a higher level than a US Federal District Court. If either party is dissatisfied with the decision of a court of appeal, that party can then appeal to the US Supreme Court by "writ of certiorari," which are just fancy words meaning a written plea, or brief, sent to the US Supreme Court asking for its opinion. But the US Supreme Court does not take all of the cases presented to it. Most of the cases described in this book went up on appeal in the courts systems for years before they ended up in the US Supreme Court (also called "the court of last resort"). Under the Supremacy Clause of the Constitution, the US Supreme Court decisions are binding upon state courts as well as upon federal courts.

From these appeals, a judge or panel of justices will issue a written "opinion." A written case opinion, especially from a high court, creates "precedent," meaning that the majority opinion is used as a future source for deciding other judicial cases. Common law is the collection of precedent. The US Supreme Court's majority opinions create precedent on Constitutional matters.

Each of the following chapters contains the stories of cases. These are the personal stories of individuals' conflicts with government. Oftentimes, one or more of the justices on the panel of justices do not agree with the majority of justices. A justice who does not agree with the majority writes a dissenting opinion. Most often a dissenting opinion at least calls attention to an opposing legal argument. A dissenting opinion might provide insight for a later argument that could overturn precedent. The following stories from federal cases hold some precedential, or at least historical value, either because of the majority opinion (meaning the winning side) or the dissent (the losing or opposing side).

Our Supreme Court Justices

The US Supreme Court does not hear every matter concerning a violation of the Constitution. It only hears a limited number of appeals of cases from lower federal courts. The US Supreme Court currently receives approximately 5,000 to 7,000 appeals a year. It typically hears only approximately 100 to 150 of those cases a year. The Supreme Court currently consists of nine justices. Four of those justices must vote to accept to hear a case.

The opinions of all the courts are to be unbiased. Each federal judge or justice has taken an oath of office, which states: "I do solemnly affirm that I will administer justice without respect to persons, and do equal right to the poor and to the rich, and that I will faithfully and impartially discharge and perform all the duties incumbent upon me . . . under the Constitution and laws of the United States. So help me God."[6]

Furthermore, all judges and justices must disclose any personal or financial relationships to any of the parties to the cases before them. They must recuse themselves (sit out) from any decision-making that would directly affect them personally. In this way, the judicial branch of government is completely different from the other branches of government. US Supreme Court justices are appointed rather than voted on. They are appointed for their history of unbiased opinions; thus they are not to be swayed by party preferences.

There are no exact requirements to becoming a justice of the Supreme Court, yet one must, obviously, have intelligence and a great understanding of the law. The terms are until death, or retirement, or if convicted of some crime by the Senate. This is meant to keep the justices free from the ever-changing mood of the public. Their opinions should only be the application of applicable law and not politics, according to the recently adopted US Supreme Court Code of Conduct.[7] The President appoints a US Supreme Court Justice whenever there is a vacancy on the Court during their term in office.

Statistics show that Justices appointed by conservative Presidents are more likely to take a more conservative point of view on the Court. Likewise, appointments made by Democratic Presidents tend to have more liberal points of view. This is not always the case though, and some justices have been called "swing justices," because their view cannot be considered either conservative or liberal. These swing justices often break the ties on the Court in close cases. Recognizing that we are a mixture of ideologies and traditionally a bipartisan voting population, this appointment process is meant to evenly distribute the US Supreme Court Justices' ideologies. As vacancies on the Court do not come up often, a President will usually only appoint one, or possibly two, Justices throughout their entire term of office. However, three vacancies on the US Supreme Court came up during President Trump's short four years in office. Since those three appointments, beginning in 2017 with the appointment of Justice Gorsuch, the Supreme Court has become more conservative.

But not all Republican appointments mean "conservative" appointments. For example, President Dwight D. Eisenhower, who was retired military, was considered a "Modern Republican." His approach was somewhat conservative and he ran on the Republican ticket. President Eisenhower appointed Justice Earl Warren. Justice Warren served on the Supreme Court from 1953 through 1969. During the "Warren Court," while Justice Earl Warren was the Chief Justice of the US Supreme Court, the Court experienced perhaps its most broadening views on the application of rights to individuals. The Court remained somewhat evenly seated with conservatives and liberals after Justice Warren's years, with general agreement on many cases. Beginning in the 1980s, perhaps, the justices' ideological leanings began to spread farther apart.

With a few exceptions, the US Supreme Court has not been known for its diversity over the years. Thurgood Marshall was the first Black person to serve as a Supreme Court Justice. He served from 1967 to 1991. Since Justice Marshall, only three other non-White justices have been appointed (Clarence Thomas, Sonia Sotomayor, and Ketanji Brown Jackson). Of the total 104 associate justices over time, only six have been women. Sandra Day O'Connor was the first female to serve as a Supreme Court Justice. She served from 1981 to 2006 and was appointed by President Regan. Those that followed are Justice Ruth Bader Ginsburg, Justice Sonia Sotomayor, Justice Elena Kagan, Justice Amy Coney Barrett, and most recently Justice Jackson. Of the seventeen Chief Justices, all seventeen have been men.

The current makeup of the US Supreme Court is:

- John G. Roberts, Jr., Chief Justice of the United States, 2005 (G.W. Bush appointment)
- Clarence Thomas, Associate Justice, 1991 (G.H.W. Bush appointment)

- Samuel A. Alito, Jr., Associate Justice, 2006 (G.W. Bush appointment)
- Sonia Sotomayor, Associate Justice, 2009 (Obama appointment)
- Elena Kagan, Associate Justice, 2010 (Obama appointment)
- Neil M. Gorsuch, Associate Justice, 2017 (Trump appointment)
- Brett M. Kavanaugh, Associate Justice, 2018 (Trump appointment)
- Amy Coney Barrett, Associate Justice, 2020 (Trump appointment)
- Ketanji Brown Jackson, Associate Justice, 2022 (Biden appointment)

The Supreme Court as composed June 30, 2022 to present

Front row, left to right: Associate Justice Sonia Sotomayor, Associate Justice Clarence Thomas, Chief Justice John G. Roberts, Jr., Associate Justice Samuel A. Alito, Jr., and Associate Justice Elena Kagan. **Back row, left to right:** Associate Justice Amy Coney Barrett, Associate Justice Neil M. Gorsuch, Associate Justice Brett M. Kavanaugh, and Associate Justice Ketanji Brown Jackson.

Credit: Fred Schilling, Collection of the Supreme Court of the United States

Whether our hybrid "code" and "common law" way of creating laws is a good system, or the best in the world, or the worst, I don't know. But I do know that it's the system that we've got, so we need to understand it and be a part of the discussion. The stories that follow show a leaning of the scales of justice to the left and to the right, from then to now, both in order to be fair, but more importantly, to demonstrate the movement of the law according to the pendulum of time and thought. As you read the stories, pay attention to when a decision was rendered because it explains the constitutional climate of the country at that time.

Some of the decisions may seem unfair or unjust according to your own moral compass. It is important to understand that just because we may not agree with something, that isn't necessarily a violation of our collective freedoms, but instead it might have been decided for the protection of freedom and democracy itself. All of the following stories are meant to provoke thought and encourage hope for a future that cultivates justice for all. As we read these stories, we must remember that Lady Justice is blind, so she is not prejudiced or biased; she cuts to the truth with the sword and weighs the inequities with her scales.

CHAPTER 1

First Amendment Right to Free Speech

What Did you Say?

"**Congress shall make no law** respecting an establishment of religion, or prohibiting the free exercise thereof; or **abridging the freedom of speech**, or of the press; or the right of the people peaceably to assemble; and to petition the Government for a redress of grievances." (ratified, December 1791)

Although there are six clauses in the First Amendment, about half of the people in America today can correctly identify free speech as a First Amendment right. But many misunderstand the right. The most frequent misconception is that the First Amendment allows anyone to say anything at any time to anyone they want. This is mostly true, but the First Amendment free speech clause only comes into play when it is the *government* that is limiting speech. The Free Speech clause only guarantees a person the right to speak freely without *government* suppression. The First Amendment has nothing to say about what private citizens say to one another most of the time. It does not prohibit private parties or corporations from creating boundaries for acceptable speech *on their own terms*!

For example, Facebook, Instagram, X (formerly Twitter), Snapchat, and other social media platforms are privately owned companies with very limited government regulations. Since they are not government owned or controlled, privately held social media can regulate content. At the moment, at least, privately held media companies control the content of these platforms, not any government entity, although government regulations have recently been proposed.

But the First Amendment right to free speech is not unlimited, even from government suppression. It does not protect certain types of speech. For example, political speech that "incites imminent lawless action" is not protected by the Constitution (*Brandenberg v. Ohio*[8] reviewed below); certain obscenities and child pornography do not enjoy a Constitutional right to free speech; fighting words, fraud, defamation (*New York Times v. Sullivan*[9] reviewed below), true threats, and speech that is integral to criminal conduct are not protected types of speech. You can't say those things!

School grounds are hot playgrounds for Constitutional issues because public school grounds are government entities run by the State. Thus, rules that limit public school students' speech might be in violation of the constitutional rights of those students. But the issue[*] in our first story isn't so much what speech is, or is not, protected by the First Amendment. The question is: *where exactly is the end of the public school grounds?*

---

[*] Most US Supreme Court cases involve only one or two "issues." An "issue" in this context means a legal question that the court will resolve.

NOW...

Mahanoy Area School District v. B.L.
(Brandi Levy, a minor) (2021)[10]

In 2017, when Brandi Levy was a fourteen-year-old freshman at Mahanoy Area High School in Pennsylvania, she tried out for the varsity cheerleading squad. She didn't make the varsity team but was offered a spot on the junior varsity cheerleading squad. That weekend, off campus at a corner grocery store, frustrated and angry that she didn't make the varsity team, Brandi and a friend took a photo of her with her middle finger up. She posted it on Snapchat with the caption that read, "fuck school fuck softball fuck cheer fuck everything."

Brandi had about 250 friends on Snapchat, some were also students at Mahanoy High School and on the cheer squad. The photo and caption were up on Snapchat for about twenty-four hours. In that twenty-four hours, another student took a screenshot of the post and shared it with other members of the cheerleading squad. The post spread. One of the students showed the photo to her mother, who was a cheerleading coach. That week, several cheerleaders and students appeared "visibly upset" by the posts. The coach discussed the matter with the principal and the other coaches. As a result, the coaches decided to suspend Brandi from the junior varsity team for a year. She later told reporters that the decision upset her greatly and that she cried the whole time. Although Brandi apologized to the school and the school's athletic director, principal, superintendent, and school board, they all affirmed Brandi's suspension from the team.

Brandi, along with her parents, filed a lawsuit in Federal District Court for violation of her First Amendment right to free speech. The panel of justices in the lower District Court sided with Brandi, but for different reasons. The majority of justices in the lower Federal Court said that the conduct was not substantially disruptive enough to warrant disciplinary action. The remaining justices said that her conduct was not on school grounds and, therefore, could not be disciplined by school authorities.

After the initial court ruling, and as part of the ruling, she was reinstated to the junior varsity cheerleading squad. But the Mahanoy School District was unhappy with the decision and appealed the court's decision to a Federal Court of Appeals. The Appeals Court also agreed with Brandi. It ruled that the disciplinary measures that the school took were in violation of her First Amendment right to free speech.

The Mahanoy School District appealed again—this time to the US Supreme Court. The school district specifically asked the US Supreme Court to decide whether *Tinker v. Des Moines*[11] (reviewed below), which holds that "public school officials may regulate speech that would materially and substantially disrupt the work and discipline of the school [*on-campus*]," applies to student speech that occurs *off campus*.

In answering that specific question, the US Supreme Court held in *Mahanoy v. B.L.* that "while public schools may have a special interest in regulating *some* off-campus student speech, the special interests offered by the school are not sufficient to overcome B.L.'s [Brandi's] interest in free expression *in this case*."[12] The Supreme Court's wording leaves the door open for schools to discipline some things said by students outside of school.

The Court's decision was premised on three points: first, schools are traditionally not "*in loco parentis*," which is a legal term meaning that schools are loath to stand in the shoes of parents. Where parents can do the disciplining, schools will not step in the way. "Geographically speaking, off-campus speech will normally fall within the zone of parental, rather than school-related, responsibility."[13]

Second, although the facts of this case took place in 2017 (pre-pandemic), take a look at when it was decided—2021. We were still in the middle of a pandemic. The prior year, all students were "off-campus." Yet, every student was "on campus" remotely everywhere! Deciding what could be regulated "off campus," especially at a time when social media was perhaps the only means of socializing for a teen, proved to be all-encompassing. Schools would need to monitor all speech of all students 24/7. The Court wisely decided that this was too much to ask of schools.

Third, and most importantly, the Court's long-standing view is that schools have a particular interest in protecting a student's "unpopular expression." The Court has often said that America's public schools are the nurseries for democracy.

Despite Brandi's vulgar language, had she been an adult there would be no question that she had a constitutional right to say what she said. Furthermore, she didn't direct it at anyone in particular. It wasn't a threat of violence. Her intended audience was only her private circle of Snapchat friends. It didn't amount to fighting words. And it wasn't really "obscene" by the Court's prior definition.

Yet in this case, the Court also said public schools may have a special interest in regulating *some* off-campus student speech. The Court listed a number of incidents where a student's speech could be regulated. Here's a checklist of instances where the Court ruled that schools *can* take disciplinary action against student speech:

1. [Unpopular] speech that others may reasonably perceive as being endorsed by the school—not okay (*Hazelwood v. Kuhlmeier*,[14] reviewed below)
2. "Indecent," "lewd," or "vulgar" speech uttered during a school assembly *on school grounds*—not okay (*Bethel School Dist. v. Fraser*,[15] reviewed below)
3. Speech during a class trip that promotes "illegal drug use,"—not okay (*Morse v. Frederick*,[16] 2007)
4. Finally, in *Tinker v. Des Moines*[17] (reviewed below), the court said schools have a special interest in regulating speech that "materially disrupts classwork or involves substantial disorder or invasion of the rights of others."[18]

In order to clarify the High Court's holding in *Mahanoy v. B.L.*, we need to step back in history a short ways to Des Moines, Iowa, 1965.

THEN . . .

Tinker v. Des Moines (1969)[19]

"It can hardly be argued that either students or teachers shed their constitutional rights to freedom of speech or expression at the schoolhouse gate."[20] ABE FORTAS

Students in America now enjoy the right to speak freely in public schools largely as a result of the actions of John and Mary Beth Tinker, who fought for their right in 1965, when John was in tenth grade and Mary Beth was in junior high in Des Moines, Iowa. *Tinker v. Des Moines* is a significant case and its reach into present day free speech rights is enormous, and yet the facts of the case are very simple.

Five students in Des Moines, Iowa, wore black armbands to school to symbolize their protest against the Vietnam War in 1965. The students were following a suggestion made by Senator Robert Kennedy and, with the approval of their parents, they wore black armbands to school as a symbol of protest. The students met in a fellow student's garage beforehand and planned their peaceful protest.

Another student from the school approached a journalism teacher and asked to write a piece on the Vietnam War. That student revealed to the journalism teacher that a number of students would wear black armbands to school. Hearing that students were planning to protest, the school administrators quickly made a "rule" banning the symbolic speech and forbidding the wearing of black armbands by threat of suspension. The students quietly, without disruption to their regular classes, wore the armbands anyway. They were suspended from school and sent home. John Tinker, age fifteen; Christopher Eckhardt, age sixteen; and Mary Beth Tinker, age thirteen brought a lawsuit against the Des Moines Independent Community School District under the free speech clause of the First Amendment, which guarantees that the government will not impede free speech.

Rules about free speech in schools are especially challenging. Schools place limits on speech because there is a need to prevent disorder in the classroom. The 1960s in America were years of civil unrest. Violent riots were daily news stories. Every day, protestors of the Vietnam War were leading a war at home against the continuing war abroad. And the Des Moines School District argued that it was the threat of violence that caused them to ban the students' symbolic speech. Initially the case was heard by the Federal District Court, which sided with the school district.

The students appealed, and the case was taken up on appeal to the US Supreme Court. The US Supreme Court is asked to review on appeal approximately 7,000 cases a year. It obviously does not hear every case that is appealed. In fact, it only issues approximately one hundred to 150 opinions a year. The petition, or appeal, to the highest court (dubbed the "court of last resort") is called a "writ of certiorari." The writ needs to be carefully written to get the Supreme Court interested in the case. Often, it's the attorney's job to clearly write the story and explain the conflict.

It is often said that the wheels of justice move slowly; so slowly that perhaps the matter gets resolved before the right is determined by justice. After a writ of certiorari is granted (meaning the US Supreme Court agrees to hear the case), the case is argued before the justices of the Court. In this case, although the students were suspended in December 1965, oral argument did not take place until November 1968, nearly three years later. If an issue is already decided by some other means and no longer needs the court's involvement, it is said to be "moot."

Concerned that the case would become moot after John, Christopher, and Mary Beth graduated from high school, the students asked for "damages" of one dollar. They would still have something that needed to be determined by the Court, even if their suspension played out and they graduated before the case was decided. At oral argument, the attorney for the Tinkers, Dan L. Johnston, had this to say in response to a question posed by Justice Earl Warren who asked, "What happens if the Vietnam War ends before we decide this case?"

> ... [M]y own experience, and I'm sure the Court's experience, is that this is not an isolated problem, that the correct balance between the interest of the school in maintaining discipline and decorum and the rights of the students who, because I believe of the improvement in American education, have increasingly moved to have opinions and to want to express opinions, that this kind of situation arises and will continue to arise.[21]

Mr. Johnston could not have foreseen how right he was and what an impact this case would have on future students! This case has become the standard to which all public schools measure tolerance of student expression.

The US Supreme Court reversed the Federal District Court's decision and sided with the students seven to two. In coming to their decision, the Supreme Court emphasized that there was no material interference with school activities and no disturbance or disorder on the school premises. The students were free to have opinions and express them at school so long as it did not disrupt learning. In fact, the Court said that they should be encouraged to discuss and exchange important ideas.

The opinion in *Tinker v. Des Moines* is a foundation for advocacy of free speech especially relevant to public schools because education is, and should be, more than just passing on knowledge from one generation to another. Education is only successful if the students can reach conclusions through an exchange of ideas. Young minds eager to learn should be free to debate the issues of the day, even if they are controversial. In an earlier case, *Keyishian v. Board of Regents*, Justice

Brennan described classrooms as the 'marketplace of ideas' on which the nation's future depends. He said:

> 'The vigilant protection of constitutional freedoms is nowhere more vital than in the community of American schools.' (citation omitted). The classroom is peculiarly the 'marketplace of ideas.' The nation's future depends upon leaders trained through wide exposure to that robust exchange of ideas which discovers truth 'out of a multitude of tongues, [rather] than through any kind of authoritative selection.'[22] (Keyishian v. Bd. of Regents)

Since it was finally decided in 1969, *Tinker v. Des Moines* has provided the backdrop for a host of cases involving schools, student, teacher, and school administrative rights, including Brandi Levy's case.

"To suppress expression is to reject the basic human desire for recognition and affront the individual's worth and dignity." JUSTICE THURGOOD MARSHALL[23]

Consider this:

Justice Stephen Breyer, who wrote the majority opinion in the *Mahanoy v. Brandi L.* case, said, "It might be tempting to dismiss B.L.'s words as unworthy of the robust First Amendment protections discussed herein. But sometimes it is necessary to protect the superfluous in order to preserve the necessary. 'We cannot lose sight of the fact that, in what otherwise might seem a trifling and annoying instance of individual distasteful abuse of a privilege, these fundamental societal values are truly implicated.' (citation omitted.)"[24]

- What do you think Justice Breyer meant by that? Why do you think he said, "it might be tempting to dismiss B.L.'s

words as unworthy of the robust protections of the First Amendment?"
- Compare and contrast the two cases on freedom of speech at school. What are the similarities? What are the differences?
- The *Brandi L.* case talks a lot about what speech the parents can control and what the school should control. In *Tinker v. Des Moines,* the focus is more on the student's *freedom* to speak. What party in each do you think is in the most control of a student's speech?
- Brandi's case took four years to finally decide. She was a freshman at the time of the incident and a senior in high school, near graduation, by the time it was all over. After the Supreme Court's decision she said that "it was a long four years." Do you think Brandi regretted saying those things on a public forum? Are the words she used commonly used at school?
- School authorities obviously disagreed with the viewpoints expressed both by Brandi L. and by the Tinkers. Do you think viewpoints should or should not be discussed at school?
- There does not seem to be any evidence that the student that took the screen shot of Brandi's post and spread the photo was disciplined. Do you think that student should have been disciplined? Or do you think that was free speech too?
- Can you think of other instances where speech should be protected from school discipline? Are there other instances where students *should* be disciplined because of speech?
- Have you witnessed, or been a part of, unpopular or political speech that led to discipline at school? Did *material interferences with school activities and disturbances or disorders on the school premises* occur? Or was it a *robust exchange of ideas*?

ADDITIONAL RESOURCES:

Chapter 1: Free Speech

- If you or one of your classmates believes that your school, school district, or its administrators have violated your First Amendment right to freedom of speech, you can contact the American Civil Liberties Union (ACLU).
- High school students can apply to join hundreds of young people for the summer in Washington, D.C., with ACLU advisors to practice advocacy and activism skills.
- Support "Every Student's Right to Learn" with the ACLU.
- See: the ACLU online resources on issues of Students' Rights: Speech, Walkouts, and Other Protests.
- Attend an ACLU event in your area.
- Listen to the podcasts about free speech to learn more about your rights. There is an excellent podcast on the ACLU website titled "Ask an Expert: What are My Speech Rights At School?"
- Look to see if there is a Junior State of America (JSA) chapter in your area. JSA is a student-led organization preparing students of all ages to participate in democracy.
- Follow reliable news sources. There are several outlets that provide truthful accounts and fact-check social media.
- Find news on free speech rights. The Knight First Amendment Institute at Columbia University has educational opportunities and provides research assistance along with news on current events concerning free speech and social media and engages in litigation for the protection of the First Amendment right to free speech.
- The Institute for Free Speech also has a legal team that defends First Amendment rights across the country and provides news, research, and commentary on free speech issues.

- The Foundation for Individual Rights (FIRE) provides advocacy for all of the First Amendment rights and works to reform legislative policies.
- Education Unlimited offers camps and programs to teach advocacy skills like debate and speech courses.
- The Institute for Citizens and Scholars provides education for democracy.
- Civics for Life is a multigenerational online resource for civics education, civil discourse, and civil engagement.
- The Sandra Day O'Connor Institute for American Democracy is a nonprofit organization founded by our first female US Supreme Court Justice, Sandra Day O'Connor.
- Visit the US Department of Education, Office of Elementary and Secondary Education, American History, and Civics for additional resources.
- Visit the National Constitution Center's Supreme Court Case library.

CHAPTER 2

Defining Freedom of the Press, and What Speech Is Free Speech?

*"***Congress shall make no law** *respecting an establishment of religion, or prohibiting the free exercise thereof; or* **abridging the freedom** *of speech, or* **of the press**; *or the right of the people peaceably to assemble; and to petition the Government for a redress of grievances."* (Ratified, December 1791)

Although closely related to freedom of speech, freedom of the press is known as the pinnacle of a free society. Without it there can be no democracy. Many sources, including the press itself, think that the spread of misinformation is eroding confidence in democracy and is a growing challenge to democracy itself. It's been said, "If you want to rule the world, buy the media."

The press goes by differing euphemisms. It's been called the "Fourth Estate" and the "Fourth Branch of Government" to express the reality of the power of the press.

The press is important to democracy because we have a right to know what the government is up to. And, we have a right to be heard and call out the government for any misdeeds. But there is also a responsibility that goes along with freedom of the press. Some of the recognized responsibilities are to research and report the truth. Until the advent of the internet, immediate dissemination of newsworthy stories was left up to a few members of the press, meaning radio, television, and newspaper reporters. The press reporters became the truth tellers, the whistleblowers, and the watchdogs of government. But social media platforms have changed what we think of as news. Anyone anywhere can report nearly instantaneously what they believe is news worthy—even "fake news." The following two cases do not take place on school grounds, but instead in the most sacred of all government offices—the office of the President of the United States. These cases set forth clearly the role that our guaranteed right of Freedom of the Press provides for democracy.

THEN . . .

New York Times v. United States, (The Pentagon Papers Case) (1971)[25]

In 1971, the Nixon Administration tried to prevent two prominent newspapers, the *New York Times* and the *Washington Post*, from publishing a report about the history of the United States involvement in Vietnam. Prevention of a newsworthy story prior to its publication is known as a "prior restraint" on the press. President Nixon said it was necessary to prevent the publication for national security. In a scathing majority opinion ruling against the suppression of the information and the prior restraint on the press by the Nixon Administration, Justice Hugo Black said,

> In the First Amendment the Founding Fathers gave the free press the protection it must have to fulfill its essential role in our democracy. The press was to serve the governed, not the governors. The Government's power to censor the press was abolished so that the press would remain forever free to censure the Government. The press was protected so that it could bare the secrets of government and inform the people. Only a free and

unrestrained press can effectively expose deception in government. And paramount among the responsibilities of a free press is the duty to prevent any part of the government from deceiving the people and sending them off to distant lands to die of foreign fevers and foreign shot and shell. In my view, far from deserving condemnation for their courageous reporting, the New York Times, the Washington Post, and other newspapers should be commended for serving the purpose that the Founding Fathers saw so clearly. In revealing the workings of government that led to the Vietnam War, the newspapers nobly did precisely that which the Founders hoped and trusted they would do.[26]

AND NOW . . .

Knight Institute v. Donald Trump[27] (2d Cir. 2019)

Keeping in mind Justice Hugo Black's sound words from 1971 in the *Pentagon Papers Case*, let's take a look at a more recent case—one involving our former President, Donald Trump. Comparing these two cases may help to demonstrate the difference between the *government* suppressing the news and a private entity suppressing the *government*.

At the same time that the *Mahanoy v. B.L. (Brandi Levy)* case was winding through the courts, this case was getting some attention and shaping the boundaries of freedom of the press in social media. In 2017, after criticizing Trump and his policies, Trump blocked seven people from his Twitter accounts @realDonaldTrump and @POTUS. The Knight First Amendment Institute of Columbia University[*] filed a lawsuit against Trump on behalf of those blocked. The lower Federal

---

[*] The Knight First Amendment Institute's stated mission is to defend the freedoms of speech and the press in the digital age through strategic litigation, research, and public education. Its aim is to promote a system of free expression that is open and inclusive, that broadens and elevates public discourse, and that fosters creativity, accountability, and effective self-government.

District Court ruled in the people's favor. Recall that in the *Pentagon Papers* case, the court emphasized that the press was there to serve the people and not to serve the government.

The issue in this case was whether or not Trump's social media accounts were "public forums." In the 1970s, the Supreme Court defined a "public forum" as a place where ideas were exchanged and politics could be debated. Historically, a traditional public forum occurred in town squares, on public streets, sidewalks and parks, and, of course, in newspapers. If an outlet for expression is considered a traditional public forum, the Supreme Court has ruled that the government may regulate content-based expression (or viewpoints) only in very limited circumstances. Restrictions on speech by any government entity may only be made if they are "necessary to serve a compelling state interest and are narrowly tailored to that end."[28] Throughout the following years, the Supreme Court has ruled that in a traditional public forum, the government may only impose reasonable time, place, and manner restrictions.

Take for instance a parade or a protest rally on a public street. The government cannot prohibit the parade or rally from taking place just because a government official does not like the cause of the protest, but it may restrict the time of the parade or rally, location, and manner of the parade or rally, but only if it is necessary to serve a compelling State interest (like traffic, for instance) and is narrowly tailored to that end. Keep in mind, however, that only peaceful exchanges are protected speech. The First Amendment does not protect any speech that incites illegal or violent action. (More on this below.)

In ruling in the people's favor, the Federal District Court reasoned that Trump's Twitter accounts should be considered "public forums" because Trump used them for official purposes where issues were often debated in the comments to his posts. Trump blocked the accounts of seven of his most outspoken critics. The District Court found that blocking those accounts prevented others from seeing differing viewpoints, and that, in his official capacity as President of the United States at the time, Trump was speaking as the government. In that capacity, Trump violated the First Amendment by suppressing the speech of his critics in a public forum.**

After the ruling in *Knight Institute v. Donald Trump*, the Knight Institute's Executive Director, Jameel Jaffer, shared this at a press statement:

> This case was about a very simple principle that is foundational to our democracy: Public officials can't bar people from public forums simply because they disagree with them. This simple principle helps ensure that people aren't excluded from the democratic process on the basis of their political views, that public officials aren't insulated from the opinions of their constituents, and that expressive forums that are important to our democracy aren't transformed into echo chambers.[29]

On January 6, 2021, a Pro-Trump mob stormed the US Capital Building while Congress confirmed President Biden's victory over him. The Justice Department, still under Trump's direction, petitioned the US Supreme Court to review the *Knight Institute v. Donald Trump* decision. But before the US Supreme Court agreed to hear the case, just one day after the violence on Capitol Hill, Twitter on its own, as a private company, permanently suspended Trump's Twitter account, citing a pattern of behavior that violated company rules "due to the risk of further incitement of violence." Now it was Trump's turn to be blocked from social media. This time, however, it was a *private company* keeping

---

** This same issue is being decided in the US Supreme Court this term (2023-2024) in two cases, *O'Connor-Ratcliff v. Garnier* and *Lindke v. Freed*. Two school board members in California blocked two parents from their social media accounts for posting criticisms. The school board members claim the social media accounts were personal, but they conducted public business on them. The court will decide whether blocking the accounts from criticism was a "state action" and therefore a First Amendment violation. These cases are still pending. Oral argument was heard October 31, 2023.

a *government official* off of its private "press," not the other way around. As such, the First Amendment right in this instance does not apply.

Even if Trump were a private citizen and not acting in his capacity as President of the United States on a public forum, the First Amendment might not protect his speech on Twitter. Trump's Tweets could be viewed as "words that incite imminent lawless activity." (See *Brandenburg v. Ohio*[30] reviewed below.) The US Supreme Court has previously ruled that certain speech can be punished and censored. Obscene material, fighting words, fraud, child pornography, and words that "incite imminent lawless activity" are punishable. Those words are not protected Free Speech.

Because Trump was no longer allowed on Twitter, regardless of a ruling from the Supreme Court, the *Knight Institute v. Donald Trump* case was considered moot. By the time it could be heard, Trump was no longer President and Twitter, as a private company, could ban whomever it chose to. Trump could no longer silence his dissenters from expressing their opinions on Twitter. Since the case never reached the US Supreme Court, it has not become precedent. But it makes clear this distinction—the government, and its public officials, cannot suppress or punish speech except for a very few important reasons (national security, preventing violence, etc.). However, private persons (and companies) can tune out and turn off government fodder if they choose.

What defines "words that incite imminent lawless activity"? Brandenburg v. Ohio (1969)[31]

Two significant cases, *Brandenburg v. Ohio* (decided in 1969) and *Hess v. Indiana*[32] (decided in 1973), define "words that incite imminent lawless activity." It is said that "sometimes good laws protect bad people," and in some cases, bad facts protect our freedoms. *Brandenburg v. Ohio* is one of those cases. In *Brandenburg v. Ohio*, the leader of the Ku Klux Klan called on a local TV station and invited a camera to film a rally. On June 28, 1964, the station complied, filmed, and reported on the rally. Portions of the film were shown on both local and national news. The speaker in the film, in Klan regalia, made the following speech:

> This is an organizers' meeting. We have had quite a few members here today which are—we have hundreds, hundreds of members throughout the State of Ohio. I can quote from a newspaper clipping from the Columbus, Ohio, Dispatch, five weeks ago Sunday morning. The Klan has more members in the State of Ohio than does any other organization. We're not a revengent (sic) organization, but if our President, our Congress, our Supreme Court, continues to suppress the White, Caucasian race, it's possible that there might have to be some revengeance (sic) taken.
>
> We are marching on Congress July the Fourth, 400,000 strong. From there, we are dividing into two groups, one group to march on Saint Augustine, Florida, the other group to march into Mississippi. Thank you.[33]

The film showed weapons that were gathered and hooded figures around a large wooden cross, which they burned while making outrageous racial insults, anti-Semitic statements, and claiming to "save America" and exclaiming "freedom for the Whites!"

In a truly ugly period of American history, this horrific display of hatred was protected by the First Amendment Free Speech clause. Although the Klansman was initially arrested, tried, and convicted of advocating violence and criminal activity, the US Supreme Court overturned the conviction of this hideous Klansman. The Court provided a two-part test for speech to be censored or punishable. First, the speech must be intended to 'incite or produce imminent lawless action,' and second, the speech must be 'likely to incite or produce such action.' This two-part test is now often referred to as "The *Brandenburg Test.*"

The Court reasoned that the Ohio law that the Klansman had been convicted of was too vague. The law made it illegal to *advocate* violence and criminal activity, but did not require further action that actually incites criminal acts or violence. In other words, words that only *might* lead to violence are protected—words that *will* lead to acts of violence are not. Unless the words are meant to turn into violent action, the words are protected free speech. The film was the only evidence that the prosecution relied on.*** The Court reasoned that the speech itself did not give instruction to others to join them in their march. The speaker only said that "if," . . . then . . . "it is possible that there *might* have to be some revengeance (sic) taken." Also, the speech would not likely incite "imminent" lawless action because the Fourth of July was six days away when the speech was made.

Ironically, just four days after that speech was aired, on July 2, 1964, President Lyndon Johnson signed the Civil Rights Act of 1964 into law, abolishing racial segregation in the United States in public schools, public accommodations and travel, and in voting registration. On July 4, 1964, Alabama Governor George Wallace, gave a speech condemning the Civil Rights Act. A large group of student activists, called the Student Nonviolent Coordinating Committee, who were instrumental and committed to the passage of the Civil Rights Act, started booing Wallace during his speech. Angry audience members attacked the students. Because of the negative publicity from the event, Governor George Wallace withdrew from the presidential race on July 19, 1964.

Hess v. Indiana (1973)[34]

Hess v. Indiana confirmed the *Brandenburg Test*. As police were clearing the street at an anti-war demonstration in the early 1970s in Indiana, Gregory Hess was overheard yelling, "[w]e'll take the fucking street again!" He was arrested and convicted of inciting a riot, but the

---

*** As of the date of oral argument before the US Supreme Court, the film had been lost and could not be located. Therefore, the US Supreme Court had not viewed it firsthand as a part of the evidence.

US Supreme Court overturned the conviction along the same lines as the *Brandenburg Test*. Hess's speech was protected under the First Amendment because he was not addressing any particular person or group and could only be seen as advocating some activity in the indefinite future. But in *Hess*, the Supreme Court recognized that words can implicitly encourage violence or lawlessness.

Consider This:

The Stanford History Education Group conducted a survey on youth's ability to evaluate information flowing from social media channels, such as Facebook and Twitter. It characterized the ability with one word—"bleak."

> Never have we had so much information at our fingertips. Whether this bounty will make us smarter and better informed or more ignorant and narrow-minded will depend on our awareness of this problem and our educational response to it. At present, we worry that democracy is threatened by the ease at which disinformation about civic issues is allowed to spread and flourish.[35]

In response, some states already require news literacy courses (Illinois, Colorado, and California).

Compare and contrast the *Pentagon Papers* case and the *Knights Institute v. Trump* case. What do they have in common? In what ways are they different?

Because of the widespread immediate dissemination of speech, should private social media companies have a responsibility to check content for abuse? Do social media companies have a duty of care to protect users from harassment, violence, and other harmful content? What about real actual threats and bullying?

Do you think all political speech should be allowed on social media, making it a "public forum," or kept off of social media by the media companies?

At least Twitter apparently thought Trump's tweets might provoke more violence and deleted his account. What do you think? Taking both *Brandenburg v. Ohio* and *Hess v. Indiana* into account, were Trump's speech on January 6, 2021, and prior Tweets, protected by the First Amendment? Were his statements, taken together with his actions and prior Tweets, intended to 'incite or produce imminent lawless action,' or 'likely to incite or produce such action?'****

Crowd of Trump supporters marching on the US Capitol on 6 January 2021, ultimately leading the building being breached and multiple deaths.

Fig. 1 Photo by TapTheForwardAssist, Reproduced with permission from Creative Commons.org License CC BY-SA 4.0 (Additional licensing information is found at the back of the book under Permissions and Licenses.)

**** While writing this section, former President Trump was indicted (meaning criminally charged) on felony charges for attempting to overturn the results of the 2020 election by fraud and inciting the violent rioting by his supporters on the Capitol Building in Washington D.C. Former President Trump relies on *Brandenburg v. Ohio* in his defense to those charges. As of today, some states have blocked him from being a presidential candidate on the 2024 ballot under Article 3, of the Fourteenth Amendment. One state—Colorado—found that he committed insurrection, meaning inciting the violent attempt to take over the government on January 6, 2021. That case was appealed to the US Supreme Court. The majority held that blocking him from the Presidential election is a federal action and cannot be decided by an individual state.

Tear gas outside of US Capitol, January 6, 2021

Fig. 2 Photo by Tyler Merbler, USA. Reproduced with permission from Creative Commons.org under Attribution 2.0 generic license (Additional licensing information can be found at the back of the book under Permissions and Licenses.)

What Is "Indecent" Student Speech?

Throughout the years, the US Supreme Court has had trouble defining exactly what is "obscene." In one famous quote in 1969, Justice Potter Stewart wrote that he wasn't exactly sure how to define obscenity, "[b]ut I know it when I see it . . ."[36] Currently, the US Supreme Court has defined obscenity as sexually explicit and grossly offensive pictures, words, videos, or movies that "lack any serious literary, artistic, political, or scientific value to a reasonable person in the local community." The court continued to grapple with the meaning of "obscene" and has largely left it up to the states to decide. But under federal law, it is illegal to distribute or exhibit obscene materials to minors,[37] including over the internet. So, naturally, states may ban obscene materials in public schools.

In the public school setting, however, the test is a little different. Instead of defining obscenity, which like Justice Stewart said, we know it when we see it, the test is more like "what is indecent?" This test takes into account the age and maturity of the audience. The case that defines what school speech is indecent is *Bethel School District v. Fraser*.

Bethel School District v. Fraser (1986)[38]

At a high school assembly of approximately 600 students at Bethel High School in a small town in Washington State, seventeen-year-old Matt Fraser gave a speech endorsing a fellow classmate who was running for vice president of the class. Students were required to attend the assembly in the large assembly hall or report to study hall. Prior to giving the speech, two of his teachers advised him against giving it. He admitted in testimony that his sole purpose in giving the speech was "to humor [his] audience in the hopes they would vote for [his] candidate."

Although the US Supreme Court found that the speech was not categorically "obscene," it did not deserve the protection of free speech under the First Amendment as in *Tinker v. Des Moines* because, unlike that case, the speech was unrelated to any important public policy or political viewpoint. The US Supreme Court opinion describes the content of the speech as "lewd" because "during the entire speech, Fraser referred to his candidate in terms of an elaborate, graphic, and explicit sexual metaphor." In deciding that public schools could indeed discipline "this confused boy" the court said:

> The process of educating our youth for citizenship in public schools is not confined to books, the curriculum, and the civics class; schools must teach by example the shared values of a civilized social order. Consciously or otherwise, teachers—and indeed the older students—demonstrate the appropriate form of civil discourse and political expression by their conduct and deportment in and out of class. Inescapably, like parents, they are role models. The schools, as instruments of the state, may determine that the essential lessons of civil, mature conduct cannot be

conveyed in a school that tolerates lewd, indecent, or offensive speech and conduct such as that indulged in by this confused boy.

The pervasive sexual innuendo in Fraser's speech was plainly offensive to both teachers and students—indeed, to any mature person. By glorifying male sexuality, and in its verbal content, the speech was acutely insulting to teenage girl students. The speech could well be seriously damaging to its less mature audience, many of whom were only fourteen years old and on the threshold of awareness of human sexuality. Some students were reported as bewildered by the speech and the reaction of mimicry it provoked . . . .

Accordingly, it was perfectly appropriate for the school to disassociate itself to make the point to the pupils that vulgar speech and lewd conduct is wholly inconsistent with the "fundamental values" of public school education.[39]

Young Mr. Fraser was suspended for three days for giving the speech. As part of the disciplinary measures against him, he was also disqualified from giving a speech at graduation. However, students wrote him in on the ballot, giving him the second highest number of votes for speakers at the high school graduation ceremony.*****

What Constitutes Fraud?

Fraud can mean a variety of things, from false advertising to misleading the public. For a public figure (political or famous figure) to claim that they have been defamed, they must show that the written or spoken words about them are not only false, but also said with "malice," meaning with harmful intent or reckless disregard for whether

---

***** Matthew Fraser is now the CEO of Education Unlimited, which provides academic camps for students in a variety of subjects, including public speaking and mock trial preparation.

the story is true or not. The most famous US Supreme Court case involving defamation is *New York Times v. Sullivan.*

New York Times v. Sullivan (1964)[40]

Prior to 1964, many political figures sued civil rights leaders, claiming that they had been defamed. This effectively silenced some activities of the civil rights movement—until in 1960, when the *New York Times* published a full-page advertisement describing civil rights protests in Montgomery, Alabama, and supporting Dr. Martin Luther King, Jr. The ad criticized Southern officials in Montgomery, Alabama, including Sullivan, the commissioner of police, for violating the rights of Blacks. The public officials sued the *New York Times* and certain civil rights leaders, claiming defamation.

The initial jury trial took place in Montgomery County, Alabama. The jury found the ad to contain some false statements and therefore found that the Alabama public officials had been defamed. The *New York Times* and civil rights leaders appealed the decision to the Alabama State Supreme Court. Whenever a case is appealed, both parties submit only the evidence that was reviewed in the lower trial court and new evidence cannot be introduced to the appellate courts. An appeals court rarely reviews the facts and generally accepts the facts as stated by the trial court. The appeal is only successful if there is an error in the application of the law.

The Alabama State Supreme Court found that the facts in the advertisement were misstated and upheld the lower court's findings. The *New York Times* was thus ordered to pay $500,000 in damages to the Montgomery commissioners for defaming them. Sullivan took particular exception to the ad, believing that the misstatements were meant to tarnish his reputation.

The *New York Times* appealed again to the US Supreme Court. The allegedly "false" advertisement stated in part:

As the whole world knows by now, thousands of Southern Negro students are engaged in widespread nonviolent demonstrations in positive affirmation of the right to live in human dignity as guaranteed by the US Constitution and the Bill of Rights . . . .

In Montgomery, Alabama, after students sang "My Country, 'Tis of Thee" on the State Capitol steps, their leaders were expelled from school, and truckloads of police armed with shotguns and tear-gas ringed the Alabama State College campus. When the entire student body protested to state authorities by refusing to reregister, their dining hall was padlocked in an attempt to starve them into submission.

Again and again, the Southern violators have answered Dr. King's peaceful protests with intimidation and violence. They have bombed his home, almost killing his wife and child. They have assaulted his person. They have arrested him seven times for 'speeding,' 'loitering.' and similar 'offenses.' And now they have charged him with 'perjury'–a felony under which they could imprison him for ten years . . . .[41]

Given only the evidence it had before it submitted by the parties from the lower trial court's hearing, the US Supreme Court said, "[I]t is uncontroverted that some of the statements contained in these paragraphs were not accurate descriptions of events which occurred in Montgomery." The US Supreme Court found the following inaccuracies:

- Although Negro students staged a demonstration on the State Capitol steps, they sang the National Anthem and not "My Country, 'Tis of Thee."
- Although nine [Negro] students were expelled by the State Board of Education, this was not for leading the

demonstration at the Capitol, but for demanding service at a [segregated "Whites only"] lunch counter in the Montgomery County Courthouse on another day.
- Some of the student body protested the expulsion by boycotting classes on a single day.
- The campus dining hall was not padlocked on any occasion.
- Although the police were deployed near the campus in large numbers on three occasions . . . . they were not called to the campus in connection with the demonstration on the State Capitol steps.
- Dr. King had not been arrested seven times [in Alabama], but only four, and although he claimed to have been assaulted some years earlier in connection with his arrest for loitering outside a courtroom, one of the officers who made the arrest denied the assault.
- On the premise that the charges . . . . could be read as referring to him, [Sullivan] was allowed to prove that he had not participated in the events described. Although Dr. King's home had, in fact, been bombed twice when his wife and child were there, both of these occasions were after Sullivan was commissioner, and the police were not implicated in the bombings, and had made every effort to apprehend those who were.

It is true that the advertisement appearing in the *New York Times* embellished the facts. But the US Supreme Court said that the factual errors found in the evidence were "constitutionally insufficient" to support the trial court's judgment against the *New York Times*. It was a huge win! In fact, *New York Times v. Sullivan*, decided in 1964, became the most significant win for the press since the Bill of Rights was ratified. In a unanimous ruling (9-0), the US Supreme Court said that in order to find the press culpable of defamation of a public figure, the statements had to be made with actual malice. Actual malice is defined as "knowledge that statements are false or in reckless disregard of the truth."

The opinion reinforced the basic tenants of freedom of speech and freedom of the press by quoting Justice Brandeis in his concurring opinion in *Whitney v. California*:

> Those who won our independence believed . . . . that public discussion is a political duty, and that this should be a fundamental principle of the American government. They recognized . . . . that it is hazardous to discourage thought, hope and imagination; that fear breeds repression; that repression breeds hate; that hate menaces stable government; that the path of safety lies in the opportunity to discuss freely supposed grievances and proposed remedies, and that the fitting remedy for evil counsels is good ones . . . .
>
> Thus, we consider this case against the background of a profound national commitment to the principle that debate on public issues should be uninhibited, robust, and wide-open, and that it may well include vehement, caustic, and sometimes unpleasantly sharp attacks on government and public officials.[42]

ADDITIONAL RESOURCES
Chapter 2—Freedom of the Press

- Be a truth teller and fact checker! Check out The *MediaWise* Teen Fact-Checking Network (TFCN) www.poynter.org/news/tfcn/, which is a "virtual newsroom made up of middle and high students from across the United States who use social media to debunk viral misinformation and share media literacy tips."
- Don't rely on social media outlets as your only news source. Whether you're pursuing a career in journalism, running a student paper, or using social media with a few friends, always consider the impact of your writing. Report with honesty, fairness, and integrity. Report the facts as they are without dramatization, prejudices, or biases. Rely on reputable news sources, such as the Associated Press, Reuters, and NPR. Investigate by checking public records.
- Use the following tools from TFCN to evaluate and consider bias or fake news in online content: Watch your emotions from posts. If the post makes you angry or scared or laugh, it's probably meant to stir those emotions and is possibly false (or "#NotLegit"). First, ask who is behind the information; next, what's the evidence; and finally, what do other sources say?
- For teachers: MediaWise hosts a series of media literacy lessons that teach specific fact-checking skills to help students sort fact from fiction online. The lessons were developed by PBS NewsHour Student Reporting Labs in partnership with MediaWise and the Teen Fact-Checking Network, which are part of the Poynter Institute.

"[F]reedom to think as you will and to speak as you think are means indispensable to the discovery and spread of political truth."[43] JUSTICE LOUIS BRANDEIS

CHAPTER 3
Defining Freedom of the Student Press

What's news at school besides sports and the prom?

THEN . . .

Hazelwood School District v. Kuhlmeier, (1988)[44]
("Hazelwood")

All of the cases we've looked at on free speech and freedom of the press provide context for the following two cases, which take place at public schools. Keep in mind that in all of the previous cases we have reviewed, the press and free speech have won out over government censorship. Even the most abhorrent messages of the Ku Klux Klan in *Brandenburg v. Ohio* were given First Amendment protection.

The main issue or question to be decided in both of the following cases is whether or not a student newspaper is a "public forum" where viewpoint content cannot be stricken except in very limited circumstances. Justice Hugo Black and the majority of the US Supreme Court, who decided on the *Pentagon Papers* case in 1971, felt very strongly that the general public was entitled to fair, accurate and responsible reporting of important issues that involved the government. But just over ten years later the court swept the rug out from under the feet of journalists—at least as to student press. *Hazelwood* is perhaps the most devastating case for student free speech, according to both students *and* educators, who are concerned that good journalism can no longer be taught at public schools under this damaging precedent.

In August 1983, Cathy Kuhlmeier worked as the layout editor for Hazelwood East's student newspaper, *The Spectrum*. She was a junior at Hazelwood East High School in Saint Louis County, Missouri. She and other students worked creating *The Spectrum* publication for class credit in the Journalism II class under the supervision of Robert Stergos for most of the year. In Journalism I, students learned good journalistic practices such as confirming sources, researching stories, writing and editing, and information on the First Amendment's freedom of the press.

Quoting directly from the Hazelwood School Board Policy, the Board promised, "School-sponsored student publications will not restrict free expression or diverse viewpoints within the rules of responsible journalism." (Board Policy 348.51) The Hazelwood East journalism students believed in the promise of the Board and stated their expectations in a Student Policy Statement of their own each year. "The *Spectrum*, as a student-press publication, accepts all rights implied by the First Amendment . . . ." The Student Policy Statement continued to include a quote directly from *Tinker vs. Des Moines*, which by that time was already the standard set by many school districts concerning free speech. "Only speech that 'materially and substantially interferes with the requirements of appropriate discipline' can be found unacceptable and therefore prohibited."

The *Spectrum* was published approximately every three weeks and distributed to approximately 4,500 subscribers in the school and in the community. It was funded partially by the school district and partially by newspaper sales. According to Kuhlmeier, the students wanted the paper to present topics of interest to students beyond "mere fluff" pieces about the prom or the latest athletic events. In order to keep it interesting, they searched for topics of importance. Earlier issues of the *Spectrum* dealt with teen pregnancy, divorce, marriage, and runaways. Those were the exact topics that the students of the 1982-1983 Journalism II class decided to research and write about. They began interviewing several students in the months prior to the publication of what was to be the last regular paper of the year.

According to Kuhlmeier, of the approximately 2,500 students at Hazelwood East, approximately thirty to forty students were pregnant at any given time during the school year. They chose three individuals who were pregnant at the time to interview. The three gave permission to use their stories and gave three differing perspectives of being pregnant in high school. One was excited that she would soon be a mother, one was seemingly neutral about her condition but would need to "deal with it," and the last thought the news was terrible and it would ruin her life. The journalists made sure the article met sound journalistic standards. The article informed the reader that the names of those quoted in the article were not their true names. The journalists made sure that each of the persons quoted had a chance to read the article for accuracy before it was sent to publication. They also asked that each of the students quoted take the article to their parents to review prior to publication. Kuhlmeier said later that she hoped that the article would enlighten teens about the consequences of teen sex, and how it affected themselves and the people around them. Another article dealt with the effect of a parent's divorce on an individual student, with the anonymous student's permission and quotes from that student, as well.

Mr. Stergos was, by all accounts, a good teacher who guided rather than dictated, counseled rather than censored, and led students to be responsible journalists rather than condemning them for voicing the truth. Years later, Kuhlmeier described Mr. Stergos as a teacher with whom most kids could connect. Then, just a month before the end of the school year, Mr. Stergos left Hazelwood East for another job. A substitute teacher, Mr. Emerson, was placed in charge of the last publication of the year. Mr. Emerson asked the principal, Robert Reynolds, to review the articles of the last publication prior to publication. Unbeknownst to the journalism students who had worked hard to make sure the articles were fair, accurate, and anonymous, Mr. Reynolds decided to pull two pages, meaning seven articles, from the paper just prior to publication. The two articles described above on teenage pregnancy and parents' divorce were pulled. The students of the Journalism II class did not learn of the exclusion of the articles until they received copies of the final publication.

After the articles were pulled, Kuhlmeier and other journalism students went to Principal Reynolds to ask why the articles were deleted. Principal Reynolds justified his actions by saying that although the students were anonymous in the articles, someone might realize their true identities. He also commented that the articles were "too mature for an immature audience." Ms. Kuhlmeier responded, "if students were old enough to get pregnant then shouldn't they be old enough to read about it?"

The journalism students collectively said they would not sell the paper if the important articles would not appear in it. In response Principal Reynolds threatened to eliminate a senior accolades paper, which was something the students looked forward to throughout high school. The newspaper staff decided to get a vote of the seniors. The seniors at Hazelwood East voted to sell the edition of the *Spectrum* without the two questionable pages in order to have the funds necessary to publish the senior accolades paper.

Ms. Kuhlmeier and other journalism students of Hazelwood East filed a lawsuit in the Federal District Court against the Hazelwood School District, Principal Reynolds, and the substitute teacher, Howard Emerson. By the time it reached the US Supreme Court, Ms. Kuhlmeier was a senior in college and was somewhat unaware of the legal life of the case. In a 5-3 decision, the US Supreme Court did not overturn *Tinker v. Des Moines,* but it certainly muddied the waters of the standard set in *Tinker v. Des Moines.*

From the very lengthy and confusing majority US Supreme Court opinion written by Justice White, the rule now is that schools can control the content of "school-sponsored expressive activities" when "reasonably related to legitimate pedagogical concerns." Other Courts have attempted to explain and respond to the ruling in *Hazelwood* in cases that followed Justice White's opinion.

The first and the most harmful leg of Justice White's analysis is the majority's characterization of public student newspapers as non-public forums. As explained above, if a news outlet is a 'public forum' the government has less control. But finding that student papers are 'non-public forums' gives school administrators authority to restrict the content of student newspapers. The decision held that:

> . . . school facilities may be deemed to be public forums only if school authorities have 'by policy or by practice' opened those facilities 'for indiscriminate use by the general public,' ...or by some segment of the public, such as student organizations. If the facilities have instead been reserved for other intended purposes, 'communicative or otherwise,' then no public forum has been created, and school officials may impose reasonable restrictions on the speech of the students, teachers and other members of the school community.[45]

Counsel for Ms. Kuhlmeier and the other journalism students of Hazelwood East pointed out during oral argument before the Supreme Court that the *Spectrum* should be considered a "public forum" because by both policy and practice it had been used by the general public as a meeting place for ideas and expressions. Hazelwood's policy, as clearly stated in its board policy, guaranteed the students that "school-sponsored student publications will not restrict free expression or diverse viewpoints within the rules of responsible journalism." The students clearly accepted that responsibility and the freedoms of the First Amendment as stated in the Student Policy Statement.

Counsel for the students also argued that by practice, the *Spectrum* was a "public forum" because the *Spectrum* was circulated to approximately 4,500 subscribers in both the school and the community. The subscriptions partially paid the newspaper's costs. The evidence also showed that earlier students had dealt with the same substantive issues in previous articles. But that did not convince the majority US Supreme Court that the *Spectrum* was a "public forum" entitled to full free speech and freedom of the press without administrative control.

So what exactly does the *Hazelwood* decision mean to student's free speech rights? The majority opinion in *Hazelwood* allows school administrators to control the content of "school-sponsored expressive activities." Does *school sponsored* mean it is paid for by the school? Not necessarily. The court indicated that, "school-sponsored expressive activities" are those that students, parents, and members of the public might reasonably perceive to bear the 'imprimatur' [meaning some acceptance, approval, or endorsement] of the school. These activities are part of the school curriculum, whether or not they occur in a traditional classroom setting, so long as they are supervised by faculty members and have audiences. That might include anything a student does off-campus! For instance, school plays can be censored, speech on a *school* website can be censored, art displays created by the student when supervised by faculty can be censored, musical performances, sporting events, speeches, and journalism.

The Supreme Court did not provide a clear meaning as to what activities are considered "reasonably related to legitimate pedagogical (meaning 'educational') concerns." It seems this is up to school administrators. But the court gave the following examples of when schools might censor student journalism as it relates to 'pedagogical concerns': ungrammatical, poorly written, inadequately researched, biased or prejudiced, vulgar or profane, or unsuitable for immature audiences.

Since the US Supreme Court's ruling in *Hazelwood*, the horrible truth is that educational administrators have censored viewpoints that they feel might tarnish the schools image by stating an article is ungrammatically correct or poorly written or just "unsuitable."

The dissent, written by Justice Brennan, is perhaps more instructive for journalism students and teachers. He said that *Tinker vs. Des Moines* still applies. And, in fact, had the majority applied the "*Tinker* test" (did the speech 'materially and substantially' disrupt school?), they would come to a result that would be fairer to the students and uphold the ideals of the First Amendment and democracy. "Materially" and "substantially" are both vague words, and their meaning is going to depend on the circumstances, but basically it would be safe to say that if student speech is so disruptive that the educators cannot gain control of the instruction, the educators would be allowed to step in and discipline the student. If there was no disruption to the students' learning, Justice Brennan felt that the students had a First Amendment right to freely publish the articles. After all, the content is not obscene, violent, or threatening.

Furthermore, Justice Brennan's dissent makes it clear that he believed that under the First Amendment, public schools cannot control student viewpoint content. He felt that writing for the school paper is not just about good grammar and punctuation, but that the students should also learn about their right to free speech and free press. They should be free to debate the issues of the day. In his dissent to *Hazelwood*, Justice Brennan wrote:

> [The Spectrum] was not just a class exercise in which students learned to prepare papers and hone writing skills, it was a public forum established to give students an opportunity to express their views while gaining an appreciation of their rights and responsibilities under the First Amendment to the United States Constitution . . . .[46]

> Public education serves vital national interests in preparing the Nation's youth for life in our increasingly complex society and for the duties of citizenship in our democratic Republic. (Citation omitted). The public school conveys to our young the information and tools required not merely to survive in, but to contribute to, civilized society.[47]

Justice Brennan's words are just what this book hopes to convey—an opportunity to cultivate justice. But in the aftermath of *Hazelwood*, students and educators are still battling for student freedom of the press.

AND SINCE THEN . . .

Since the *Hazelwood* ruling, no high school student paper censorship case has reached the US Supreme Court again. How could it, when schools now have the authority to wield the censorship sword if their reputation in the community might be tarnished? Students have been censored when exposing scandals at school or criticizing school administration. In one such instance, a principal of Saint Charles East High School in Illinois sought to suppress a story concerning students who described widespread hazing in school athletics. In another instance, the principal of Madison County High School in Madison, Virginia, confiscated the student newspaper, the *Mountaineer*, when students sought to expose unsafe conditions in their school. School administrators at a public school in Lenoir City, Tennessee, removed a student's opinion piece titled "No Rights: The Life of an Atheist"[48] from the student paper because the district superintendent said that the article would be "distracting" and might provoke "passionate conversations."

Frank D. LoMonte, the executive director of the Student Press Law Center, believes that *passionate conversation* about social and educational issues *should be* a central purpose of the school day, but *Hazelwood* is responsible for making it a distraction instead. "Policymakers say they want civically aware students who graduate ready for meaningful participation in their government. But *Hazelwood* censorship undermines civic learning by teaching young people that the government gets to decide how and when it may be criticized."[49]

School administrators as well as students continue to be confused about what speech is acceptable on campus and off campus. Often, administrators are trying to do the right thing, but seem to be misguided because of the difficulty in balancing students' rights to exchange differing ideas on the one hand against community values on the other. Teachers and administrators are told to allow student diversity, for instance, and yet at the same time to "uphold the community values," which may or may not comport to student diversity.

In one such example, students from the Shawnee Mission School District filed a lawsuit against the school district for infringing on their First Amendment rights during a school assembly. Students across the country organized a national walkout on April 20, 2018, to advocate reforms to reduce gun violence in the wake of the Columbine High School shootings. The Shawnee Mission School District in Kansas organized an assembly to coincide with the walkout. But school district employees began to interfere with student speeches shortly after the assembly began. The school district sought to "encourage the students to keep the topic to school safety" (meaning bullying) and to steer the student's speeches away from gun control because the school district administration believed that as a public institution it could not "take a stand one way or the other on Second Amendment rights." Some of the brave and enlightened students resisted the District's efforts to censor them. One of the students' speeches began, "The school administration wants us to keep this about *school* violence [bullying] and not about the real issue here. The real issue is *gun* violence."

When students resisted the District's efforts at censorship, District officials interrupted students, ordered them to stop speaking, threatened students with discipline, and, in some cases, confiscated the tools that students were using to document the protests.

Another backlash from the *Hazelwood* ruling is that schools are losing good journalism advisers and teachers. In Virginia, the Madison County High School *Mountaineer* adviser was removed after students published an opinion piece exposing unsafe conditions of the school. (The opinion piece did eventually get published in the *Mountaineer*, but it was highly censored.) In commenting on the removal of the journalism teacher and advisor, the *Mountaineer's* editor that year said that "retaliation" might not be the right word, but the superintendent of Madison County clearly did not like the articles because of a possible negative light on the school. And in Lenoir City, Tennessee, a high school English teacher was transferred to middle school because of strong reactions from community members against publication of a yearbook article featuring an openly gay student. The community members circulated a letter demanding others to "take a stand for our faith." (The Lenoir City High School was none other than the very same that refused for publication the editorial "*No Rights; The Life of an Atheist*," by Krystal Myers.)

CLOSER TO NOW . . .

Dean v. Utica Community Schools (E.D. 2004)[50]

The list of censorship of students' press and school-related speech after *Hazelwood* goes on and on, and the battle for student freedom of the press is not entirely won. Although still fighting the impact of *Hazelwood*, some guidance has been provided by other Federal District and Circuit Courts. In a very important win for student press, this Federal District Court rejected censorship by a Michigan school district of the student newspaper, the *Arrow*.

In 2002, the *Arrow* had approximately twenty students enrolled in journalism who staffed the school-sponsored newspaper for Utica High School. The newspaper was published monthly, funded by advertising sales. The students were responsible for all editorial decisions and signed contracts with advertisers, determined the advertising rates, decided what topics to cover, developed story ideas, and set the newsstand price for the paper. Neither the superintendent of the school nor the principal or faculty regulated the subjects covered. The faculty adviser, Ms. Olman, taught journalism and provided counseling on which stories she thought would be of interest to the readers. She also checked the articles written for grammar, spelling, etc.

The school district sought to censor an article written and investigated by Katherine ("Katy") Dean and Dan Butts. The article was the result of a student investigation after learning of a lawsuit filed by local citizens against the school district. The local citizens lived near the school district's bus garage and claimed that the fumes from the bus garage contributed to their poor health. Katy and Dan researched and wrote the article citing both supporting and conflicting findings of facts. They contacted the school superintendent for comment, but the school superintendent declined to comment. Katy also contacted the principal to comment, and he stated that he did not know anything about the case but thought that it was an interesting story to cover. Nevertheless, after the article was written and reviewed by the superintendent, the principal ordered the journalism adviser to pull the article, claiming that the story was based on unreliable sources, contained a number of inaccuracies, and "would be inappropriate for the school newspaper to comment on [the litigation]." The students were not given an opportunity to revise the article.

The *Arrow* staff complied, and instead placed an editorial on censorship in the article's place. Next to the editorial was a black box with "Censored" stamped in white lettering.

The reviewing court found that the *Arrow* was a "limited" public forum and that censorship of the article was a violation of the First Amendment right of freedom of the press. Judge Tarnow, of the United States District Court, E.D. Michigan, Southern Division obviously disagreed with *Hazelwood*. But because this case was decided in a Federal District Court and did not reach the US Supreme Court, it does not create new precedent, but supplements the *Hazelwood* ruling instead. It also provides instruction to journalism classes so that they too can be considered public forums, narrowing school administration's power to regulate content. Judge Tarnow began his opinion in this case with the following quote from Harry S. Truman:

> Once a government is committed to the principle of silencing the voice of opposition, it has only one way to go, and that is down the path of increasingly repressive measures, until it becomes a source of terror to all its citizens and creates a country where everyone lives in fear.
> *Harry S. Truman, Special Message to the Congress on the Internal Security of the United States, August 8, 1950.*[51]

In further discussion Judge Tarnow said:

> The newspaper class at Utica High School is intended to teach journalism. A core value of being a journalist is to understand the role of the press in a free society. That role is to provide an independent source of information so that a citizen can make informed decisions. It is often the case that this core value of journalistic independence requires a journalist to question authority rather than side with authority. Thus, if the role of the press in a democratic society is to have any value, all journalists—including student journalists—must be allowed to publish viewpoints contrary to those of state authorities without intervention or censorship by the authorities themselves. Without protection,

the freedoms of speech and press are meaningless and the press becomes a mere channel for official thought.[52]

Unlike The *Spectrum* at issue in *Hazelwood*, the ruling in *Dean v. Utica* found the *Arrow* to be a limited public forum, where "the government may impose only reasonable time, place, and manner regulations, and content-based regulations that are narrowly drawn to effectuate a compelling state interest." The following factors supported the District Court's ruling that the *Arrow* in *Dean v. Utica* was a limited public forum:

- The course was offered as an extracurricular course because students could take the class for credit more than once
- The student staff managed all of the paper's affairs
- The students were expected to sell advertising and use the revenue to cover the costs for the publication (meaning the students were directly involved and communicated with the community, not just school officials, as a part of the course)
- With the sole exception of this one issue, the administration and faculty exercised little or no control for nearly twenty-five years prior to that over the content of the paper
- The curriculum guidelines said that students were expected to "employ an understanding of the rights and responsibilities that accompany the First Amendment"
- The masthead for the Arrow stated: "Our main purpose is to (1) inform the students, faculty and community of school related news; (2) broaden the range of thinking of staff members and readers; (3) provide a forum for readers; (4) train the students in the function of the press in a democratic society; and (5) provide entertaining features of interest to the students"

The court also found other reasons that this case was different from *Hazelwood*. It found that the journalism instruction was continuous and experienced. Unlike the *Spectrum* in *Hazelwood*, the *Arrow* was not subject to mandatory pre-publication review by any faculty or principal. There was no indication that the articles were not well-written or that they contained grammatical errors. The District Court found the article to be well researched, did not contain any biases or prejudices, and was accurate. In fact, in a footnote in the opinion, the Court noted that a former publisher and president of the *Detroit Free Press* reviewed the article and said that the story "is a perfectly legitimate news story for any newspaper, and certainly is excellent news reporting for a high school level newspaper."[53] The Court also indicated that publication of the stories would not have prevented the school from performing its normal functions.

Finally, the Court found that the censorship was "viewpoint" based, which is a violation of the First Amendment, even under *Hazelwood*. The Court said that the only reasonable conclusion for pulling the article is that the superintendent disagreed with the local residents' viewpoint as to their lawsuit against the school district.

Consider this

In 1973, before the conflict in *Hazelwood* even began, the Robert F. Kennedy Memorial Foundation created a commission to inquire into high school journalism. The Commission wrote a report of its findings, titled "Captive Voices: The Report of the Commission of Inquiry into High School Journalism," by Jack Nelson. The Commission concluded that low priority is given to journalism education in high schools and that applicants often experienced racial, cultural, and ethnic discrimination in joining journalism staff. The Commission then recommended that a national center to help student journalists be established. In 1974, the Kennedy Memorial Foundation and Reporters Committee for Freedom of the Press created the Student Press Law Center (www.splc.org) "The Student Press Law Center promotes, supports, and defends the First Amendment and free press rights of student journalists and their advisors."

The impact of the *Hazelwood* ruling on student journalism has been nothing short of devastating. Constitutional scholars, journalists, and college and high school students agree. Without freedom of speech and freedom of the press being protected at public schools, we are doing a disservice not only to students, but also to the very foundation of democracy. David Cuillier, the director of the University of Arizona's journalism school, said that one of the main problems with *Hazelwood* is that many educational administrators do not understand that the purpose of teaching journalism is not to correct grammar, spelling, or typos, but "that we teach [students] to learn to challenge to get the information that people need."

Ted McConnell, the Campaign for the Civic Mission of Schools' executive director and a Student Press Law Center board member, said, "A half century ago, high school students were required to take multiple courses on civic issues before graduating; now they might take one. Then, students were encouraged to discuss contemporary issues, even when they were controversial. Not anymore," he said. "We're falling down on educating the next generation in how their rights and responsibilities as citizens in this country work."

Effective, high-quality student journalism is an "essential component" of civic learning that helps develop democratic communities. Without allowing students to "take government out for a test drive," students get the wrong impression of democracy.

ADDITIONAL RESOURCES

Chapter 3—Defining Freedom of the Student Press

- Fight back against the *Hazelwood v. Kuhlmeier* decision and censorship of student journalism! The country needs good journalism, and we need good journalists who are trained to recognize the truth and have the ability to inform the people about what is happening at every level.
- If your school does not have a journalism class, talk to a counselor, teacher, principal, or school board and educate them on the need for journalism as a tool for civics education.
- Volunteer to staff a student-run newspaper.
- Speak out! If your high school or university will not print an article because it might tarnish or embarrass the school's reputation, don't be afraid to voice your discontent with the violation of your First Amendment rights to free speech and freedom of the press.
- The factors that the District Court in *Dean v. Utica* listed provide an outline for good journalism practices that will bode well in an argument for First Amendment rights. Make sure the articles are well investigated and researched, do not contain any biases or prejudices, and are accurate and well written.
- Contact the Student Press Law Center for help and research your First Amendment rights there. The Student Press Law Center's online library is a great source for student press legal rights.
- If there is a request to pull an article, be prepared to defend it by asking yourself ahead of time: is it libelous, defamatory, indecent, possible that it could incite lawless activity, or just untrue? Can it be edited to rectify mistakes or inaccuracies?

Can you provide an equal opportunity for a counterpoint article?
- Research the laws in your state. Prior to *Hazelwood,* in 1977, the California Education Code adopted Section 48907, which provides the *student editors* with the exclusive power for assigning and editing the news, editorials, and feature content of their publications, so long as it is not obscene, libelous, slanderous, or incites a substantial disruption. That California state law supplants *Hazelwood* and clarifies that the students are in charge of student press. At the time of this writing, seventeen states since *Hazelwood* have adopted similar laws putting student editors in charge of their publications. To research the laws related to student press in your state, locate the online law library of the Student Press Law Center (www.splc.org/law-library/).
- If your state has not passed a protective law for freedom of student press, New Voices can provide you with guides on introducing a bill in your state that will protect student freedom of the press. Be sure to check the New Voices website to seek guidance specific to your state. Many have already introduced a bill, but need advocates of Freedom of the (Student) Press to get the bills passed. Contact New Voices (www.splc.org/new-voices/) "New Voices is a student-powered nonpartisan grassroots movement of state-based activists who seek to protect student press freedom with state laws."
- Be like Quinn Mitchell, a fifteen year old who asked a pointed question to Governor Ron DeSantis of Florida. Early in 2023, in New Hampshire, while Governor DeSantis was still in the race for the Republican Party Presidential Candidacy, Quinn asked DeSantis whether he believed "that Trump violated the peaceful transfer of power, a key

principle of American democracy that we must uphold?" The candidate squirmed and evaded the question. Quinn was escorted out of the event, as well as the next event he attended. In response, Quinn posted the following on X, "Really stupid they did it again. Believe me, if I disrupted an event my mom would never ever take me to another one—not my style."

- Ask pointed questions. Demand answers. Demand to be taken seriously. And report the truth.

"The right to think is the beginning of freedom, and speech must be protected from the government because speech is the beginning of thought."[54] JUSTICE ANTHONY KENNEDY

CHAPTER 4

Book Burning: The Right to Read

More on Free Speech and Freedom of the Press

No review of students' First Amendment rights to free speech and freedom of the press would be complete without discussing the right to read. *National Geographic* reports that, "book challenges are more common than ever. Between July 1, 2021 and March 31, 2022 alone, there were 1,586 book bans in 86 school districts across 26 states—affecting more than two million students."[55]

But book banning is nothing new. According to the *National Geographic* article, book banning started in Great Britain, continued in the colonial era, and "[b]y the 1920s, Boston was so notorious for banning books that authors intentionally printed their books there in the hopes that the inevitable ban would give them a publicity boost elsewhere in the country."

A litany of books have been challenged throughout history—titles of great novels such as *The Great Gatsby* by F. Scott Fitzgerald, *The Catcher in the Rye* by JD Salinger, *The Grapes of Wrath* by John Steinbeck, *To Kill a Mockingbird* by Harper Lee, *The Color Purple* by Alice Walker, *The Lord of the Flies* by William Golding, and *1984* by George Orwell, just to name just a few.

But historically, neither good teachers, librarians, nor educators have been responsible for book bans. Textbooks and school curriculum is traditionally left up to state governments and school boards to decide. Unless there is a claim that a matter is unconstitutional, federal courts do not normally get involved. When the matter has been brought to court, however, several lower courts have upheld a constitutional "right to read," concerning books such as *Oliver Twist* by Charles Dickens; *The Merchant of Venice* by William Shakespeare; *Slaughterhouse Five*, *God Bless You Mr. Rosewater*, and *Cat's Cradle* by Kurt Vonnegut; and *Catch-22* by Joseph Heller. And the United States Supreme Court has rarely spoken on the issue.

The following case, decided in the 1970s by a lower federal court, demonstrates book banning motivated by political power.

The Right to Read Defense Committee v. School Committee, City of Chelsea (D. Mass. 1978)[56]

This case concerns a poem, "The City to a Young Girl," by Jody Caravaglia, appearing in the book *Male and Female Under 18*. Jody, who was fifteen years old at the time, wrote a sixteen-line poem about being hassled on the street by a group of men. The poem begins, "The city is; One million horny lip-smacking men; Screaming for my body." Jody never travelled to the small town of Chelsea, but her poem did. The poem raised objections from the school board committee. Mr. Quigley, who was at one time both the mayor and state senator, and a figure in Chelsea politics for more than half of his fifty-one years, raised the loudest objections.

The poem was picked up and included in an anthology of students' works and was circulated to high schools throughout the country. The paperback book, *Male and Female Under 18*, had been in the Chelsea

High School library for several months before anyone noticed Jody's poem.

Mr. Quigley said he read "The City to a Young Girl" and found it "objectionable, salacious, and obscene." He wrote an article condemning both the book and the school librarian in the city's only daily newspaper, *The Chelsea Record*, which he publishes. He referred to the teachers who opposed his action as "insubordinate" and suggested that they look elsewhere for employment. He described the poem as vulgar and objected to the content because he believed "it targeted all men," apparently believing that all males act in the same manner that Jody described in her poem.

Mr. Quigley kept the copy of the poem from two of the three female members of the committee because he 'knew they would accept my word that it was garbage.' A third woman on the committee, Lucy Brown, testified that she asked Mr. Quigley for a copy of the poem and he refused, saying she 'was too young to see it.' Mrs. Brown appeared to be in her early fifties at the time. The US District Court said:

> [T]he library is 'a mighty resource in the marketplace of ideas.' There a student can literally explore the unknown, and discover areas of interest and thought not covered by the prescribed curriculum. The student who discovers the magic of the library is on the way to a life-long experience of self-education and enrichment. That student learns that a library is a place to test or expand upon ideas presented to him, in or out of the classroom. The most effective antidote to the poison of mindless orthodoxy is ready access to a broad sweep of ideas and philosophies. There is no danger from such exposure. The danger is mind control. The committee's ban of the anthology Male and Female is enjoined.[57]

The judge in the case allowed students to observe the court proceedings. News coverage described the courtroom as "jammed" with students. Some students were witnesses. The female students especially related to the poem and said that the writer was "courageous" in describing how it felt to be treated like an object by some men. The students of Chelsea felt vindicated and heard. They were treated to a firsthand lesson on the First Amendment's freedom of speech. All because of a sixteen-line poem written by a fifteen-year-old girl expressing her feelings. She received only $10 for publication of the poem and a copy of the book.

THEN . . .

Then, in 1982, the United States Supreme Court finally weighed in on book banning. The decision was a close call; 5 to 4 upholding the First Amendment's protection of free speech and freedom of the press in a book banning case.

Island Trees School District v. Steven Pico (1982)[58]

Island Trees School District is a small school district located about thirty-one miles east of New York City on Long Island. In 1975, a politically conservative organization of parents published a list of books it described as "objectionable." In 1976, the Island Trees School District Board gave an "unofficial direction" to the principals of the high school and the junior high "that all copies of the library books in question be removed from the libraries." The "questionable books" in the high school library were *Slaughter House Five* by Kurt Vonnegut, Jr.; *The Naked Ape* by Desmond Morris; *Down These Mean Streets* by Piri Thomas; *Best Short Stories of Negro Writers* edited by Langston Hughes; *Go Ask Alice* of anonymous authorship; *Laughing Boy* by Oliver LaFarge; *Black Boy* by Richard Wright; *A Hero Ain't Nothin' But A Sandwich* by Alice Childress; and *Soul On Ice* by Eldridge Cleaver. The book in the junior high school library was *A Reader for*

Writers, edited by Jerome Archer. Still another listed book, *The Fixer* by Bernard Malamud, was found to be included in the curriculum of a twelfth grade literature course.

The board demanded to review the books from the conservatives' list. When the public became aware that the board pulled the books from the school libraries, they addressed it with the school board. The board justified its action in a press release by characterizing the removed books as "anti-American, anti-Christian, anti-Semetic (sic), and just plain filthy," and concluded that, "[i]t is our duty, our moral obligation, to protect the children in our schools from this moral danger as surely as from physical and medical dangers."

When asked to give an example of "anti-Americanism" in the removed books, two people on the school board pointed to the book *A Hero Ain't Nothin' But a Sandwich,* Childress, which states that George Washington was a slaveholder. One member of the board said, "I believe it is anti-American to present one of the nation's heroes, the first President . . . in such a negative and obviously one-sided light. That is one example of what I would consider anti-American."

High school students Steven Pico, Jacqueline Gold, Glenn Yarris, and Russell Rieger, and a junior high student, Paul Sochinski, filed a lawsuit against the school board, claiming that the censorship of these books was a violation of their First Amendment rights. The students and the board pretty much agreed that the reason for pulling the books off the school library shelves was "content-based." In other words, the board simply didn't like the content and the viewpoints expressed. The evidence showed that the school board had no other legitimate reason to pull the books.

Prior to this case, the United States Supreme Court had not gotten involved in the book banning discussion because "by and large, 'public education in our nation is committed to the control of the state and local authorities,'" and that federal courts should not ordinarily "intervene in the resolution of conflicts which arise in the daily operation of school systems" (quoting *Tinker v. Des Moines* (1969). But the Supreme Court suggested that this case was different because of the fact that this involved discretionary books—books from the school library that were made available only if a student *wanted* to read them.

Although the Supreme Court majority was in "full agreement" that school boards are permitted "to establish and apply their curriculum in such a way as to transmit community values," and that "there is a legitimate and substantial community interest in promoting respect for authority and traditional values be they social, moral, or political," the US Supreme Court also needed to make sure that the so called "community interests" and "community values" were not so limiting that it cut off the Constitutional rights of the students.

The US Supreme Court narrowed the case down to two questions. First, are there any limitations to a school board's discretion to remove school library books under the First Amendment? Second, if so, is there evidence that the Island Trees School Board exceeded those limitations?

As to the first question, the majority of the US Supreme Court said: Yes! There are limits! School boards cannot just arbitrarily exercise their "discretion" to remove school library books. As to the second question, the US Supreme Court remanded the case, meaning it handed the case back down to the lower court, to answer the second question. Did the Island Trees School District exceed those limitations? Here is the direction the US Supreme Court gave the lower court as to what limitations apply to enable it to decide:

> Although school boards may exercise discretion in deciding school curriculum, **"that discretion may not be exercised in a narrowly partisan or political manner. If a Democratic school board, motivated by party affiliation, ordered the removal of all books written by or in favor of Republicans, few would doubt that the order violated the constitutional rights of the**

students denied access to those books. The same conclusion would surely apply if an all-White school board, motivated by racial animus, decided to remove all books authored by blacks or advocating racial equality and integration. Our Constitution does not permit the official suppression of ideas. Thus, whether petitioners' removal of books from their school libraries denied respondents their First Amendment rights depends upon the motivation behind petitioners' actions. If petitioners intended by their removal decision to deny respondents access to ideas with which petitioners disagreed, and if this intent was the decisive factor in petitioners' decision, then petitioners have exercised their discretion in violation of the Constitution."[59] (Emphasis added.)

Wow! The US Supreme Court ruling in *Island School District v. Pico* is still the precedential opinion providing all school boards guidance in exercising their discretion in deciding First Amendment rights to read at school. The above paragraph from the majority opinion highlighted here should not be forgotten. If book removal is motivated to prevent access to ideas that school administrations disagree with, it is a violation of students' First Amendment rights. That case was decided in 1982, but we're still dealing with politically charged book banning in 2024.

The Dissent

The Supreme Court was almost equally divided in this case. Four out of the nine US Supreme Court Justices disagreed. They said that the school boards, elected by the parents and at the direction of the parents, were in the best position to decide what books should be in the school libraries. The dissent said it should not be left to the students—or, and especially, for the federal courts to decide. The dissent also said that the books are, after all, available to the students at bookstores and public libraries, and that the Constitution does not require school libraries to carry all books or require school boards to justify to its teenage pupils the decision to remove a particular book from a school library. Parents of young children especially should guide their children on books appropriate for the age of the child, both in terms of content and the child's abilities and curiosities.

AND NOW . . .

Book banning is *still* a part of current topic-based politics despite the majority opinion in *Island Trees School District v. Pico*. Here are a few more examples of book banning court cases in the states since the *Island Trees v. Pico* decision: *Annie on My Mind* by Nancy Garden, *Heather Has Two Mommies* by Lesléa Newman, *Daddy's Roommate* by Michael Willhoite, and *Harry Potter and the Sorcerer's Stone*, by J.K. Rowling.

Lower courts and federal courts have thus far protected the right to read. Courts have applied *Tinker v. Des Moines* and *Island Trees School Dist. v. Pico*, determining that these books would not cause disruption and that these restrictions were on the basis of the ideas expressed and therefore violated the First Amendment.

The unfortunate reality is that school boards don't want to be accused of promoting "immorality and vulgarity" by any parent, so it is easier to stand down and avoid the fight by not putting a challenged book in the public school library. Follett School Solutions is one of the country's largest providers of books to schools in grades Kindergarten through twelfth grade. The CEO of content, Britten Follett recently commented on the belief that book banning is still driven by politics, "And in the end, the librarian, teacher, or educator is getting caught in the middle."

According to PEN America: The Freedom to Write,[60] presently, Texas, Florida, Georgia, North Carolina, and Arkansas lead the nation in attempts to keep certain books off the shelves.

In June 2023, the governor of Texas signed a bill banning "explicit books" in Texas schools. It is dubbed part of his "parental empowerment" plan. He said, "Some school libraries have books with sexually explicit and vulgar materials. I'm signing a law that gets that trash out of our schools." But the ban does not give parents the responsibility for reviewing what their children read. Instead, it puts the responsibility on book vendors to rate the content they sell to libraries and catalog a list for the Texas Education Agency. If the Texas Education Agency disagrees with the rating, it can override it with its own rating. Booksellers, vendors, publishers, and authors object. Under the new proposed law, The Texas Education Agency has authority to exclude any vendors who do not comply. Additionally, school districts must review their content and submit compliance reports to the Texas Education Agency. As such, the state of Texas has literally put itself in control of what students can and cannot read. This is a flagrant violation of the First Amendment Free Speech clause.

Val Benavidez, executive director of Texas Freedom Network, said in a public statement, "All the alarm bells should be going off when state leaders use their elected power to control our children's ideas and erase the historical experiences of our communities. [The new law] restricts our children's ability to read freely by allowing politicians to interfere with our education system when parents already have a system that works."

The alarm most definitely sounded and two bookstores, book groups, and sellers sued the State of Texas to block the law. The complaint, filed in the federal court, US District Court, Western Division Texas (*Book People, Inc. v. Wong*[61]), alleges that the new law "grants the government unchecked licensing authority to dictate which books are allowed in public schools and which booksellers can conduct business with public schools."[62]

The Texas book ban law will never be enforced. The federal judge assigned to the case blocked the law from enforcement until the case proceeds by issuing a preliminary injunction. The hearing on the preliminary injunction took place on August 31, 2023, just one day before the law was to take effect on September 1, 2023. And the US Court of Appeals for the Fifth Circuit later agreed that the Texas law is a violation of First Amendment rights.[63] Similar lawsuits have been filed recently in Florida and Arkansas aimed at new state legislatures that ban viewpoints.

BOOKS ARE NOT TRASH!

As demonstrated in the closely divided majority and dissent in the *Island Trees School District v. Steven Pico* case, school districts are between a rock and a hard place on this issue. Parents might be threatened by social change. Often, the first encounter of changing social norms is in books and other media, and some (even if only a few) may overreact. They blame the school districts. The school districts answer to the parents and the "community values" while trying to advocate for students, too. It's not always easy—or clear cut.

One school district's fight against banning books offers a positive result. Instead of filing a lawsuit under First Amendment rights, those objecting to pulling books from the schools' libraries in Forsyth County Schools in Georgia made a complaint to the US Department of Education, Office for Civil Rights (the OCR). The OCR's mission is "to ensure equal access to education and to promote educational excellence through vigorous enforcement of civil rights in our nation's schools."[64] The OCR makes sure that students' equal rights under the Fourteenth Amendment and the 1964 Civil Rights Act are protected.

A group of parents objected to certain books they felt were offensive, mostly given the books' inclusion of LGBTQ+ discussions. The superintendent of schools opted to have the books pulled. With that, the complaint was filed with the OCR. The complaint alleged that the Forsyth County School District discriminated against students on the basis of sex, race, color, or national origin.

The OCR conducted an investigation of the complaint and reported its findings in a letter to the district.[65] The OCR's investigation revealed that after the books were removed, certain students felt harassed, fearful, and "expressed the belief that the district does not care about diversity." The OCR concluded that it was "concerned" that the school district had created a hostile environment that needed to be ameliorated.

The school district was offered an agreement, which "requires the district to issue a statement to students in the district explaining the book removal process and offering supportive measures to students who may have been impacted by the book removal process." The agreement also requires the district to administer a climate survey of the student bodies at each of the district's middle and high schools to assess whether additional steps need to be taken.

What's good about this solution is that it does not point fingers at anyone—not the concerned parents nor the school district nor the students. The letter simply recognizes a difference in family values. And, most importantly, the Office for Civil Rights prompted communication between the differing groups. In the end, that is what we want most out of our First Amendment rights. We want to be able to express differing ideas without fear of retaliation or harassment. We simply want to be better understood so that we all can empathize with one another. In any disagreement with schools over these issues, we might do better to see that the school officials are trying their best to be supportive to all sides, rather than combative. They too are struggling to find themselves and find creative solutions. Admittedly, not everyone "wins" in a workable solution, but everyone loses in a heated battle for control.

More to Consider:

The majority opinion in *Island Trees School District v. Steven Pico* is one of the best protections students have to keep books on the shelves at their school libraries. This doesn't mean the US Supreme Court won't take another case about book banning in the future, but for now, *Island Trees School District v. Steven Pico* is the definitive law on the subject. How do you think the language from *Island Trees School District v. Steven Pico* affects your ability to read the books you want?

Do you agree with the dissent in *Island Trees School District v. Pico* that parents and school districts, and not federal justices, or the students themselves, should determine what is appropriate for young readers?

Without access to certain books on a variety of conversational topics, are you being denied an education equivalent to the rest of the world to be able to enter a worldwide marketplace?

Are state legislators, "motivated by party affiliation," telling you implicitly that you are denying the word of God by believing in science or gender equality? Are state legislators, "motivated by racial animus," deciding to remove all books authored by Blacks or advocating racial equality and integration?

Students at Xavier High School in New York were given an assignment. They were to write a persuasive letter to their favorite author asking the author to visit the school. Five students chose to write to Kurt Vonnegut, who is one of the most frequently challenged authors of banned books of all time. (The most banned book of all time, however, is *1984* by George Orwell. How ironic!) According to the book *Letters of Note, Vol. 2* by Shaun Usher, Vonnegut never made the trip to Xavier High School, but wrote back to the students. He was the only author to reply to the students' request. Here is Vonnegut's letter:

228 E 48 NYC 10017 212-688-2682 November 5, 2006

Dear Xavier High School, and Ms. Lockwood, and Messrs Perin, McFeely, Batten, Maurer and Congiusta:

I thank you for your friendly letters. You sure know how to cheer up a really old geezer (84) in his sunset years. I don't make public appearances any more because I now resemble nothing so much as an iguana.

What I had to say to you, moreover, would not take long, to wit: Practice any art, music, singing, dancing, acting, drawing, painting, sculpting, poetry, fiction, essays, reportage, no matter how well or badly, not to get money and fame, but to experience <u>becoming</u>, to find out what's inside you, <u>to make your soul grow.</u>

Seriously! I mean starting right now, do art and do it for the rest of your lives. Draw a funny or nice picture of Ms. Lockwood, and give it to her. Dance home after school, and sing in the shower and on and on. Make a face in your mashed potatoes. Pretend you're Count Dracula.

Here's an assignment for tonight, and I hope Ms. Lockwood will flunk you if you don't do it: Write a six line poem, about anything, but <u>rhymed.</u> No fair tennis without a net. Make it as good as you possibly can. But don't tell anybody what you're doing. Don't show it or recite it to anybody, not even your girlfriend or parents or whatever, or Ms. Lockwood. OK?

Tear it up into teeny-weeny pieces, and discard them into widely separated trash recepticals. You will find that you have already been gloriously rewarded for your poem. You have experienced becoming, learned a lot more about what's inside you, and you have made your soul grow.

God bless you all!

Kurt Vonnegut

ADDITIONAL RESOURCES

Chapter 4—Right to Read

- Be proactive in your community and in your school district. Ask the school board for the school district's policy on purchasing, distributing, and eliminating books. If the policy needs some revisions, ask if you can serve on the committee to revise the policy. If not, why not?
- Stage a debate at your own school on the best way to handle "challenged books" (books that some people feel are inappropriate for the school library). Make sure all sides of the debate are represented.
- See if the student press would like to summarize and publish your findings in the school paper.
- Learn more about book banning and how you can help with PEN at https://pen.org or at https://pen.org/how-to-fight-book-bans-a-tip-sheet-for-students/.
- Write a book, a poem, or an essay expressing your own point of view on a topic of debate. Now imagine someone having the right to call it "trash." Use that feeling to fight against book banning.
- Follow Kurt Vonnegut's suggestion: "Write a poem, tear it up, and discard it at widely separated trash receptacles. Feel the reward of knowing yourself better and having your soul grow just from having written it."
- Read a book. In fact, read a lot of books. Select a book on the challenged list. In fact, select several books on the challenged list—especially if you have an opposing viewpoint currently or know nothing about the topic. As you read, keep an open mind. After you've read a book on the challenged list, ask yourself if you learned anything, if you have a different perspective on the subject, or if you enjoyed it.

- Start a student book club. Meet once a month with friends and discuss differing points of view.
- Go to your local library and read, read, read.
- Many colleges have libraries open to the public. It may be a trip worth taking.
- Write to your representative asking them to prevent book banning in your state. http://action.everylibrary.org

CHAPTER 5

The Establishment Clause and Freedom of Religion

Religious Teachings and Prayer in Public Schools Understanding The Separation Between Church and State (PART I)

"Congress shall make no law respecting an establishment of religion, or prohibiting the free exercise thereof; *or abridging the freedom of speech, or of the press; or the right of the people peaceably to assemble; and to petition the Government for a redress of grievances."* (Ratified, December 1791)

Although the First Amendment is probably best known as the amendment that gives us the right to free speech, it also limits the government's involvement in our freedom to believe or not believe in any religion. Perhaps no other subject concerning public schools has been on the US Supreme Court's docket more often than those dealing with the sensitive issues concerning religion's place at schools. As shown in the following cases, there is so much tension at this line between the freedom of expression of one's religious beliefs in government settings (e.g., public school settings) and the establishment of religion by the government that it is difficult to discuss one clause without the other.

On the one hand, the Free Exercise Clause gives us the right to freely exercise the religion of our choosing, or to choose no religion. On the other hand, the Establishment Clause prevents the *government* from establishing religion. They are two individual but equally important clauses of the First Amendment. Justice Breyer recently wrote that the purpose of the two clauses is to "allow for an American society with practitioners of over one hundred different religions, and those who do not practice religion at all, to live together without serious risk of religion-based social divisions." *Carson v. Makin* (2022) dissent, J. Breyer.[66]

We all understand that we want to be free to practice our religious faith without government interference. But in what circumstances is the government so biased, so lenient, so accommodating to religious preferences that it begins to "establish" religion? The question that comes up most often for the US Supreme Court to determine is: where is the line between the meaning of the Establishment Clause of the First Amendment and the Free Exercise Clause?

The following stories all concern a right to public education free from religious overtones. For the last half of the twentieth century, the US Supreme Court has been strict in its application of a "wall of separation between church and state." However, beginning in the year 2000 and since, the discussion of the tension between the Establishment Clause and the Free Exercise Clause demonstrate a shift to a more Christian universal and conservative point of view in the Supreme Court. As you read the following stories, keep in mind these sound words, written in 1947 by Justice Black:

> The 'establishment of religion' clause of the First Amendment means at least this: neither a state nor the federal government can set up a church. Neither can pass laws which aid one religion, aid all religions, or prefer one religion over another. Neither can force nor

influence a person to go to or to remain away from church against his will or force him to profess a belief or disbelief in any religion. No person can be punished for entertaining or professing religious beliefs or disbeliefs, for church attendance or non-attendance. No tax in any amount, large or small, can be levied to support any religious activities or institutions, whatever they may be called, or whatever form they may adopt to teach or practice religion. Neither a state nor the federal government can, openly or secretly, participate in the affairs of any religious organizations or groups, and vice versa. In the words of Jefferson, the clause against establishment of religion by law was intended to erect **'a wall of separation between church and State.'** *Reynolds v. United States, supra*, at 98 U. S. 164. (*Everson v. Board of Education of the Township of Ewing* (1947)[67]

THEN . . .

Scopes trial (1925)

Science, history, and reproductive rights are some of the classroom subjects where freedom of expression of religious beliefs and the Establishment Clause bump along on a sea of troubled waters. But students are not the only ones who have historically been banned, reprimanded, or shamed for speaking out in schools. Teachers are both encouraged to shepherd the "marketplace of ideas" and restricted by being government workers. On the one hand, they must maintain peace and order in schools, and on the other hand allow new and innovative ideas to emerge. Yet, as government employees, they must teach the curriculum they are given in public schools, even if that does not match their personal religious views.

In 1925, schools were reluctant to teach Darwin's theory of evolution because the theory directly contradicts any literal interpretation of the Bible. Several states' legislatures even proposed bills to make it illegal to teach the theory of evolution in regular biology classes. These laws came to be known as "the monkey laws." In Tennessee, a bill was introduced and passed making it a crime "to teach any theory that denies the story of divine creation as taught by the Bible and to teach instead that man was descended from a lower order of animals." A substitute biology teacher in Tennessee named John Scopes admitted to teaching the theory of evolution in a biology lesson. He was defended in a criminal trial by the most famous attorney of the time, Clarence Darrow.

The trial became a spectacle. Darrow and his client were painted as anti-Christians opposed to all of the teachings of the Bible. But Darrow was convincing in his cross-examination of the prosecution's star witness. The witness was "an expert in the religious interpretation of the Biblical story of our origin." Darrow convincingly made the witness squirm on the stand and ended up admitting that the Bible might not need to be taken literally to explain the origin of humans. Nevertheless, the jury eventually found Scopes guilty and he was fined one hundred dollars. The case was eventually dismissed on a technicality, and an appeal was therefore impossible. Thus, the issue was still not permanently decided for another forty years . . .

AND THEN . . .

Epperson v. Arkansas (1968)[68]

In a bit of irony, another case decided on the very same day on which the oral argument took place in *Tinker vs. Des Moines* had a huge impact on public school's freedoms. The case *Epperson v. Arkansas* also involved the First Amendment, but it was decided on a different clause of the First Amendment—the Establishment Clause. *Epperson v. Arkansas,* decided in 1968, had a long history that dates back to 1859, when Darwin first published his work *Origin of the Species*. It was not until 1968, more than one hundred years after Darwin first published his theory of evolution, that the Supreme Court ruled that any law that prohibits teaching other theories of evolution besides the Bible violates the Establishment Clause of the First Amendment.

Epperson v. Arkansas involved a young teacher in Little Rock, Arkansas. She was just twenty-four years old, barely out of college herself, and a newlywed. Susan Epperson obtained a master's degree in zoology and was hired by the Little Rock public schools to teach tenth grade biology in 1964. Although the science of Darwin's theory of evolution was widely accepted as a theory by 1964, Arkansas (and one other state, Mississippi) still had an anti-evolution statute making it illegal to teach the theory in public schools. According to the law in Arkansas, it was unlawful for Ms. Epperson "to teach the theory or doctrine that mankind ascended or descended from a lower order of animals," or "to adopt or use in any such institution a textbook that teaches" this theory. "Violation is a misdemeanor and subjects the violator to dismissal from his position."[69]

After one year of teaching biology without incident, Ms. Epperson reported for class the next school year. She was given a new textbook to teach from that taught Darwin's theory of evolution. Not wanting to lose her job for teaching from the "illegal" chapter, and not wanting to lose her job for *not* teaching the chapter from the textbook she was assigned, she applied to the court for a determination that the Arkansas law was a violation of the Establishment Clause. In legal parlance, the application to the court before a legal action is taken is called a "declaratory relief" action. At the beginning of a declaratory relief action, the parties preserve the status quo. In other words, the parties cannot take any action until the court makes a final determination on the merits of the case. In this case, Ms. Epperson would not lose her job while the court decided whether she could teach the subject matter out of the textbook she was given. The case took four years to be resolved.

Ms. Epperson was raised in a Presbyterian household. Her father was also a biology teacher and an elder of the church. He taught at Ozark College, which is affiliated with the Presbyterian Church. Ms. Epperson said she never viewed the science of evolution to conflict with her faith. In fact, along with the views of her family, teaching science seemed *natural*. But at the time that the suit was filed, critics suggested Ms. Epperson was doing the devil's work. In an interview with Ms. Epperson in 2021, at age eighty, she recalled that "[she] got letters telling [her] that [she] was going to hell." She said she would rather pray for her critics than argue with them. She said, "I kind of knew who makes the decision about who goes to hell. And it was not the person who wrote that letter."

The state court found the Arkansas anti-evolution statute to be in violation of the First Amendment and stated that the law "tends to hinder the quest for knowledge, restrict the freedom to learn, and restrain the freedom to teach."[70]

The State of Arkansas appealed the decision to the Supreme Court of Arkansas. The Arkansas Supreme Court reversed the lower court's decision. The Arkansas Supreme Court ruled that the statute was within the powers of the State to specify the curriculum in public schools. It was a very vague ruling and the statute itself, Ms. Epperson's attorney argued, was just as vague. Did it make it illegal to teach that the theory of evolution was "true," or was it illegal to even educate students as to the existence of any scientific theory of the origin of humans other than the Bible?

After losing at the state level in the Supreme Court of Arkansas, Ms. Epperson then appealed the case to the US Supreme Court. The US Supreme Court granted review. In oral argument to the US Supreme Court, the attorney for Ms. Epperson, Eugene Warren,* said that he found that teachers in the State of Arkansas were avoiding the topic altogether. The teachers were frightened to teach biology and science for fear of losing their jobs.

In his argument before the US Supreme Court, Mr. Warren said, "When the teacher reaches that chapter [in the biology textbook] the

---

* No relation to the Chief Justice of the US Supreme Court sitting at that time, Justice Earl Warren.

teacher simply skips it, unless the teacher happens to be one of those ingenious people that wants to be sure that the student actually reads it. That teacher announces that the reading of the chapter is illegal. And, of course I think all of the children would immediately run to read it and probably get more from that chapter than from any other chapter in the book." [71]

The comment is both humorous and accurate. It is human nature that we want to read and see and do what is forbidden. But this was not just book banning; this was *textbook* banning. Scientific theory is essential knowledge. As we learn how much our human footprint impresses upon our world and the science behind it, we learn new solutions. Without it societies fail. Humanity fails.

Mr. Warren took exception especially to the second phrase in the Arkansas law making it illegal to "use" any textbook that teaches the theory of evolution. He suggested that the way the law was written would effectively eliminate all books in any school library that mentioned any theory of evolution, which would include encyclopedias, dictionaries, general reference books, and even the Bible. Mr. Warren concluded his argument by saying, "If the Act has that sort of meaning, then that means that every school has got to rid its libraries of all these books, and that's just plain ridiculous. That's book burning at its worst."

Ms. Epperson won her case. The US Supreme Court majority struck down the Arkansas law. Over fifty years later, Ms. Epperson is still a noteworthy speaker. She taught science at Pike's Peak Community College and then at University of Colorado, Colorado Springs. She delivered the commencement speech at the University of Ozarks in 2016, and spoke at the site of the original Scopes trial in Dayton, Tennessee. In her talks, she still speaks about her faith in connection with science. In an article appearing in the Arkansas Democrat-Gazette in 2021, she commented on her own faith.

"Whenever I speak, I talk about my faith," she said. "You're talking to a bunch of science teachers or science people. Some of them may be believers, some are not, but the door is open for me because of the [Supreme Court] case. And so I can just stand there and talk about my faith and say that I see no conflict."

"If I have a mission in life, it is to try, and you're really hitting your head on a brick wall, I think, to . . . . convince people that evolution is not anti-biblical, it's not anti-faith [or] anti-religion," she said.[72]

THEN . . .

Barnette v. School Board of West Virginia (1943)[73]

Imagine you were in a classroom and forced to recite something that was abhorrent to your conscious. For example, imagine you were in Germany during World War II and you were compelled to pledge allegiance to Hitler or salute his army when you knew you're your friends and family were being slaughtered based on Hitler's systematic discrimination.

For two children attending a public elementary school in Charleston, West Virginia, the situation must have felt very similar to the experiences of others in Europe at the very same time. Marie Barnette, eight years old, and her sister, Gathie, ten years old, were expelled from school after their winter break just after the bombing of Pearl Harbor and the beginning of the US involvement in World War II.

Under a new law in West Virginia in 1942, students in public schools were required to stand, face the flag with their right arm fully extended toward the flag with the palm up, and recite: "I pledge allegiance to the flag of the United States of America and to the republic for which it stands, one nation under God** with liberty and justice for all."

** Although the phrase "one nation under God" appeared in West Virginia in 1942, it was not adopted nationwide until 1954.

72　CULTIVATING JUSTICE

Students stand to salute the American flag in class. (Circa 1942)

Marie and Gathie were expelled for not saluting the flag or reciting the pledge of allegiance.

Marie and Gathie's faith, Jehovah's Witness, believes in a literal interpretation of the Bible that does not allow them to pledge their faithfulness to, or worship, symbolism of any kind. Their failure to conform to the law of the State of West Virginia rendered them "insubordinate." They were expelled from school and declared "unlawfully absent" and "delinquent" until such time that they would comply.

If their parents were convicted of keeping them from attending school, the parents would be subject to jail time and fines. Moreover, other children of the faith of Jehovah's Witness were being expelled and excluded from public schools for no other reason except for their faith. In a documented interview in 2003 with Gathie Barnette, she explained that her parents avoided prosecution for causing delinquency by having Marie and Gathie go to school in the morning until the flag salute occurred. When Marie and Gathie refused to join in the salute, the school sent them home. Gathie believed her elementary school teacher at that time had empathy for her and her parents' position but had to obey the laws of the State.

Marie and Gathie's parents instructed them not to salute the flag. But it was clearly not the parents' intention to prevent their children from attending school. Under the First Amendment, they believed they were allowed freedom to believe and practice the religion of their choosing. This, they believed, is the true intent of the "Free Exercise Clause" of the First Amendment. It was the school's position that because the children refused to pledge their allegiance to the flag, they could *not* attend public school.

With threats of being sent to criminal juvenile reform schools for their non-compliance, and threats to their parents for criminal prosecution for causing delinquency, Marie and Gathie's parents sued the West Virginia State Board of Education on their behalf on First Amendment rights to free speech and freedom of religion.

The US District Court for the Southern District of West Virginia ruled that the law was unconstitutional because it violated the First Amendment rights to the free exercise of religion and freedom of speech. The Board of Education exercised its right to appeal the decision to the US Supreme Court.

The US Supreme Court sided with Marie and Gathie Barnette and their parents. Justice Robert Jackson wrote the opinion for the majority of the court. Justice Jackson recognized that the nationalism expressed by the pledge of allegiance was an honored form of patriotism, much like our national anthem is now. Nevertheless, he was also aware of the atrocious acts in the name of "nationalism" taking place in Europe under Hitler at the same time. Masses of people were being annulated because of the biases of a few against certain heritage or religious beliefs. Expression of differences to patriotism could lead to one's death under Hitler's regime. Taking this into account, Justice Jackson expressed his chilling concerns about requiring unified patriotism. He said,

> Those who begin coercive elimination of dissent soon find themselves exterminating dissenters. Compulsory unification of opinion achieves only the unanimity of the graveyard.... [T]he Bill of Rights denies those in power any legal opportunity to coerce that consent.[74]

The opinion goes on to say that freedom will not disintegrate nationalism.

> To believe that patriotism will not flourish if patriotic ceremonies are voluntary and spontaneous, instead of a compulsory routine, is to make an unflattering estimate of the appeal of our institutions to free minds. We can have intellectual individualism.[75]

And finally, one of the most often quoted compliments to the First Amendment is the following from the US Supreme Court majority opinion in the *Barnette v. School Board of W.V.* case:

> If there is any fixed star in our constitutional constellation, it is that no official, high or petty, can prescribe what shall be orthodox in politics, nationalism, religion, or other matters of opinion, or force citizens to confess by word or act their faith therein.[76]

A string of cases followed, holding that religious teachings in public schools violates the Establishment Clause.

McCollum v. Board of Education (1948)[77]

In 1940, members of the Jewish, Roman Catholic, and Protestant faiths formed a voluntary association that they called "the Champaign Council on Religious Education" (The Association). The Association received permission from the Board of Education of Champaign, Illinois, to offer religious teaching to students in public schools. The Association employed religious teachers at their own expense. The religious teachings were conducted in the regular classrooms of the public school buildings. Students who did not choose to take the religious instruction were told to leave their classroom and go "some other place" in the school to continue with their regular curriculum.

The US Supreme Court held that it did not matter that more than one religion was represented. Personal beliefs were just that—personal to each individual—and religious teachings were simply forbidden in public schools under the First Amendment. The Court made the following findings: (1) the Protestant groups, being larger in number, obtained an "overshadowing advantage" to control and spread their message over other faiths; (2) the program was voluntary in name only—students faced subtle pressure to participate; and (3) the power given to the school superintendent and the "Council on Religion" to reject certain teachers and decide which faiths could participate was censorship.

The court opinion reads in part:

> This is beyond all question a utilization of the tax-established and tax-supported public school system to aid religious groups to spread their faith. And it falls squarely under the ban of the First Amendment. . . .
>
> Here not only are the State's tax-supported public school buildings used for the dissemination of religious doctrines. The State also affords sectarian groups an invaluable aid in that it helps to provide pupils for their religious classes through use of the State's compulsory public school machinery. This is not separation of Church and State.[78]

Engel v. Vitale (1962)[79]

Government officials of the State of New York's public school system composed a prayer that they recommended and published as a part of their "statement on Moral and Spiritual Training in the Schools." The prayer read as follows:

> Almighty God, we acknowledge our dependence upon Thee, and we beg Thy blessings upon us, our parents, our teachers and our Country.[80]

The State of New York recommended that each school district in New York adopt the prayer and have it recited at the commencement of each school day. The State officials defended the prayer because they viewed it as being only "non-denominational" in nature, which they claimed would not be objectionable to "all men and women of good will." They also defended the prayer because they only "recommended" saying it every day at the beginning of the school day—therefore it was only "voluntary."

The "non-denominational" prayer immediately outraged parents and students throughout New York. Soon a lawsuit against the school districts and New York officials was filed. The highest court in New York agreed to allow schools to recite the prayer. The case was then appealed to the US Supreme Court.

The parents who objected to the prayer did not object specifically to the words of the prayer. They simply believed in the freedom of religion and that religious activity such as this should not be incorporated into public schools. They had two specific legal arguments. One, the parents argued that it was a violation of the Establishment Clause, because the State provided the words to the prayer. And two, the prayer also violated the Free Exercise Clause because the students were subtly being coerced into a faith other than their own firmly held beliefs. They were required to stand and say the prayer, just stand silently, or, if the student refused to stand, would be singled out to leave the room while the prayer was being said. For many students, being singled out to leave the room while others stood and prayed was a bitter punishment for their non-belief.

The majority opinion of the US Supreme Court said that the fact that the prayer was meant to be "non-denominational" and only "voluntary" did not make it any less of a violation of the First Amendment's Establishment Clause. Moreover, it is not necessary to show that the government directly compelled students to pray for courts to find a violation of the Free Exercise Clause. Justice Black, writing for the majority, wrote:

> [T]he State's use of the Regents' prayer in its public school system breaches the constitutional wall of separation between Church and State. . . . We think that the constitutional prohibition against laws respecting an establishment of religion must at least mean that, in this country, it is no part of the business of government to compose official prayers for any group of the American people to recite as a part of a religious program carried on by government. . . .
>
> **When the power, prestige and financial support of government is placed behind a particular religious belief, the indirect coercive pressure upon religious minorities to conform to the prevailing officially approved religion is plain.**
>
> But the purposes underlying the Establishment Clause go much further than that. Its first and most immediate purpose rested on the belief that a union of government and religion tends to destroy government and to degrade religion. The history of governmentally established religion, both in England and in this country, showed that whenever government had allied itself with one particular form of religion, the inevitable result had been that it had incurred the hatred, disrespect and even contempt of those who held contrary

beliefs. That same history showed that many people had lost their respect for any religion that had relied upon the support of government to spread its faith. **The Establishment Clause thus stands as an expression of principle on the part of the Founders of our Constitution that religion is too personal, too sacred, too holy, to permit its "unhallowed perversion" by a civil magistrate.**

The judgment of the Court of Appeals of New York is reversed.[81] (Emphasis added.)

Santa Fe School District v. Doe (2000)[82]

In the year 2000, headlines read things like, "They Haven't Got a Prayer," and "The US Supreme Court Rules it's Illegal to Pray at School." But, headlines and the media sometimes distort much. Let's see if we can put the ruling in *Santa Fe School District v. Doe* (2000) in its proper perspective.

In Santa Fe, Texas, prior to 1995, students elected a student council "chaplain" who conducted a Christian prayer over the loudspeaker at every game of the Santa Fe High School varsity football team. Traditionally, the high school graduation also included a prayer from the podium.

At the 1994 graduation ceremony, the senior class president delivered this invocation:

> Please bow your heads.
> Dear heavenly Father, thank you for allowing us to gather here safely tonight. We thank you for the wonderful year you have allowed us to spend together as students of Santa Fe. We thank you for our teachers who have devoted many hours to each of us. Thank you, Lord, for our parents, and may each one receive the

special blessing. We pray also for a blessing and guidance as each student moves forward in the future. Lord, bless this ceremony and give us all a safe journey home. In Jesus's name we pray.[83]

The Santa Fe Independent School District had a population of approximately 4,000—overwhelmingly Southern Baptist. One Mormon parent and student, and one Catholic parent and student, brought a lawsuit under the Establishment Clause in the Federal District Court against the Santa Fe Independent School District in opposition to the practice of student-led prayer at the high school. They claimed that this official prayer violated the Establishment Clause of the First Amendment. They sued under the anonymous names as "Jane Does" to protect their families and the students from intimidation and harassment. The District Court recognized that many officials of the Santa Fe School District did not respect or honor the anonymity of these families and therefore issued the following order while the lawsuit was pending:

… ANYONE TAKING ANY ACTION ON SCHOOL PROPERTY, DURING SCHOOL HOURS, OR WITH SCHOOL RESOURCES OR APPROVAL FOR PURPOSES OF ATTEMPTING TO ELICIT THE NAMES OR IDENTITIES OF THE PLAINTIFFS IN THIS CAUSE OF ACTION, BY OR ON BEHALF OF ANY OF THESE INDIVIDUALS, WILL FACE THE HARSHEST POSSIBLE CONTEMPT SANCTIONS FROM THIS COURT, AND MAY ADDITIONALLY FACE CRIMINAL LIABILITY. (Emphasis in original Order of the Court.)[84]

In their complaint, the Jane Does alleged that the school district had engaged in "several proselytizing practices, such as promoting attendance at a Baptist revival meeting, encouraging membership in religious clubs, chastising children who held minority religious beliefs, and distributing Gideon Bibles on school premises."

While the lawsuit was pending, the school district changed its policy to allow the students (1) to vote by secret ballot to allow a pre-game ceremony invocation or message and an invocation at graduation; and (2) to vote by secret ballot what student from a list of volunteers should give the invocations.

The District Court ruled that the Establishment Clause was violated by both of these policies because public prayer at school is a Constitutional invasion of the freedoms of others. The school district appealed to the US Supreme Court, asking the High Court to decide this question: "whether petitioner's policy permitting student-led, student-initiated prayer at football games violates the Establishment Clause." (The school district apparently abandoned its argument in favor of prayer at graduation, based on the US Supreme Court's opinion in *Lee v. Weisman* (1992),[85] which held that prayer at a public school graduation violated the Establishment Clause.)

The US Supreme Court ruled six to three that the invocation policies of the Santa Fe School District did indeed violate the Establishment Clause. One of the main purposes of the Establishment Clause, the Court reasoned, was to protect a minority from a majority's attempts to convert people's religious beliefs. A vote of the *majority* of students to allow student-led prayer, to be led by a student who earned the *majority* of votes, by its very definition does not protect the *minority* of students who did not want to allow student-led prayer and were not of the same religious faith as the majority.

The ruling did not make student prayer at school "illegal," as some of the headlines of the day suggested. It simply held that prayer in public schools over a loud speaker at a ceremony or event that encourages, or even requires, student participation is a violation of the Establishment Clause.

> The delivery of a message such as the invocation here on school property, at school-sponsored events, over the school's public

address system, by a speaker representing the student body, under the supervision of school faculty, and pursuant to a school policy that explicitly and implicitly encourages public prayer-is not properly characterized as 'private' speech.[86]

The school district then argued that students are not "required" to attend football games or even graduation. But the Court's decision explained that while attendance at these events are not mandatory, they are important events for every high school student, and denying them access based on their religious choice is further proof of the Constitutional violations.

> The second part of the district's argument-that there is no coercion here because attendance at an extracurricular event, unlike a graduation ceremony, is voluntary—is unpersuasive. For some students, such as cheerleaders, members of the band, and the team members themselves, attendance at football games is mandated, sometimes for class credit. The district's argument also minimizes the immense social pressure, or truly genuine desire, felt by many students to be involved in the extracurricular event that is American high school football. The Constitution demands that schools not force on students the difficult choice between attending these games and avoiding personally offensive religious rituals.[87]

The Court then reiterated its long-held belief that the Free Exercise clause does not surpass the limits of the Establishment Clause,

> The principle that government may accommodate the free exercise of religion does not supersede the fundamental limitations imposed by the Establishment Clause. It is beyond dispute that, at a minimum, the Constitution guarantees that government

may not coerce anyone to support or participate in religion or its exercise, or otherwise act in a way which 'establishes a [state] religion or religious faith, or tends to do so. Id. at 587 (citations omitted) (quoting *Lynch v. Donnelly*, 465 U. S. 668, 678 (1984)).[88]

The Dissent

Chief Justice Rehnquist, joined by Justice Thomas and Justice Scalia, wrote the dissent:

> The [majority] Court distorts existing precedent to conclude that the school district's student-message program is invalid on its face under the Establishment Clause. But even more disturbing than its holding is the tone of the Court's opinion; it bristles with hostility to all things religious in public life. Neither the holding nor the tone of the opinion is faithful to the meaning of the Establishment Clause, when it is recalled that George Washington himself, at the request of the very Congress which passed the Bill of Rights, proclaimed a day of "public thanksgiving and prayer, to be observed by acknowledging with grateful hearts the many and signal favors of Almighty God."[89]

Both the majority holding and the dissent left the door open for the possibility of true "private" prayer in schools, also with the possibility of implementation of reasonable restrictions of any such organized "private" prayer. But as the lower court's initial order as well as the bickering tone of the dissent illustrate with crystal clarity, the potential for harassment, intimidation and coercion exist when there is a public display of personal privately held religious beliefs in public schools—a place where diversity is meant to be encouraged, not discouraged. As shown in all of the cases above, the wall between church and state is best left erect in public schools so that playgrounds do not become battlegrounds for religious persecution.

More to the Story . . .

What follows is a very tragic additional story that took place at the very same high school in Santa Fe, Texas, eighteen years later. On May 18, 2018, a gunman opened fire at Santa Fe High School, killing ten people—eight of them high school students—and injuring thirteen others. In the days following, the town did what it always did—it prayed together. Two weeks later, the First Baptist Church hosted the town's annual baccalaureate service for the high school's graduating seniors. About one hundred graduates attended. The school superintended was there. And the county's district attorney, who was responsible for prosecuting the suspected seventeen-year-old high school senior gunman, was also there. He spoke from the pulpit, where he said, "You are entering into a war zone, and it's a spiritual war zone . . . . And you are entering into an area where you will have to deal with—and you are already dealing with—the full effects of sin in our world."

Santa Fe High School did not sponsor the baccalaureate service and students were not compelled to attend; thus the service was within Constitutional boundaries.

Billy Graham Ministries came to Santa Fe and placed white crosses on the grounds—one for each student and teacher killed.*** One of the crosses was placed for Sabika Sheikh, a foreign exchange student from Pakistan killed in the shooting. Sabika was a Muslim. She was selected to attend high school in America for one year on an exchange study program established by Congress after the 9/11 attack to strengthen cultural ties with the Muslim world, called the Kennedy-Lugar Youth Exchange and Study Program.

Sabika did not choose Santa Fe High School. She was placed at this notably Southern Baptist public school to deliver a different message of love and peace. When Sabika was selected for the program to come to America—a land where she believed everything was possible—she said

---

*** There is no indication that the shooting was religiously motivated.

she wanted to show people that the vast majority of Pakistanis were not supporters of terrorism, that they were friendly and accommodating, and that there was nothing to fear about their Islamic faith. But she did not lead prayer over the loudspeaker at football games. She shared it one-on-one with Jaelyn Cogburn.

While at Santa Fe High, Sabika was known as smart, kind, tolerant, and a beautiful soul. Soon after her arrival, Sabika and Jaelyn became best friends. Sabika said she wanted the *real* American experience, so when she was invited to move into the Cogburn home with her best friend, Jaelyn, she jumped on it. Ms. Cogburn took them to the movies, high school football games, and high school plays. Sabika dressed up for Halloween, ate pizza, and snapped photos of her American experience. Sabika was described as a great student, making nearly perfect grades in physics, reading all the American classic novels, and writing a research paper on the #MeToo movement. She volunteered for community service at the library and a nursing home. She made a lot of friends at Santa Fe High School and was described as a "peacemaker," and the "Nelson Mandela" of the class.

While at the devout Christian Cogburn home, Sabika continued to roll out her prayer rug in the evenings, being sure to face toward Mecca, and recite her daily prayers from the Quran. Sabika also attended the non-denominational Christian church services with the Cogburns. She celebrated Christmas with her best friend's family. Sabika and Jaelyn shared on a very personal level about their religious beliefs and what that meant to them. Outside of school, Jaelyn told Sabika about the Bible and its teachings, while Sabika told Jaelyn about the Quran and its teachings. The two became inseparable, yet they kept their individual faith viewpoints without infringing upon one another's. They learned to respect one another's faith without trying to change each other. They found that they had more in common than anything different.

On May 12, 2018, Sabika and Jaelyn went to the prom. Sabika had never been to a dance before and loved it. The school year was about to end and Sabika was due to go home, but she never made it. Six days after the prom and just days before the end of the school term, on the morning May 18, 2018, a gunman came into Sabika's first-period art class just minutes after it began and starting shooting. Jaelyn and Sabika had arrived there together, but didn't share the same first-period class. When it was clear to Jaelyn what was happening, she searched for Sabika. Jaelyn's heart began to break the moment that she realized she would never see her friend alive again. A memorial service was held for Sabika at the Brand Lane Islamic Center near Houston, Texas. More than two thousand people were in attendance. Jaelyn told the crowd that Sabika was "loyal to her faith and her country. She loved her family, and she couldn't wait to see them. She was the most amazing person I've ever met. I will always miss her."[90]

After the shooting and the death of their daughter, the white cross, placed at Santa Fe High for Sabika, did little to comfort her family in Pakistan, who had to mourn their daughter's death from afar. It is heartbreaking irony that Sabika was sent to a predominantly Christian community to demonstrate that there is nothing to fear from Muslims, yet she had everything to fear. Let's make sure that her story is retold again and again—not for the violence, but to honor her message of acceptance, friendship, and faith.

After the shooting, Jaelyn decided to leave Texas to attend high school in Belize as an exchange student, an inspiration that she says came from the God of her understanding. There, she wrote a poem about her best friend Sabika:

I'm an American girl in Belize living her life alone.
You've never seen me. I'm unheard of and unknown.
I swear I've never been closer to a person. Nor will I ever be.
She was like an angel sent from God and came to set me free.
A boy went to school with a gun in his hand.

He started shooting. And I just ran.
I know what it's like to hurt, to have pain, to gain, to lose.
I know what it's like to live when death has come so close.

Jaelyn and Sabika on Snapchat, 2017

Fig. 3 Photo courtesy of Cogburn Family

Jaelyn and Sabika ready for the prom, May 12, 2018

Fig. 4 Photo courtesy of Cogburn Family

Kennedy v. Bremerton School District (2022)[91]

As many of the US Supreme Court justices have said throughout history, from Justice Black to Justices Stevens, Ginsburg, Breyer, Sotomayor, and others, personal spiritual beliefs must sometimes give way to others' beliefs if we are to truly give credence to our collective value of being "One Nation under God," remaining faithful not to one God; but rather to One Nation, under whatever God we believe in, or none at all. To hold to that ideal, the government, in whatever form, must remain neutral. It cannot give preference to one religion, or the "God" of one understanding. It cannot establish religion, nor prohibit the free exercise of ALL religions. This case asks: *can we truly be free to practice our individual religious faiths, whatever they are without government intrusion?*

You might already be familiar with this case, or have had a similar experience at your high school—the football coach leading the team in prayer. A football coach in Bremerton, Washington, claims he was "fired" because he engaged in private prayer at football games. The Bremerton School District first counseled Coach Kennedy not to give locker room talks that were religiously related and not to pray at the fifty-yard line immediately after the game concluded while he was still on duty. The school district cautioned him that this could be viewed as an endorsement of a particular religious belief at a public school, and therefore a violation of the Establishment Clause, exposing the district to a potential lawsuit.

Coach Kennedy would not comply with the school district's request. Instead, he rallied the media to support his "religious freedom." He was placed on administrative leave and given a poor performance evaluation because he refused to comply with the district's request that he simply pray in private instead of involving the students. After further noncompliance, the school district eventually declined to renew Coach Kennedy's contract. He then sued the school district, seeking exemplary damages, for violating his rights and "discriminating" against him on the basis of his religious leanings.

The Federal District Court held that his suspension was justified because he put the school district at risk for liability under the Establishment Clause. The lower Federal District court relied on *Garcetti v. Ceballos* (2006),[92] which held that speech by a government employee is government speech when it is made "pursuant to [the employee's] official duties." As the high school coach, Kennedy was conducting prayer in his official duties because he was still in uniform after the games. He was there to assist his team, respond to parents and the public as the coach, and was required to remain on the field until all of the players and attendees had left. The US Court of Appeals for the Ninth Circuit affirmed. Coach Kennedy then appealed to the US Supreme Court.

The majority on the US Supreme Court disagreed with the lower courts' rulings and the school district's decision to reprimand Coach

Kennedy. These are the facts of the case according to the majority opinion delivered by Justice Gorsuch:

> Joseph Kennedy lost his job as a high school football coach because he knelt at midfield after games to offer a quiet prayer of thanks. Mr. Kennedy prayed during a period when school employees were free to speak with a friend, call for a reservation at a restaurant, check email, or attend to other personal matters. He offered his prayers quietly while his students were otherwise occupied. Still, the Bremerton School District disciplined him anyway. It did so because it thought anything less could lead a reasonable observer to conclude (mistakenly) that it endorsed Mr. Kennedy's religious beliefs. That reasoning was misguided. Both the Free Exercise and Free Speech Clauses of the First Amendment protect expressions like Mr. Kennedy's. Nor does a proper understanding of the Amendment's Establishment Clause require the government to single out private religious speech for special disfavor. The Constitution and the best of our traditions counsel mutual respect and tolerance, not censorship and suppression, for religious and nonreligious views alike.[93]

And now, here is a portion of the facts reconstructed in Justice Sotomayor's dissent, joined by Justices Breyer and Kagan:

> To the degree the Court portrays petitioner Joseph Kennedy's prayers as private and quiet, it misconstrues the facts. The record reveals that Kennedy had a longstanding practice of conducting demonstrative prayers on the fifty-yard-line of the football field. Kennedy consistently invited others to join his prayers and for years led student athletes in prayer at the same time and location. The Court ignores this history. The Court also ignores the severe disruption to school events caused by Kennedy's conduct, viewing

it as irrelevant.... As the majority tells it, Kennedy, a coach for the district's football program, 'lost his job' for 'pray[ing] quietly while his students were otherwise occupied.' The record before us, however, tells a different story...."[94]

Richard B. Katskee is a lawyer for Americans United for Separation of Church and State. He argued for the school district in support of the decision to discipline Coach Kennedy. In his argument to the justices of the Supreme Court he said, "No one doubts that public school employees can have quiet prayers by themselves at work even if students can see." But, Katskee said, that is not what Kennedy had engaged in. Instead, Katskee argued, Kennedy "insisted on audible prayers at the fifty-yard line with students.... (and) announced in the press that those prayers are how he helps these kids be better people."

To Katskee, the coach could just as easily have prayed quietly to himself alone on his way home after the game, without influencing or involving students.

Justice Sotomayor's dissent compiles a complete review of the evidence. This work is painstaking. Remember that no new evidence is admitted on an appeal. The evidence in these cases literally arrives in a box from the initial trial court. It is up to the reviewer to comb through the many documents, including prior testimony, through transcripts, and all of the other evidence submitted at trial, to reveal the true factual story. This evidence is, of course, available for review by all of the justices and their clerks. They are not allowed, however, to support their review by obtaining information outside of the trial court's record. If they had been allowed, a simple web image search would have revealed photographs of many of the instances Coach Kennedy conducted "quiet private prayer."

Nevertheless, Justice Sotomayor's dissent *did* include photographs from the trial court's pile of evidence. The following three photographs appear in Justice Sotomayor's dissent to demonstrate that Coach

Kennedy's representation of "quiet private prayer" is a misrepresentation of the facts.

Photograph of J. Kennedy standing in group of kneeling players.
SOTOMAYOR, J. dissenting 597 US ___ (2022)

Photograph of J. Kennedy in prayer circle (Oct. 26, 2015).
SOTOMAYOR, J. dissenting 597 US ___ (2022)

THE ESTABLISHMENT CLAUSE AND FREEDOM OF RELIGION   91

Photograph of J. Kennedy in prayer circle (Oct. 16, 2015).
SOTOMAYOR, J. dissenting 597 US ___ (2022)

The media attention did nothing to promote Coach Kennedy's stated cause. It only brought attention to the division caused by public display of personally held beliefs. After Coach Kennedy's portrayal of a lack of religious tolerance at Bremerton High School, a Satanist group came to a Bremerton High School football game. The group showed up to the game wearing Satanic horns and emblems to demonstrate that they too have been persecuted and that they too should be allowed to demonstrate their religious beliefs on the football field during the post-game events. Parents and students were now in the middle of a religious disagreement and upheaval that need not occur on public school grounds.[95]

The following short piece of Justice Sotomayor's dissent explains the chaos that began with Coach Kennedy's call for media attention,

> On October 16, after playing of the game had concluded, Kennedy shook hands with the opposing team, and as advertised, knelt to pray while most BHS players were singing the school's fight song. He quickly was joined by coaches and players from the opposing team. Television news cameras surrounded the group. Members

of the public rushed the field to join Kennedy, jumping fences to access the field and knocking over student band members. After the game, the district received calls from Satanists who 'intended to conduct ceremonies on the field after football games if others were allowed to.' To secure the field and enable subsequent games to continue safely, the district was forced to make security arrangements with the local police and to post signs near the field and place robocalls to parents reiterating that the field was not open to the public.[96]

Attorney Katskee believed this event was disruptive enough to demonstrate the inappropriateness of Coach Kennedy's actions. Katskee argued at the hearing before the US Supreme Court that Coach Kennedy was not being singled out because of his religious beliefs; he was simply being required to be faithful to his obligations under his employment and the Establishment Clause as a government employee at a public school.

But the majority of the Supreme Court saw the school district's actions as inhibiting Coach Kennedy's freedom of religion. The Court instructs school districts and lower courts to now apply a "history and traditions" test to determine an Establishment Clause versus Free Exercise challenge. The exact meaning of that test is yet to be determined. However, Justice Sotomayor's dissent attacks the "history and traditions" test because school administrators would find it impossible to apply.

As to the history and traditions of the Establishment Clause, we need look no further than *Everson v. Bd. of Ed. of Ewing* (1947) (reviewed below). The reason that the Establishment Clause appears as the very first clause of the First Amendment is to protect an individual's freedom from government established religious teachings. In 1947, the US Supreme Court stated, "A large proportion of the early settlers of this country came here from Europe to escape the bondage of laws which compelled them to support and attend government-favored churches...."⁹⁷ So it is difficult to reconcile the majority holding even with its own test. The only answer to this radical change of heart of the Supreme Court seems to be its current make up of conservative justices.

Justice Sotomayor's dissent is filled with frustration. What really seems to upset her about the majority opinion is that it is all about the "rights" of one person—a government school employee—whereas the rights of the *students* are not prioritized in the majority opinion. Earlier cases which held that religious prayer had no place in public schools focused on each individual *student's* religious freedom.

Although coercion is still an important factor to consider, the majority found that because Coach Kennedy prayed *after* the games, the students were not coerced into joining him. And that those who did join him in prayer did so of their own free will. But the dissent sees Coach Kennedy's actions as a means of subtly pressuring students to pray alongside him. A player who would not participate is excluded from the camaraderie of the team, said the dissent, which is subtle coercion. The dissent points out that indirect and subtle coercion is still coercion. Justice Sotomayor's dissent concludes:

> ...Today's decision is particularly misguided because it elevates the religious rights of a school official, who voluntarily accepted public employment and the limits that public employment entails, over those of his students, who are required to attend school and who this Court has long recognized are particularly vulnerable and deserving of protection. In doing so, the Court sets us further down a perilous path in forcing States to entangle themselves with religion, with all of our rights hanging in the balance. As much as the Court protests otherwise, today's decision is no victory for religious liberty. I respectfully dissent.[98]

More to the Story

But that's not the end of the story. The relevant facts of this case took place in 2015. The US Supreme Court's decision was not handed down until 2022. That means that seven years went by as Kennedy continued to "fight to get his job back." In the meantime, he moved to Florida, wrote a book, appeared and spoke at a Trump rally, and reportedly was asked by Republican Florida Governor Ronald DeSantis to assist in his 2024 presidential election campaign, which Kennedy allegedly declined, stating he was loyal to Trump.

And in 2022, the Bremerton School District rehired Coach Kennedy as assistant coach and approved a settlement of the case to him of nearly $2 million. He accepted. He appeared at the first game of the 2022 season at Bremerton High School. After the game, he was observed walking to the fifty yard line and knelt for approximately ten seconds. No one joined him. Kennedy then quit and did not return to Bremerton High School again.

Consider this:

Does belief in science mean we must abandon all faith in religion or spiritual beliefs? And does religion obligate one to deny scientific advancements? Or can the two coexist, as they do for the science teacher Ms. Epperson?

Do you think it is possible that through that comingling of science and faith we can rid ourselves of famine, disease, and war?

Is there a place for true private prayer at public school?

We hope to trust our teachers and government employees, including the judges and justices of our courts, to leave behind their biases, prejudices, and preferences and to treat everyone as equals, especially in this highly sensitive area of religious preferences. Do you think the US Supreme Court is leading us to one national religion? If so, why? If not, why? Do you think the existence of one national religion would be dangerous to democracy?

Recall that NFL player Colin Kaepernick knelt in support of Black Lives Matter as a form of peaceful protest in 2016. Do you see the *Barnette v. West Virginia* case as similar or different? Why or why not? Do you see the *Kennedy v. Bremerton* case as similar or different? Why or why not? Does the fact that the NFL is a private entity support your position?

Do you believe that nationalism, patriotism, and religion are one and the same?

Do you think the outcome of the *Kennedy v. Bremerton* case would be the same if the coach led the students in a Buddhist chant, Muslim prayer, or Satanic ritual?

This nation's history and origin is predominantly some form of Christianity, which still holds true today.**** However, interestingly, about three in ten adults in the United States report that they are now religiously unaffiliated.[99] Rather than being "One Nation under God," are we now becoming one nation losing faith? Or does this case suggest our highest court would prefer a return to a belief in one Christian religion, rather than one nation for all?

A Gallup poll found the majority of individuals in America are not affiliated with a church or churches for the first time since these statistics have been recorded.[100] Do you think this fact is due to a lack of religious teaching or too much religious preaching?

"Political freedom cannot exist in any land where religion controls the state, and religious freedom cannot exist in any land where the state controls religion." SEN. SAM J. ERVIN JR.

**** In research conducted in 2021, it was estimated that 63 percent of the 330 million people in the United States are some form of Christian faith.

CHAPTER 6
The Establishment Clause and Freedom of Religion

Public Funding of Private Schools and the Establishment Clause

Understanding The Separation Between Church and State (PART II)

To provide freedom of religion beyond the constraints of government, religious organizations do not pay taxes, and the IRS may not review their bookkeeping records. On the other hand, under the Establishment Clause, taxpayers are also not required to support religious organizations. After *Brown v. Board of Education* (1954)[101] (reviewed below under the discussion of the Fourteenth Amendment) every child is entitled to a free and equal *public* education in the United States. Every child is *not*, however, entitled to free religious education under the Establishment Clause of the First Amendment. Just as prayer in public schools is a violation of the Establishment Clause, funding to religious schools is a violation of the Establishment Clause, as well.

Everson v. Board of Education of Ewing (1947)[102]

This case examines whether or not state taxes that assist private religious schools assist in the "establishment" of religion. Parents received refunds from the State of New Jersey for the cost of busing children to and from both private and public schools. Ninety-six percent of the children in a particular school district in New Jersey attended Catholic school. Taxpayers sued the State under the Establishment Clause of the First Amendment. They argued that the taxes they paid were going to the Catholic Church and, therefore, contributed to the establishment of the Catholic Church.

The US Supreme Court looked at the equities being served and held that reimbursement to the parents for busing was for a public purpose and did not violate the Establishment Clause. The Court reasoned that all parents of all religions, or of none, equally benefited. But the opinion in this case is very cautious and sought to limit the reach of their decision rather than broaden it. To emphasize the concern of allowing the government to assist religious instruction, the Court explains in vivid detail why the "anti-establishment" of religion was so important to early Americans.

> A large proportion of the early settlers of this country came here from Europe to escape the bondage of laws which compelled them to support and attend government-favored churches.
>
> The centuries immediately before and contemporaneous with the colonization of America had been filled with turmoil, civil strife and persecutions, generated in large part by established sects determined to maintain their absolute political and religious supremacy.... In efforts to force loyalty to whatever religious group happened to be on top and in league with the government of a particular time and place, men and women had been fined,

cast in jail, cruelly tortured, and killed. Among the offenses for which these punishments had been inflicted were such things as speaking disrespectfully of the views of ministers of government-established churches, non-attendance at those churches, expressions of nonbelief in their doctrines, and failure to pay taxes and tithes to support them.

These practices became so commonplace [prior to the restrictions of the Bill of Rights] as to shock the freedom-loving colonials into a feeling of abhorrence....

The people there, as elsewhere, reached the conviction that individual religious liberty could be achieved best under a government which was stripped of all power to tax, to support, or otherwise to assist any or all religions, or to interfere with the beliefs of any religious individual or group.[103]

The court then stated unequivocally and without dissent:

No tax in any amount, large or small, can be levied to support any religious activities or institutions, whatever they may be called, or whatever form they may adopt to teach or practice religion. (*Reynolds v. US* (1878).)[104]

Lemon v. Kurtzman (1971)[105]

In 1971, Pennsylvania and Rhode Island enacted statutes that provided monetary benefits to non-public schools, including church-related elementary and secondary schools. Both state statutes were meant to provide only enough assistance to religious institutions to put them on an even keel with public schools and no more. But state residents filed lawsuits to block the statues as being a violation of the Establishment Clause.

The US Supreme Court held that financial assistance provided to parochial schools violated the Establishment Clause. But the Court recognized that there was "some play in the joints" where a benefit might be allowed under the Establishment Clause if it was universal. The Court's decision in this case established the three-part *"Lemon Test"* to define when the government's assistance would not violate the Establishment Clause.

Under the *Lemon Test*, government action that incidentally assists religion is not a constitutional violation if it (1) has a secular (non-religious) purpose; (2) the principle or primary effect of the statute, or government action, does not advance or inhibit religion; and (3) the statute or government action does not result in "excessive government entanglement" with religion. If any of these prongs are violated, the statute or government action is unconstitutional and a violation of the Establishment Clause.

The Court explained the third prong of "excessive government entanglement." The majority felt that providing financial aid to parochial schools is not only objectionable to non-believers, but would be objectionable to believers as well when financial aid requires government oversight. The choice of religious teachings would be left up to the government. Similarly, the choice in textbooks, expenditures, teachers, would now be in the hands of the government. In the concurring opinion Justice Brennan, Jr. wrote:

> . . . [G]overnment and religion have discrete interests which are mutually best served when each avoids too close a proximity to the other. It is not only the nonbeliever who fears the injection of sectarian doctrines and controversies into the civil polity, but, in as high degree, it is the devout believer who fears the secularization of a creed which becomes too deeply involved with and dependent upon the government.

... At some point, the school becomes 'public' for more purposes than the Church could wish. At that point, the Church may justifiably feel that its victory on the Establishment Clause has meant abandonment of the Free Exercise Clause.[106]

Although the *Lemon Test* has been applied in many Establishment Clause cases since then, it is also continuously criticized. Many legal scholars believe that the application of the *Lemon Test* has created a rule where the Establishment Clause obliterates the Free Exercise Clause instead of defining the line between the two. In some cases, the Supreme Court continues to recognize some "play in the joints" between the Establishment Clause and the Free Exercise Clause. This allowed states to permit some financial aid to private schools so long as the benefit is not 'religious' aid.

Zelman v. Simmons-Harris (2002)[107]

The start of something BIG: In 2002, Chief Justice Rehnquist wrote the majority opinion in *Zelman v. Simmons-Harris.* The US Supreme Court was almost evenly divided in this case, voting 5-4 to allow a school voucher program in Ohio to include religious schools. Justices O'Connor, Scalia, Kennedy, and Thomas joined Justice Rehnquist in his majority decision. Justices Stevens, Souter, Ginsburg, and Breyer joined in a dissent.

Cleveland, Ohio, was facing a major crisis in education. The students were dropping out or failing out before reaching their senior year in high school at an "unprecedented" rate. The US Supreme Court found that, "Of those students who managed to reach their senior year, one of every four still failed to graduate. Of those students who did graduate, few could read, write, or compute at levels comparable to their counterparts in other cities."[108] The majority of students were from low-income and minority families. Most did not have the means to afford private schooling.

To address the problem, Ohio developed a pilot voucher program for the 1999-2000 school year in Cleveland. Any private school, whether religious or non-religious, could participate in the program so long as the school met educational standards. Eligibility for the program was first based on need. The eligible families would receive a "voucher" and were able to choose which participating school the student would attend. The program was meant to enhance the educational options by providing a variety of participating schools.

Taxpayers, including Simmons-Harris, argued it was unconstitutional under the Establishment Clause. They criticized the voucher system, concerned that the majority of this huge tax expense was going to religious institutions. But Zelman, the superintendent of instruction in Ohio, argued that because of the educational crises, the Ohio program was constitutional because it was a neutral program that offered private choice to parents—the funds did not go directly to religious institutions.

Although the Supreme Court was nearly evenly divided, in the end, the majority found that Ohio's program passed the constitutional objection. The majority opinion said,

> "In sum, the Ohio program is entirely neutral with respect to religion. It provides benefits directly to a wide spectrum of individuals, defined only by financial need and residence in a particular school district. It permits such individuals to exercise genuine choice among options public and private, secular and religious. The program is therefore a program of true private choice."[109]

Justice Souter wrote one of the dissents, joined by Justices Stevens, Ginsburg, and Breyer. Justice Stevens wrote an additional dissent. He believed that the effect of providing a massive amount of money to religions for educational purposes would advance religion. He was also concerned that it was not a true "neutral program" with "true private choice" and that the amount that was provided through the vouchers only assisted a small percentage of people whose children already attended established religious private schools. To back this, he cited the number of students using the vouchers during the test period. Only 5 percent chose to use the vouchers, and of that five percent, 96 percent used the vouchers at private religious schools in the 1999-2000 year pilot program.

While everyone clearly sees the need and wants the students of Cleveland, Ohio, to succeed, Justice Steven's dissent seems to ask: Why can't the money used for the voucher system instead be used to improve the public school system? And, once again, he articulates the dangers of providing public funds for religious instruction and denounces Ohio's voucher program as a violation of the Establishment Clause.

Justice Stevens points out that if only 5 percent of the students in the selected district used the vouchers, the other 95 percent of students were not being assisted. "The solution to the disastrous conditions that prevented over 90 percent of the student body from meeting basic proficiency standards obviously required massive improvements unrelated to the voucher program." Next, the voucher program "may have given some families a powerful motivation to leave the public school system and accept religious indoctrination that they would otherwise have avoided . . ." thus *establishing* religion.

And he points out that whether parochial education is voluntary or not, the State is still required to provide a *public* education, which the voucher program is not supporting. Justice Stevens' dissent reads in conclusion:

> The Court seems to have decided that the mere fact that a family that cannot afford a private education wants its children educated

in a parochial school is sufficient justification for this use of public funds.

... I am convinced that the Court's decision is profoundly misguided. Admittedly, in reaching that conclusion I have been influenced by my understanding of the impact of religious strife on the decisions of our forebears to migrate to this continent, and on the decisions of neighbors in the Balkans, Northern Ireland, and the Middle East to mistrust one another. Whenever we remove a brick from the wall that was designed to separate religion and government, we increase the risk of religious strife and weaken the foundation of our democracy.[110]

AND NOW . . .

This year, 2023, Cleveland, Ohio, still has the voucher program. And . . . it is still being litigated. This time, by public school districts and public school advocates. The voucher program was expanded in the years since *Zelman v. Simmons-Harris* was decided. The program is no longer based on low-income status. It is now a statewide program, which allows all families, regardless of income, to apply for scholarships for more than $8,000 per student. Every student in the State of Ohio can be subsidized by the State to attend religious schools. Parochial schools are at an advantage because many have already been in existence for some time. They also have the additional backing of their congregations. Yet, the congregations do not pay taxes, nor are they required to submit to public oversight. Teachers and public school districts claim that the voucher system is depleting Ohio's public funds that should be available to the public school system. Nearly one-third of all the public school districts (approximately 250 public schools, meaning about 230,000 public school students) in Ohio have now joined the lawsuit against the State.

The public school districts claim that the voucher system violates the Ohio State Constitution, which states that "The General Assembly shall make such provisions, by taxation, or otherwise, [which] will secure a thorough and efficient system of common schools throughout the State; but no religious or other sect, or sects, shall ever have any exclusive right to, or control of, any part of the school funds of this State."

The lawsuit *Columbus City School Dist. v. Ohio*, filed in the Court of Common Pleas, Franklin Ohio, alleges that the voucher program cripples public school districts' resources by taking hundreds of millions of dollars of taxpayer money into private, mostly religious, institutions. The school districts allege that the result discriminates against minority students and increases segregation in Ohio's public schools.

The complaint alleges that in some school districts, private schools receive more state funding through vouchers from the few students that use them than an entire school district receives for all of its public school students. The numbers are staggering. It is alleged that 23,500 vouchers were issued in 2019 at a cost to the State of Ohio of 113 million dollars. 30,000 vouchers were issued in 2020 at a cost of 149 million dollars. And 32,600 vouchers were issued in 2021 at a cost of 163 million dollars.

Mark Wallach, lead attorney for the public school districts, teachers, and students said, "Public school students are increasingly faced with overcrowded facilities, inadequate materials, and insufficient learning support. Private schools, in contrast, receive a disproportionate share of Ohio's public tax dollars, allowing them to expand, build, and grow, while eluding any accountability for how they spend taxpayer dollars.* This diversion of funds to EdChoice causes the most harm to the most vulnerable students, including minority children, disabled pupils, and those from less affluent communities."

---

* Trial is set in the matter (Columbus City School District vs. State of Ohio, Case No. 22 CV-000067) for November 2024. No doubt it will be a case that many states and many school districts, as well as private schools, will be watching closely.

Many of the private schools receiving the vouchers, including religious schools, are allowed to discriminate. Private schools are not required to enroll students with disabilities—physical, mental, or emotional disabilities. On the other hand, public schools are required to enroll all children throughout the state. The cost to teach children with handicaps, whether those are physical, mental, or emotional, are much greater than for the average student. This leaves a population in the public schools of students with greater challenges. The result is that education becomes economically, intellectually, and behaviorally divided.

Dan Heintz, an Ohio public schoolteacher and elected member of the Cleveland Heights-University Heights Board, estimates that the state spends around $3,000 to educate a student in his school district. But through the new voucher program, the state will spend $8,400 to educate the same student. He believes that families earning $30,000 a year should not be required to subsidize private school tuition for families earning ten times that. Although public education is meant to be free, and free from political and religious overtones, more money is spent on each student to attend private, mostly religious, schools. The more money spent on each student to attend private schools; the less money spent on public education.

Espinoza v. Montana Department of Revenue (2020)[111]

Parents of students attending a private Christian school brought this lawsuit against the State of Montana. The parents here claimed that their faith dictates that their children *must* be educated at a Christian school. A tax credit program gave scholarships to a few students. Ninety-four percent of the program's few scholarship students attended religious private schools. The Montana tax board wanted the program reviewed to determine whether the program violated Montana's

Constitution, which forbids public money assistance to any church or religious school.

The Montana State Supreme Court first decided the case. It held that the tax credit program violated the Montana State constitution. The Montana State Supreme Court ordered the entire scholarship program to be abolished. The parents of students attending a Christian school claimed that the Montana Supreme Court violated their First Amendment right to free exercise of religion. In other words, when the faith-based students' benefit was taken away, they filed a lawsuit claiming that their faith was impinged now that they would not receive the aid.

The US Supreme Court (nearly split 5-4) held that Montana's prohibition of this aid to private religious schools is unconstitutional under the Free Exercise Clause. Justice Ginsburg's dissent, joined by Justices Breyer, Kegan, and Sotomayor, says that the Free Exercise Clause requires that *no burden* be placed on the free exercise of religion; but it does not require *benefits* to exercise religious choice. Justice Ginsberg explains that these parents were not being required to give up their faith, nor were they required to send their children to non-parochial schools—they were simply not given any additional funding to do so at the state's expense. Her dissent reads, in part:

> Recall that the Montana court remedied the state constitutional violation by striking the scholarship program in its entirety. Under that decree, secular and sectarian schools alike are ineligible for benefits, so the decision cannot be said to entail differential treatment based on petitioners' religion. Put somewhat differently, petitioners argue that the Free Exercise Clause requires a State to treat institutions and people neutrally when doling out a benefit—and neutrally is how Montana treats them in the wake of the state court's decision.

Accordingly, the Montana Supreme Court's decision does not place a burden on petitioners' religious exercise. Petitioners may still send their children to a religious school. And the Montana Supreme Court's decision does not pressure them to do otherwise.[112]

Carson v. Makin (2022)[113]

Again, this lawsuit was brought by parents (petitioners) whose child was denied the tuition to attend religious school under Maine's constitution, which explicitly prohibits state tax dollars to benefit religions. The US Supreme Court saw it as a Free Exercise Clause case and not an Establishment Clause case. The majority held that Maine's constitutional resistance to supporting sectarian schools discriminates *against* religion and is unconstitutional under the Free Exercise Clause.

Justice Breyer's dissent, and even some of his questions during oral argument, recognized many of the problems that may come with the majority's holding. He explained that some (maybe most) religions are inherently biased. In his dissent he said:

> This potential for religious strife is still with us. We are today a nation with well over one hundred different religious groups, from Free Will Baptist to African Methodist, Buddhist to Humanist. (citation omitted.) People in our country adhere to a vast array of beliefs, ideals, and philosophies. And with greater religious diversity comes greater risk of religiously based strife, conflict, and social division. The Religion Clauses were written in part to help avoid that disunion. As Thomas Jefferson, one of the leading drafters and proponents of those Clauses, wrote, 'to compel a man to furnish contributions of money for the propagation of opinions which he disbelieves, is sinful and tyrannical.'[114]

Consider This:

In *Brown v. Board of Education*[115] (reviewed below under the Fourteenth Amendment), our public education shall not be segregated or divided. That means that our free education shall not be divided on religious grounds as well as on racial grounds. The use of public funds in private schools has spawned a lot of debate. The executive secretary of the Detroit branch of the NAACP, William H. Penn Sr., criticized what he calls "parochiaid" (meaning public taxpayer assistance to private religious education) for promoting segregation of Black children and disadvantaging the poor. "In part, this is a deliberate attempt to provide an escape for those who are fleeing the inner-city in an effort to avoid integration. . . . The key question is 'how can Government prohibit racial segregation in public schools and then foster private schools which are nothing more than segregated institutions?'"

Do you agree that voucher programs contribute to re-segregation? If so, do you believe it separates us along just along racial lines or along religious and economic lines as well? Why? Or why not?

Recent research suggests that states' economies improve as a state improves its financial support to public education in K-12 grades.[116]

Do you agree with this conclusion?

ADDITIONAL RESOURCES

Chapters 5 and 6—Separation of Church and State

- Join the discussion of religious liberty. We Dissent (www.We-dissent.org) is a monthly podcast hosted by secular women who are also attorneys at major organizations in the United States. They discuss religious liberty in federal and state courts and their work to keep government and religion separate.
- Research your rights at the US Department of Education "Guidance on Constitutionally Protected Prayer and Religious Expression in Public Elementary and Secondary Schools," May 15, 2023.
- If you live in the State of Ohio, research "Vouchers Hurt Ohio." (www.vouchershurtohio.com)
- If you live in any one of the other forty-nine states, research funding for both private and public schools in your state.
- If you are of voting age, consider the long-term effect of passage of voucher programs or other state supported private schools and vote accordingly.

"Believing with you that religion is a matter which lies solely between Man & his God, that he owes account to none other for his faith or his worship, that the legitimate powers of government reach actions only, & not opinions, I contemplate with sovereign reverence that act of the whole American people which declared that their legislature should 'make no law respecting an establishment of religion or prohibiting the free exercise thereof,' thus building a wall of separation between church and State." THOMAS JEFFERSON

CHAPTER 7

The First Amendment: The Right to Assemble Peacefully

*"***Congress shall make no law** *respecting an establishment of religion, or prohibiting the free exercise thereof; or* **abridging the freedom** *of speech, or of the press; or* **the right of the people peaceably to assemble**; *and to petition the Government for a redress of grievances." (Ratified December 1791)*

Have you ever attended a free music festival? Or a parade? Or maybe a holiday celebration in the community park? A rally, a walk-a-thon, or a march for a cause? Most of us, at one time or another, have gathered with like-minded people for a cause or just a get-together on public property. If so, you have been exercising your First Amendment right to peaceably assemble. You largely owe this right to one member of the Communist Party and to an abundance of Civil Rights activists of the 1960s, and as a result of the Civil Rights Act of 1964.

DeJong v. Oregon (1937)[117]

In 1934, Dirk DeJong was arrested for speaking about communist ideas to a group of 150 to 300 people in Portland, Oregon. It appears that all that DeJong did was speak to a public group. He did not advocate violence, nor promote illegal activity. He spoke to protest recent police brutality in confrontations with striking union workers and jail conditions. Police raided the meeting during his speech and he was arrested. He was convicted under a State statute making "criminal syndicalism" illegal, which was defined as anything that *"advocates crime, physical violence, sabotage, or any unlawful acts or methods as a means of accomplishing or effecting industrial or political change or revolution."* DeJong was sentenced to seven years in jail for assisting in conducting the public meeting.

While this case also contains an element of Free Speech, the focus of the decision rested on the right to assemble. The US Supreme Court held that the State statute was unconstitutional because it denied citizens the right to peaceably assemble, which is a First Amendment right. This was the first case to apply the right to assemble to the states under the Fourteenth Amendment. (The Fourteenth Amendment "incorporates" all the freedoms of the Bill of Rights to the individual states by providing all citizens with due process and equal protections under the laws.) A huge victory for parades, music festivals, and, of course, protests.

Edwards v. South Carolina (1963)[118]

One morning in the spring of 1961, 187 Black high school and college students met at the Zion Baptist Church in Columbia, South Carolina. At about noon they began to walk in groups of about fifteen to the State Capitol grounds. Each group carried signs saying, "I am proud to be a Negro," and "Down with segregation." The state grounds encompass an area of two blocks. The area is open to the public. Their stated purpose was "to submit a protest to the citizens of South Carolina, along with the Legislative Bodies of South Carolina, our feelings and our dissatisfaction with the present condition of discriminatory actions against Negroes in general, and to let them know that we were dissatisfied, and that we would like for the laws which prohibited Negro privileges in this State to be removed."

Police officers were already present because they had advance knowledge of the students' planned protest. Police told the students that they "had a right, as citizen(s), to go through the State House grounds, as any other citizen has, as long as they were peaceful."

The protestors walked through the state grounds for about forty-five minutes. A group of onlookers of about 200 to 300 people formed on the sidewalk. But there was no evidence of any hostility from either the onlookers or the protestors. Neither pedestrians nor vehicles were obstructed by the march.

Nevertheless, police told the protestors that they would be arrested if they did not disperse within fifteen minutes. Instead of dispersing, the protestors began to sing loudly. They sang "The Star Spangled Banner" and other patriotic and religious songs, while stamping their feet and clapping their hands. After the fifteen minutes had passed, the police arrested the protestors and marched them off to jail. The State trial court convicted each of the protestors of "breach of the peace" and imposed sentences ranging from a $10 fine or five days in jail to a $100 fine or thirty days in jail. In affirming the judgments, the Supreme Court of South Carolina said that, under state law, the offense of breach of the peace "is not susceptible of exact definition," but provided the following general definition:

> In general terms, a breach of the peace is a violation of public order, a disturbance of the public tranquility, by any act or conduct inciting to violence.... it includes any violation of any law enacted to preserve peace and good order. It may consist of an act of violence or an act likely to produce violence. It is not necessary that the peace be actually broken to lay the foundation for a prosecution for this offense. If what is done is unjustifiable and

unlawful, tending with sufficient directness to break the peace, no more is required. Nor is actual personal violence an essential element in the offense. . . .[119]

The protestors appealed the decision to the US Supreme Court and Justice Stewart wrote the majority opinion, which said in part:

> These petitioners were convicted of an offense so generalized as to be, in the words of the South Carolina Supreme Court, "not susceptible of exact definition." And they were convicted upon evidence which showed no more than that the opinions which they were peaceably expressing were sufficiently opposed to the views of the majority of the community to attract a crowd and necessitate police protection.
>
> The Fourteenth Amendment does not permit a State to make criminal the peaceful expression of unpopular views.
>
> [A] function of free speech under our system of government is to invite dispute. It may indeed best serve its high purpose when it induces a condition of unrest, creates dissatisfaction with conditions as they are, or even stirs people to anger. Speech is often provocative and challenging. It may strike at prejudices and preconceptions, and have profound unsettling effects as it presses for acceptance of an idea. That is why freedom of speech . . . is . . . protected against censorship or punishment, unless shown likely to produce a clear and present danger of a serious substantive evil that rises far above public inconvenience, annoyance, or unrest. . . . There is no room under our Constitution for a more restrictive view. For the alternative would lead to standardization of ideas either by legislatures, courts, or dominant political or community groups.[120]

Consider This:

Many others, like these 187 brave students, realized that collectively, peacefully, their voices could be heard and changes could take place. For further proof of Black Americans' place in this nation's history, while preserving our right to peacefully assemble, look to these additional cases:

> *Henry v. City of Rock Hill* (1964)[121] The US Supreme Court held that the "Fourteenth Amendment does not permit a State to make criminal the peaceful expression of unpopular views."
>
> *Cox v. Louisiana* (1965)[122] The Baton Rouge police arrested twenty-three members of Congress of Racial Equality (CORE) for illegal picketing, which prompted a *march* and a demonstration of 1,500 to 3,800 people in front of the courthouse during the hearing of the twenty-three arrested.
>
> *Shuttlesworth v. City of Birmingham* (1965)[123] In 1962, Black citizens of Birmingham, Alabama, were arrested for boycotting downtown department stores.
>
> *Gregory v. City of Chicago* (1969)[124] Protestors in Chicago marched from city hall to the mayor's residence for desegregation of public schools.
>
> *NAACP v. Clairborne Hardware Co.* (1982)[125] The NAACP organized a boycott of White merchants to promote equality and racial justice.

Each of these cases involves racial disparity. Each time, the Court upheld rights to assemble in peaceful protest. Notice the dates and their struggles. It took years of protesting to make changes. These people fought for their freedoms and yours. The key to these decisions is peace.

ADDITIONAL RESOURCES

Chapter 7—The Right to Assemble Peacefully

- Exercise your right! Picket, protest, run, rally, march, or gather for a cause you are passionate about—so long as it is peaceful.
- Make peace part of your plan.
- If you plan to picket, protest, demonstrate, march, or rally, be sure to review local laws ahead of time. Obtain a permit. Remember that the government can place *reasonable* restrictions related to the time, place, and manner of protests without running afoul of your Constitutional rights to Free Speech and to Peaceable Assembly. This applies to peaceful protests at public universities as well as on high school campuses and in our cities and towns.

"I was once asked why I don't participate in anti-war demonstrations. I said that I will never do that, but as soon as you have a pro-peace rally, I'll be there." MOTHER TERESA

CHAPTER 8

The First Amendment: The Right to Petition

*"***Congress shall make no law** *respecting an establishment of religion, or prohibiting the free exercise thereof; or* **abridging the freedom** *of speech, or of the press; or the right of the people peaceably to assemble; and* **to petition the Government for a redress of grievances.***" (Ratified, December 1791)*

The First Amendment contains six clauses that describe six different privileges we enjoy. Perhaps the most far-reaching of all the freedoms guaranteed in the First Amendment is the least known. Our First Amendment provides, among the other freedoms, for the right to petition the Government for a redress of grievances. Although it has been defined differently in different contexts, it is most universally accepted as being a part of protests. But as we just learned in the last chapter, the right to protest is given to us under the right to peaceably assemble. So, what is the right to petition? The right to petition is probably best described as equivalent to a right to court access in cases *against* the government and present day lobbying *directing* legislators to adopt laws.

Initially, this clause was interpreted to mean that anyone could send a "petition" to Congress making a request. This was the procedure for a myriad of grievances for about 150 years. From the beginning of the formation of Congress, petitions were received for women's rights, Black rights, Native American rights, foreign rights and children's rights. All petitions were reviewed and decided on by Congress. It did not matter who, or how many, signed a petition. Each petition was considered.

We no longer petition the government directly to change laws through a "grievance" process. At some point, groups formed banding together to request new laws. These are our current lobbyists. We also sue the government in litigation for violating our rights under established laws. The result is many of the laws explained by the stories in this book. This is why we have both a "code" system, meaning statutes and laws, and a "common law" system, meaning precedent from cases like the stories contained in this book. Statutory law is created in Congress. Bills are introduced, debated, and voted on by the House of Representatives and the Senate.

Maggie Blackhawk, an assistant professor at University of Penn Carey Law School, has been researching the "Petition Clause" of the First Amendment since 2013.[126] After conducting her extensive research, she concluded that our current lobbying system, without offering the public a more formal, public, and equal means of access, is a violation of the right to petition. Blackhawk believes that Congress violates the Petition Clause by not reforming the current lobbying system. Anyone can still propose a bill through their congressional representatives, but lobbying groups are largely in control of bill presentation and passage now. As an expert on the subject, Professor Blackhawk points out that big corporations with extreme wealth and resources are in more control of bill presentation and passage than individuals and organizations with less capital. Moreover, lobbying groups are not subject to anti-trust laws even if their efforts are for an anti-competitive motive.

The bills that pass become the statutes or code laws. In addition to these statutes, there have been bills introduced to amend the Constitution. To confirm an amendment, a proposal is made to Congress to ratify by vote. It takes many years to get Congressional approval. Congress has not approved most proposed amendments. The reason for this is to prevent departure from the original Bill of Rights and preserve consistency. Nearly 12,000 proposals have been made to amend the Constitution since its ratification, and only seventeen have passed. Once ratified, the National Archivist must affirm ratification. There are now twenty-seven Amendments, including the Eighteenth Amendment, establishing the prohibition of the sale of alcohol, and the Twenty-First Amendment, repealing the Eighteenth Amendment prohibition of alcohol.

Proposals have been made to amend the Constitution, for example, concerning voting rights, defining human life, proposing a ban on flag desecration, campaign finance reform, proposing an amendment preventing a President of the United States to be able to pardon himself for crimes against the United States, proposing a parental rights amendment (which opponents argue is a disguise for denying minors their Constitutional rights), a proposal to adopt school prayer, establishing a Christian State, and a variety of other proposed additional amendments to the Constitution.

Five Constitutional Amendments remain that have been adopted by Congress but have not yet been ratified by the required number of states. Recently (June 2023), the Governor of California, Gavin Newsom, proposed a gun control amendment. The Equal Rights Amendment, which will be discussed in a later chapter, also hangs in limbo, awaiting the National Archivist to affirm ratification.

The Federal Tort Claims Act also prompted the avoidance of the clear path directly to Congress by petition. The Federal Tort Claims Act replaces petitioning for changes in the government with lawsuits *against* the government. In 1946, the Federal Tort Claims Act gave jurisdiction to federal courts to resolve grievances against the government. Some legal scholars believe that this adversarial system better flushes out the inequities in our laws. Most people recognize that there are ambiguities in most of our laws, including the Constitution. Often, when the Constitution or other written laws are applied to real life situations, conflicts arise about *how* the Constitution or law is applied. It may depend on the facts and evidence of the circumstances and situations presented.

Another hurdle to overcome, which some argue is a complete barricade to accessing the law, is the cost of litigation. Carol R. Andrews, Associate Professor of Law, University of Alabama School of Law, wrote a law review article describing the economic barriers some face in gaining access to the courts.[127] Additionally, as noted elsewhere, the length of time a court action takes to seek relief may be a prohibiting factor in obtaining justice.

Consider This:

Since *we* are the government, it is both our right and our duty to stay informed of current legislative proposals so we can have a voice in the matters that matter to all of us.

ADDITIONAL RESOURCES

Chapter 8—The Right to Petition

- Read more on the history of the right to petition: Congressional Management Foundation, A Brief History of the First Amendment Right to Petition Government, by Kathy Goldschmidt, February 25, 2022, found at: www.congressfoundation.org/news/blog/1904-a-brief-history-of-the-first-amendment-right-to-petition-government.
- Stay informed. Learn about how to write and introduce a bill, the legislative process, lobbying, and the judicial system. Read more on how bills become laws at www.house.gov/the-house-explained/the-legislative-process.
- Sign up for a free account to learn about bills that have been introduced that you are interested in and track their progress through www.fastdemocracy.com. "Fast Democracy" is a database of all bills that are currently proposed. www.FastDemocracy.com can also track state bills. You can search the website for topics of interest. The website data describes a proposed bill and provides the text of the bill. It provides the timeline of the bill's passage (when it was introduced, when it was submitted to a committee, or to the House, etc.). It even allows interaction where you can express your opinion on the bill and see what others have expressed. For instance, searching bills proposed on the subject of education led to US—HR 5326 (118 legislative session). This bill proposes "to amend the Higher Education Act of 1965 and the Elementary and Secondary Education Act of 1965 to provide rules of construction that nothing in those Acts requires the use, teaching, promotion, or recommendation of any academic discipline, program, or activity that holds that the United States is a Nation founded on white supremacy and

oppression, or that these forces are at the root of American society." This bill was introduced on September 1, 2023. It was referred to the House Committee on Education and Workforce. At the time of writing this, no other action has been taken on this bill. While it is written in a manner that suggests it is race neutral, historians might oppose passage of this law because it might limit their usage of education materials concerning slavery, the American Civil War, or the Civil Rights movement of the 1960s.

- Find out who is behind certain bills that have been proposed. Opensecrets.org is an organization that tracks the lobbying groups involved in federal bills. www.opensecrets.org/federal-lobbying/bills. They keep statistics on spending, such as the spending for and against legislation. For example, you can view the top spenders on legislation, what industries spend on lobbying campaigns, and search by issue. For instance, a simple search reveals that pro-gun ownership organizations spent over 15 million dollars on lobbying for pro-gun legislation from 2009 to 2022. That was over five times greater than gun *control* lobbyists and over seven times what was spent that same year by gun manufacturing.
- To find out more about what amendments have been proposed throughout history, visit the National Archives at www.archives.gov/open/dataset-amendments.html.
- Learn all you can about the bills proposed and your representatives from these and other sources. Review proposed bills and what money is backing the representatives on the ballot at EVERY ELECTION (federal, state and local elections all matter to YOU) and VOTE! VOTE, VOTE, VOTE!

"Our lives begin to end the day we become silent about things that matter." MARTIN LUTHER KING, JR.

CHAPTER 9

The Second Amendment: Guns–Our Right, or Our risk?

A well regulated Militia, being necessary to the security of a free State, the right of the people to keep and bear Arms, shall not be infringed. *(Ratified, December 1791)*

On February 14, 2018, a nineteen-year-old gunman entered Marjory Stoneman Douglas High School and began shooting with a semi-automatic weapon. Within six minutes, he killed fourteen students and three teachers. He severely injured seventeen others. On March 24, 2018, an estimated 1 to 2 million people demonstrated throughout the United States in support of gun control legislation, making it one of the largest-ever protests in the United States. Many carried signs that said: "Love Children More Than You Love Your Guns."

The "March for Our Lives" was led and organized by surviving students of the Parkland, Florida, shooting. Those students and others formed Never Again MSD (#NeverAgain, aka #MarchforOurLives), a political action committee for gun control.* In a nationally televised town hall hosted by CNN on February 21, 2018, X Gonzales, at age

---

* Students also co-authored two books: *We Say #Never Again*, by the Parkland Student Journalists; and *Glimmer of Hope*, by the founders of March For Our Lives.

nineteen, criticized the National Rifle Association ("NRA") and conservative politicians who have received money from gun lobbyists, saying, "You're either funding the killers, or you're standing with the children."

Hundreds of thousands of people gathered in Washington, DC for the March for Our Lives rally, protesting gun violence and demanding action by elected officials to enact common-sense gun control laws. 24 March 2018, 09:23
(Source, March for Our Lives)

Fig. 5 Photo by Phil Roeder, from Des Moines, IA. Reproduced with permission from Creative Commons.org under Attribution 2.0 generic license (Additional licensing information located under Permissions and Licenses.)

Gonzales also sharply criticized the State of Florida for not having any gun control measures. The student-led groups demanded that Florida pass a law to ban assault weapons; stop the sale of high-capacity magazines, restricting the amount of ammunition; require background checks on every gun purchase, including those online and at gun shows; and increase the age to be able to purchase a gun from eighteen to twenty-one.

A Florida bill titled The Marjory Stoneman Douglas High School

Public Safety Act was passed just weeks after the shooting through the student groups' efforts. Although not all of their demands were met, one gun control measure passed. The legislation increased the legal age to purchase a gun in Florida from eighteen to twenty-one. But on June 23, 2022, the US Supreme Court affirmed *New York State Rifle and Pistol Association, Inc. v. Bruen.*[128] That decision held that requiring an applicant to show that they had a special need to carry a concealed weapon is unconstitutional. Because of that decision, the Florida Governor backed a bill to lower the legal age for purchase of a gun back down to eighteen years of age. His reasoning? An eighteen year old may voluntarily serve in the armed forces. That same eighteen year old might carry weapons in war zones, so why not at home?

Only a few US Supreme Court cases throughout history deal with the right "to keep and bear arms" under the Second Amendment. For the first one hundred years of our nation, there were no decisions about the Second Amendment. In the next one hundred years, between 1876 and 1980, four cases seem to limit an individual right to carry guns and use them for purposes outside of a "militia" (or army) of the state. In the last fifteen years, however, starting with the 2008 case *District of Columbia v. Heller,*[129] the US Supreme Court holdings concerning the Second Amendment have gone helter-skelter to expand the use of firearms. Below is a summary timeline, including the eight major cases from the US Supreme Court on the issue of the constitutionality of the right to bear arms:

> 1876—*US v. Cruikshank*[130]—The Court said the right to bear arms is not granted by the Constitution. The Second Amendment means no more than that it shall not be infringed by Congress, and has no other effect than to restrict the powers of the national government. States, it reasoned, have the power to form laws restricting their population, and can restrict a state militia, or army, to keep the state safe.

1886—*Presser v. Illinois*[131] - This decision held that state legislatures could enact statutes to control militia organizations in their state, except for the federal defense organizations.

1939—*United States v. Miller*[132]—In the 1930s, the nation was outraged by the violent acts of gangsters, including the Valentine's Day Massacre, where seven men were killed with submachine guns and shotguns execution-style. In response, in 1934, the National Firearms Act was passed. The law required semi-automatic weapons and shotguns with a barrel of less than eighteen inches to be registered at the time of purchase or resale. The issue in this case was whether a sawed-off shotgun, transported between states, was protected under the Second Amendment. The court held it was NOT protected under the Second Amendment. "Only weapons that have a reasonable relationship to the effectiveness of a well-regulated militia under the Second Amendment are free from government regulation." It also found that, "The Court cannot take judicial notice that a shotgun having a barrel less than eighteen inches long has today [1939] any reasonable relation to the preservation or efficiency of a well-regulated militia, and therefore [we] cannot say that the Second Amendment guarantees to the citizen the right to keep and bear such a weapon."

[1968—Gun Control Act of 1968 was enacted. The Gun Control Act of 1968 is a US federal law that regulates the firearms industry and firearms ownership.]

1980—*Lewis v. United States*[133]—The court held that "any felony conviction, even an allegedly invalid one, is a sufficient basis on which to prohibit the possession of a firearm," which Congress can impose.

2008—*District of Columbia v. Heller*[134]—The court held that "private citizens have the right under the Second Amendment to possess an ordinary type of weapon and use it for lawful, historically established situations such as self-defense in a home, even when there is no relationship to a local militia." It also held that, "the Second Amendment extends, prima facie, to all instruments that constitute bearable arms, even those that were not in existence at the time of the founding." This, the majority held, was the correct linguistic interpretation of the meaning of the confusing language of the Second Amendment. The decision has been sharply criticized and blamed for escalating gun violence in America. Justice Stevens, who wrote the dissent along with three other justices, called it "unquestionably the most clearly incorrect decision . . . announced during my tenure on the bench." His dissent relied on the notion that, at the time that it was written, the phrase "the right to bear arms" meant a collective right for a "militia," not an individual right. He continued to criticize the decision until his death in 2019. (See discussion below.)

2009—*United States v. Hayes*[135]—The majority concluded that an offense need only include the use of force as an element of a crime to fall within the Gun Control Act of 1968, which is a federal law prohibiting certain convicted criminals, including some convicted of misdemeanor crimes, from owning guns.

2010—*McDonald v. City of Chicago*[136]—The Fourteenth Amendment incorporates the Second Amendment right to keep and bear arms for the purpose of self-defense. In other words, the right is protected from state as well as federal interference. On the last day of Justice Stevens's work with the US Supreme Court, he wrote the dissent in this case as well, again expressing doubt that the Second Amendment protects an individual right to modern firearms.

2016—*Caetano v. Massachusetts*[137]—This case came out of the State of Massachusetts Supreme Court. The State tried to legislate stun guns and argued that stun guns were not readily adaptable to use in the military and, therefore, not constitutionally protected. While the US Supreme Court had an opportunity to clarify or rectify its holding in *District of Columbia v. Heller,* instead it reiterated its holding that "the Second Amendment extends, prima facie, to all instruments that constitute bearable arms, even those that were not in existence at the time of the founding."

2022—*New York State Rifle and Pistol Association, Inc. v. Bruen*[138]— New York's requirement that an applicant for an unrestricted license to "have and carry" a concealed pistol or revolver must prove "a special need for self-protection distinguishable from that of the general community" is held unconstitutional. The majority called on lower courts to find that *any* restriction on carrying firearms is unconstitutional unless the regulation is consistent with the nation's "historical and traditional" regulations of the Second Amendment. Critics of the decision include judges who are tasked with applying the precedent of the US Supreme Court in their rulings. Many say that the majority's opinion in this case allows even convicted felons (of felonies not in existence in 1791) to argue that they have a constitutional right to possess firearms. District Court Judge Carlton W. Reeves said, "We are not experts at what White, wealthy, male property owners thought about firearm regulations in 1791. Yet now we're expected to play historian in the name of constitutional adjudication." Another District Court judge accused the Supreme Court of creating a "historical Where's Waldo" to determine what regulations on gun violence might be held Constitutional by the current US Supreme Court.

Between 2019 and 2021 alone, the death rate among children due to gun violence doubled.¹³⁹ But gun violence is not just mass shootings. It includes accidental shootings, interactions with police, protests becoming violent, road rage, gang shootings, domestic violence (women are five times more likely to die from domestic violence if their partner owns a firearm), and suicides (men who own guns are three times more likely to commit suicide; women seven times more likely).

In the days after the March for Our Lives, Justice Stevens called on YOU, America's youth, to take radical action against an individual right to bear arms. He called on you to demand a repeal of the Second Amendment. Justice Stevens has called the *District of Columbia v. Heller* the worst decision to come out of the US Supreme Court during his tenure. Justice Stevens was appointed by Gerald Ford in 1975, and retired from the Court in 2010. He served for thirty-five years. Three days after the March for Our Lives, Justice Stevens wrote a letter to the editor of the *New York Times* calling for a repeal of the Second Amendment. Every legislator, every senator, every congressperson, every student, every teacher, every school administrator, and every American should read the letter written by Justice Stevens.** ¹⁴⁰

But some believe that Justice Stevens's view is too simplistic. Amendments to the Constitution are rarely achieved, and only the prohibition of alcohol has ever been repealed. In fact, some believe that Justice Stevens's approach fuels Americans who believe that "it is our Constitutional right to carry a gun and damn those who want to take away my Constitutional rights!" The NRA TV host, Grant Stinchfield, called on Justice Stevens to be "ashamed of himself" and said he was "a disgrace to America." But Justice Stevens noted, "*Your* interest in

---

** New York Times, Op Ed. Contributor, John Paul Stevens, Repeal the Second Amendment, By John Paul Stevens, March 27, 2018 www.nytimes.com/2018/03/27/opinion/john-paul-stevens-repeal-second-amendment.html

keeping and bearing a certain firearm may diminish *my* interest in being and feeling safe from armed violence."[141]

Justice Breyer, who recently retired from the bench, has written several books about his own term on the Supreme Court. He suggests that the Court look to the intent of written law, rather than the pure text. If the intent of the Second Amendment was to make American citizens safe by allowing an armed militia, or state police, perhaps *D.C. v. Heller* was wrongly decided, as Justice Stevens suggests.

Instead of a dramatic removal of a constitutional right, many hope that legislation to control firearms will gain favor and that the Second Amendment right to bear arms can coexist with gun control. Duke Law School students sent a copy of a book they authored about the Second Amendment to Justice Stevens. In it, they remained hopeful and "positive" that gun control through legislation, rather than litigation, could make the change to end, or at least curb, gun violence. Justice Stevens wrote back. He thanked them for the book, which he read "with interest and admiration," but was "puzzled" by their positive views. He said "In my opinion the main purpose of the amendment is to enhance the appeal of NRA's arguments against additional regulations. No other civilized country has such an amendment or a comparable number of gun-related tragedies. I am convinced that the country would be better off if the Second Amendment were repealed."

Justice Stevens's interest in the Second Amendment and the *District of Columbia v. Heller*[142] decision did not end when he retired from the Court. In fact, it haunted him. In his autobiography, *The Making of a Justice*, released just before his death at age ninety-nine, he called the *Heller* decision, "the worst self-inflicted wound in the Court's history."

In one of his last interviews he said, "These mass shootings are peculiar to America and are peculiar to a country that has the Second Amendment, so I think that interpreting the Second Amendment to protect the individual right to own firearms is really just absurd, and it's also terribly important. It happens over and over and over again. I think I should have been more forceful in making that point in my *Heller* dissent."[143]

AND NOW . . .

US v. Rahimi (pending, 2023-2024)[144]

The US Supreme Court is set to hear the case *US v. Rahimi* in the 2023-2024 term. This case will decide if someone who is subject to a domestic violence protective order can be prohibited from owning a gun. Zackey Rahimi argues that the prohibition placed on him is a violation of his Second Amendment rights. But Rahimi is not like the respondent in Heller. Heller was a Washington, D.C., special police officer who applied for a gun permit to keep a handgun while off-duty at home for self-defense. Heller's gun-handling training far exceeded the typical gun-owning American. Rahimi, on the other hand, is by all accounts a bad actor. He is not one that the NRA would select as a poster child to gain support for keeping an individual right to bear arms.

In 2019, Rahimi argued with his ex-girlfriend about their son in a parking lot, knocked her down, and dragged her to his car. When he noticed a witness, he shot at the witness. He threatened to shoot his ex-girlfriend if she reported the abuse. His ex-girlfriend obtained a domestic violence restraining order against him. Under federal law, he was then prohibited from possessing a gun. Undeterred, he fired an AR-15 at the house of someone who posted something he took offense to on social media. He shot at another driver of a car when he was involved in an accident, which he caused. He shot at a car in a road rage scene. He fired several shots into the air at a fast food drive-up window that denied his friend's credit card for payment. After these shootings, a federal investigation ensued and his home was searched, where a pistol, rifle, and ammunition were found. He was then charged with violating the federal law prohibiting people subject to a domestic violence protective order from possessing a gun.

Rahimi argued before the US Supreme Court that under *New York State Rifle and Pistol Association, Inc. v. Bruen*[145] he has a Constitutional right to possess a gun because there is no "history or tradition" dating back to the enactment of the Second Amendment regulating firearms because of protective orders for victims of domestic abusers. But of course not. Women and children have historically had few rights against domestic abusers. In some states, a domestic abuser is not criminally charged. Many times, a domestic violence proceeding is not a felony but only a misdemeanor.

Oral argument took place in November 2023. The decision will probably be announced a few months after publication of this book. Based on oral argument, it is doubtful that domestic abusers subject to protective orders will have an individual right to bear arms. Justice Roberts, known as a conservative justice, implied that if the subject is shown to be sufficiently dangerous, they should have their firearms taken from them and that should be the end of the case.

This is completely in alignment with the majority holding in the case *United States v. Hayes* (2009).[146] That case decided that any offense that included the use of force falls within the Gun Control Act of 1968, even a misdemeanor. What is interesting to note is that when *United States v. Hayes* was decided in 2009, Justice Roberts wrote a dissent. There, he criticized not the meaning or language of the Second Amendment, but the wording and meaning of the prohibitions of the Gun Control Act of 1968. Perhaps Justice Roberts is feeling some of the regret of the *Heller* decision like Justice Stevens. Perhaps he is questioning the application of the history and traditions test to the modern world.

Experts agree that this is the Supreme Court's chance to clarify

New York State Rifle and Pistol Association, Inc. v. Bruen.[147] It would be easier for judges to determine if the party before them is potentially dangerous, considering the evidence related to *that party*, than to determine whether or not there was some equivalent firearm regulation for the crime charged in our "history and tradition."

Cargill v. Garland, Attorney General (pending 2023-2024)[148]

Also before the US Supreme Court in the 2023-2024 term is the issue of regulations applied to "bump stocks." In *Cargill v. Garland,* as US Attorney General, the single question is whether or not a "bump stock" is a "machine gun," under 26 USC § 5845(b), subject to federal regulation by the Bureau of Alcohol, Tobacco, Firearms and Explosives (ATF).

> **26 USC § 5845 (b) Machinegun**
> The term "machine gun" means any weapon which shoots, is designed to shoot, or can be readily restored to shoot, automatically more than one shot, without manual reloading, by a single function of the trigger. The term shall also include the frame or receiver of any such weapon, any part designed and intended solely and exclusively, or combination of parts designed and intended, for use in converting a weapon into a machine gun, and any combination of parts from which a machine gun can be assembled if such parts are in the possession or under the control of a person.

Stephen Paddock was a quiet businessman and video poker player, and for several decades, he stockpiled weapons and ammunition. On the last day of the Highway 91 Music Festival in Las Vegas, Nevada, on October 3, 2017, he opened fire on concertgoers killing fifty-eight

THE SECOND AMENDMENT: GUNS—OUR RIGHT, OR OUR RISK?   133

(three more died in the aftermath) and wounding approximately 500 more. This lone shooter owned forty-seven guns—legally. Twenty-three guns were found in his hotel room at Mandalay Bay, where he knocked out a window to shoot into the crowd below. Twenty-four more guns were found between his two homes nearby after the shooting. Multiple calls to 9-1-1 were received from various locations as the injured concertgoers fled the scene searching for cover. Authorities first believed that there were multiple shooters. Not just because there were multiple calls and multiple injuries, but also because the shooting spree happened so quickly harming so many, all within ten minutes. Twelve of the guns he had in the hotel room were equipped with a "bump stock," which is a device that allows a semiautomatic rifle to fire 400 to 600 rounds of ammunition per minute.***

In 1934, Congress first regulated the sale and possession of machine guns by the National Fire Arms Act. Then, in 1968, Congress amended the law, making it a crime to transfer or possess a machine gun. The ATF is a federal agency responsible for classifying firearms. Before a manufacturer goes through the trouble and expense of mass-producing a firearm that cannot be sold under the National Fire Arms Act, it may voluntarily submit the firearm to the ATF for classification. In 2002, a manufacturer submitted a device that was attached to a standard semiautomatic rifle and used a spring to harness the recoil energy of each shot, causing the firearm to cycle back and forth, impacting the trigger finger repeatedly after the first pull of the trigger. The bump stock gets its name because the shooter pulls the trigger once, the stock bumps up against the shooter and rocks back and forth, bumping into the trigger finger to initiate each shot. Thus, by pulling the trigger once, the shooter initiated an automatic firing sequence that was advertised as firing "approximately 650 rounds per minute."

*** To see and hear an analysis of how fast the shots occurred in the Las Vegas Massacre, see the following *New York Times* article: https://www.nytimes.com/interactive/2017/10/04/us/bump-stock-las-vegas-gun.html

The ATF initially did not classify the bump stock as a machine gun. Although one pull of the trigger with a bump stock automatically caused the finger to engage more shots, the ATF initially decided that the finger still needed to "engage" for each shot, which takes it out of the definition of a "machine gun." In 2006, the ATF re-classified the device as a "machine gun," noting that if the spring device is removed it would not be classified as a machine gun. The inventor manufacturer challenged ATF's classification (*Akins v. United States*[149]). The US Court of Appeals Eleventh Circuit upheld the ATF's classification that the bump stock attached to a semi-automatic weapon is a machine gun. That Court interpreted the phrase 'single function of the trigger' in Section 5845(b) to mean 'single pull of the trigger,' and said this meaning is consistent with the statute and its legislative history. That Court also said that "[t]he plain language of the statute defines a machine gun as any part or device that allows a gunman to pull the trigger once and thereby discharge the firearm repeatedly." (*Akins v. United States*)

The ATF soon received classification requests for bump stock devices that did not include an internal spring. The new bump stock, without the internal spring, works with one pull of the trigger when the shooter maintains constant forward pressure on the weapon's barrel-shroud or fore-grip. The weapon slides back along the bump stock, causing the trigger to "bump" the shooter's stationary finger and fire another bullet. Even without the internal spring, one pull of the trigger is all that is needed to fire approximately 400 to 800 rounds in a minute. In comparison, an AR-15 can fire approximately sixty rounds a minute without a bump stock. In a series of classification letters between 2008 and 2017, ATF concluded that such devices did not enable a gun to fire 'automatically' and were, therefore, not "machine guns."

After the Las Vegas shooting, the National Rifle Association (NRA) urged the ATF to reclassify any bump stock as a machine gun. You read that right. The NRA urged the ATF to reclassify and regulate the bump stock as a machine gun. Public outcry demanded that the NRA do something about mass shootings across the country. In the days following the Las Vegas killing spree in 2017, the NRA called on the ATF to review whether 'bump stocks' without the internal spring—similar to the devices used in the Las Vegas shooting massacre—comply with federal law. The NRA issued the following statement:

> The NRA believes that devices designed to allow semi-automatic rifles to function like fully-automatic rifles should be subject to additional regulations.

Many became suspicious of the NRA's position. Congress was already poised in 2017 to create legislation dealing with mass shootings and gun violence. It appeared to some that the NRA's statement was made to head off gun control in Congress, preferring new regulations from the ATF related to the single issue of the bump stock rather than having Congress debate more stringent gun control such as universal background checks on gun sales, a ban on assault weapons, and limits on high-capacity ammunition magazines. The statement feels even more disingenuous than it did in 2017, especially since the NRA was blocking proposals to curb transport of concealed weapons between states at the same time. And the NRA continues to lobby heavily *for* gun rights. (See the information concerning the Right to Petition.) But in 2018, at the NRA's urging after the 2017 Las Vegas massacre, the ATF reclassified the "bump stock" as a "machine gun," making it illegal to possess.

The current case before the US Supreme Court this term is not a case directly related to the Las Vegas shootings and killings. This case involves Michael Cargill, who purchased a bump stock in 2018 before the ATF re-classified the device as a machine gun. That classification then prohibited the possession of a bump stock. Cargill surrendered his bump stock device after reclassification and brought the lawsuit against the US Attorney General. He argues that the non-mechanical bump stocks are not machine guns under the federally regulated definition. In his brief to the US Supreme Court, he states that "three appeals courts, including the court below, agree with ATF's pre-2018 position that non-mechanical bump stocks are not machine gun[s]." But he admits that two other appeals courts agree with ATF's present-day interpretation that a bump stock is correctly classified as a machine gun.

The association for manufacturers and retailers of guns, the NSSF Firearm Industry Trade Association, filed an *amicus curiea* (meaning "friend of the court") brief supporting Michael Cargill. The NSSF argues that the action to reclassify the bump stock as a machine gun in 2017 was an "unlawful agency action." It accuses the ATF of making a hasty decision based on public outcry after the Las Vegas massacre. It also argues that the ATF exceeded its authority and that only Congress could make such a regulation.

It will be interesting to see if the NRA supports its earlier statement hoping that the ATF *would* regulate the bump stock, or if it will back the gun manufacturers and retailers on this issue.

National Rifle Association (NRA) v. Vullo (pending 2023-2024)[150]

One more bizarre case is headed to the US Supreme Court this term—*National Rifle Association (NRA) v. Vullo*. This case is a free speech case brought by the NRA. In 2017, before the Las Vegas massacre, the NRA announced its "Carry Guard" insurance program at the NRA Annual Convention in April of that year. Carry Guard is advertised as "self-defense insurance protection." The NRA sold and advertised insurance, which would cover legal fees (both civil and criminal) and any liability for anyone using licensed firearms. The lower court found that the NRA's insurance coverage applied "even in circumstances where the insured intentionally killed or injured someone or otherwise engaged in intentional wrongdoing."[151] (*Nat'l Rifle Ass'n of Am. v. Vullo*, 49 F.4th 700, 706 (2d Cir. 2022).)

> Carry Guard provided coverage for losses caused by licensed firearm use, including criminal defense costs resulting from using a firearm with excessive force to protect persons or property, even if the insured was found to have acted with criminal intent. In other words, it insured New York residents for intentional, reckless, and criminally negligent acts with a firearm that injured or killed another person. (*Nat'l Rifle Ass'n of Am. v. Vullo*, 49 F.4th 700, 707 (2d Cir. 2022).)

The NRA contracted with three insurance companies to underwrite this insurance. The New York State Department of Financial Services (DFS) regulates banking and insurance in the State of New York. In 2017, the New York DFS, led by Maria Vullo, began a criminal investigation of the NRA related to the NRA's Carry Guard insurance program because payment to another for the killing of a human life is a felony.

After the Parkland shooting, Vullo sent a recommendation letter to banks and insurance companies doing business in New York, encouraging them to "continue evaluating and managing their risks, including reputational risks, that may arise from their dealings with the NRA or similar gun promotion organizations, if any, as well as continued assessment of compliance with their own codes of social responsibility."

The same day, Governor Cuomo issued a press statement announcing that he had directed DFS to:

> ... urge insurers and bankers statewide to determine whether any relationship they may have with the NRA or similar organizations sends the wrong message to their clients and their communities who often look to them for guidance and support. *(per the press release)*

Vullo was quoted in the press release as stating that:

> ... business can lead the way and bring about the kind of positive social change needed to minimize the chance that we will witness more of these senseless tragedies, [and urging] all insurance companies and banks doing business in New York to join the companies that have already discontinued their arrangements with the NRA, and to take prompt actions to manage these risks and promote public health and safety. *Nat'l Rifle Ass'n of Am. v. Vullo*, 49 F.4th 700, 707 (2d Cir. 2022).

Then, in 2020, the NRA settled with the DFS with regard to the criminal investigation of the Carry Guard insurance program. The settlement included a penalty payment from the NRA of $2.5 million. The NRA was also banned from doing any insurance business in New York for five years. The three insurance companies involved also settled with the State of New York, paying a total of $13 million in penalties. The NRA no longer sells Carry Guard anywhere in the nation, but may provide other insurance products in some states.

Although that should be the end of the story, it is only the beginning of the case currently before the US Supreme Court. The NRA sued Vullo in 2022 on First Amendment grounds for the statements attributed to her (*Nat'l Rifle Ass'n of Am. v. Vullo*). The trial court dismissed the case on a motion to dismiss, believing that the NRA had not made sufficient factual allegations to state a case. The NRA appealed that decision, which was reversed in the District Court. The case was appealed again and the US Supreme Court, which will now decide whether the NRA's allegation that by pressuring banks and insurers to avoid doing business with affiliates of the NRA, Vullo, acting for the DFS, "stifled the ability of the NRA to exercise the NRA's free speech rights" sufficient to make a First Amendment claim.

Consider This:

The Second Amendment has been criticized for its lack of clarity, and over-punctuation: **A well regulated Militia, being necessary to the security of a free State, the right of the people to keep and bear Arms, shall not be infringed.**

It does not say that each individual has a right to bear arms, but that is the current interpretation. Does it mean that only "a well regulated militia" shall have a right to bear arms? Who is this, "*well regulated militia*"? Even if we assume that we individuals could all potentially be called upon to serve in this phantom "militia," doesn't it say that some regulation is necessary "to the security of a free State"?

How would the Second Amendment be written if it were written today?

How would you re-write the Second Amendment?

What legislation would you propose to end gun violence?

ADDITIONAL RESOURCES

Chapter 9—Second Amendment Right to Bear Arms

- Join March for Our Lives: www.marchforourlives.org/what-we-want/. Since the mass shooting in Parkland, Florida, this youth organization has organized hundreds of chapters across the country fighting for sensible gun prevention policies that will save lives.
- Demand a world free of gun violence with March for Our Lives. Young people have a vital interest in ensuring that the Constitution is interpreted correctly to allow the enactment of gun violence prevention measures that will protect themselves, their peers, and all Americans.
- Do not underestimate the power of your voice; it can effect change. Be a part of the record turnouts of youths voting for gun safety laws.
- In 2023, with the constant encouragement from March for Our Lives, President Biden created the White House Office of Gun Violence Prevention. Be a part of the discussion at every opportunity to speak out about how it feels to be hiding under a desk during a lock down drill and demand a better world.
- Support efforts to pass gun legislation, including an additional amendment to the constitution, as Governor Newsom (CA) proposed, which raises the federal minimum age to purchase a firearm from eighteen to twenty-one, mandates universal background checks to prevent dangerous persons from purchasing guns, institutes a reasonable waiting period for all gun purchases, and bars civilians from the purchase and ownership of assault weapons that are designed to kill as many people as possible in a short amount of time.

- Read the Amicus Curiae (or Friends of the Court) Brief in the *US v. Rahimi* case before the US Supreme Court. www.marchforourlives.org/wp-content/uploads/2023/09/US-v.-Rahimi-MFOL-Amicus-Brief-8.21.23.pdf
- Read the appeal of Justice John Paul Stevens to repeal the Second Amendment: www.nytimes.com/2018/03/27/opinion/john-paul-stevens-repeal-second-amendment.html
- Create an event with Walls of Demand to end gun violence. Walls of Demand uses urban art and nonviolent creative confrontation to expose the effects of mass shootings. Walls of Demand was formed by activist/artivist Manuel Oliver and Patricia Oliver, parents of Joaquin Oliver, who was one of the 17 lost at MSD. www.wallsofdemand.com They also formed Change the Ref, whose mission is "to empower our next generation so they can fight for their values, have their voices heard, and impact change for their future."
- There are many people in America that support an individual's right to carry weapons of war. But as Justice Stevens points out, those that demand to uphold the Second Amendment's right to bear arms have a very loud voice, which often muffles the sound of voices that cry out for silencing gun violence. What reasons do you have not to join the voices of victims and their families and friends who cry for their losses and for change? What accommodations would you give victims, their families, or future victims of gun violence? What regulations would satisfy both points of view?
- Read more about the history of firearm regulations www.justice.gov/archive/opd/AppendixC.htm

"If there is any justice in this country, the politicians who do nothing to protect us from gun violence will be voted out." X GONZÁLEZ

CHAPTER 10

The Third and Fourth Amendments: Rights to Privacy

The Third Amendment

No Soldier shall, in time of peace be quartered in any house, without the consent of the Owner, nor in time of war, but in a manner to be prescribed by law. *(Ratified, December 1791)*

As of now, the Third Amendment has never been the basis of any decision in the US Supreme Court. It just hasn't been an issue. It is thought, however, to provide some protection of the homes of individuals, as we will see in a few of the following cases on the right to privacy under the Fourth Amendment.

The Fourth Amendment

The right of the people to be secure in their persons, houses, papers, and effects, against unreasonable searches and seizures, shall not be violated, and no Warrants shall issue, but upon probable cause, supported

by Oath or affirmation, and particularly describing the place to be searched, and the persons or things to be seized. *(Ratified, December 1791)*

The Fourth Amendment is an important protection for our right to privacy. It protects against "unreasonable searches and seizures" of personal property. Students have a right to their privacy as well as adults, but that right is diminished while the student is on school grounds.

New Jersey v. T.L.O. (1985)[152]

Two girls were found smoking in the bathroom in Piscataway High School in Middlesex County, New Jersey. One of the girls was fourteen years old. The court records refer to her only as "T.L.O." T.L.O. and her companion were taken to the principal's office because smoking in the bathroom is a violation of school rules. While the companion student admitted to smoking in the bathroom, T.L.O. denied it. In fact, she said that she "did not smoke at all." The vice principal asked her to come into his office and demanded that she open her purse. He removed cigarettes from her purse and noticed rolling papers. He then searched the purse more thoroughly. In it, he found a small amount of "marijuana, a pipe, a number of empty plastic bags, a substantial quantity of money in one dollar bills, an index card that appeared to be a list of students who owed T.L.O money, and two letters that implicated T.L.O in marijuana dealing."

T.L.O.'s mother was called to take her to the police station. At the police station, T.L.O. confessed to selling marijuana. She was then charged with delinquency in juvenile court.

A bit of "legalese" on criminal procedure is needed to explain the ruling in this case. Items that are concealed and out of "plain view" cannot be searched or confiscated without a search warrant. That is, personal items contained in a place where society has an "expectation of privacy" may not be searched. A suitcase, for instance, keeps items out of plain view and cannot be searched without probable cause—EXCEPT at an airport before allowing the suitcase to be handled and carried by the aircraft. Why? Because there is no legitimate expectation of privacy when you are requiring others to handle your luggage on an airplane. Besides, the need to ensure public safety outweighs the need for privacy in that case.

If something is concealed, not in plain view, within an item where there *is* a legitimate expectation of privacy, a search of that item without a search warrant might be an illegal search *unless* there is "probable cause." Probable cause is loosely defined as reasonable grounds for suspicion. A search warrant can only be issued if there is some degree of suspicion that some specific evidence of a violation of law will be found. Confiscating anything contained within the concealing item without a warrant or probable cause may be an illegal seizure.

The privacy rights guaranteed by the Fourth Amendment requires fair investigating. To that end, a defendant to criminal charges may apply to the court to remove, or "move to suppress," evidence that is obtained through an "illegal search and seizure." This is known as the "exclusionary rule." Said differently, if an official search violates constitutional rights, the evidence is not admissible in criminal proceedings. Furthermore, any additional evidence derived from the illegal search is also inadmissible. This is known as the "fruit from the poisonous tree" doctrine.[153] (*Wong Sun v. United States* (1963).) In this case, T.L.O. argued that the search of her purse was a violation of the Fourth Amendment right. Furthermore, she argued that not only should the evidence found in her purse not be used in the proceedings against her, but also her confession should not be used. She argued that the confession obtained (the "fruit") could not be used against her because it was derived from the illegal search (the "poisonous tree").

The question in this case was whether school authorities are limited under the Fourth Amendment, just as police and other public officials are in conducting searches. The Supreme Court held that they are. The court said, "The Federal Constitution, by virtue of the Fourteenth Amendment, prohibits unreasonable searches and seizures by state officers," which includes public school officials. The court reasoned that "[i]f school authorities are state actors for purposes of the constitutional guarantees of freedom of expression and due process, it is difficult to understand why they should be deemed to be exercising parental rather than public authority when conducting searches of their students."

But the Court didn't end the analysis there. The Court said that the requirement is that searches and seizures are to be "reasonable" under the Fourth Amendment and that "reasonableness" depends on the context of the search. The Court applied a balancing test:

> On one side of the balance are arrayed the individual's legitimate expectations of privacy and personal security; on the other, the government's need for effective methods to deal with breaches of public order.[154]

The State of New Jersey argued that "a child has virtually no legitimate expectation of privacy in articles of personal property 'unnecessarily' carried into a school." The Court disagreed with the State's argument. The Court said:

> Students at a minimum must bring to school not only the supplies needed for their studies, but also keys, money, and the necessaries of personal hygiene and grooming. In addition, students may carry on their persons or in purses or wallets such nondisruptive yet highly personal items as photographs, letters, and diaries. Finally, students may have perfectly legitimate reasons to carry with them articles of property needed in connection with

extracurricular or recreational activities. In short, schoolchildren may find it necessary to carry with them a variety of legitimate, noncontraband items, and there is no reason to conclude that they have necessarily waived all rights to privacy in such items merely by bringing them onto school grounds.[155]

But on the other hand,

> The child's interest in privacy must be [balanced against] the substantial interest of teachers and administrators in maintaining discipline in the classroom and on school grounds. Maintaining order in the classroom has never been easy, but in recent years, school disorder has often taken particularly ugly forms: drug use and violent crime in the schools have become major social problems.[156]

The Court concluded that warrants would unnecessarily burden school administrators, and that warrantless searches on school grounds should not require the same level of "probable cause" that allow police to search without a warrant. Instead, the Court concluded that on school grounds, school administrators should apply the "special needs doctrine," where there is a relaxed application of the Fourth Amendment protections. The special needs doctrine examines the "reasonableness" of the search, which depends on two factors:

Was the search justified from the beginning?

Was the search reasonable in light of the circumstances?

In the case of T.L.O., the majority of the Court found that the initial search of T.L.O.'s purse was justified because she was found smoking in the bathroom but she denied smoking at all. Her possession of cigarettes, clutched in the only thing that she was holding—her purse—was relevant and gave rise to the initial search. It showed that she lied about smoking "not at all," and implicated her in breaking the "no smoking in the bathroom" rule. Then, when the vice principal picked up the cigarettes from the purse and noticed the rolling papers, he had reason to look for marijuana. Finding it, and the money, and the log of who owed her money and the letters "implicating her drug dealing" she was pretty much up a creek. The Court found that the continuing search was "reasonably related to the circumstances."

So in what instances would the search of a student at school *not* be reasonable?

Stafford Unified School District #1 v. Redding (2009)[157]

A strip search of a thirteen year old at middle school for ibuprofen is unreasonable. In this case, one student said they got a pill from another student that made him sick. That student said that he got the pills from "Marisa" and she was going to distribute them among other students. Marisa was confronted. She spilled the pills, which she said that she got from "Redding." Redding had a party the week before at her house where students consumed alcohol.

This gave the school enough information to be suspicious of Redding. Even though the pills (from Marisa) were confirmed to be four prescription strength ibuprofen and one other anti-inflammatory over the counter drug, the school administrator pulled Redding out of class and confronted her. She denied any knowledge of the pills. He then searched her backpack. Finding nothing, he ordered an assistant to take Redding to the school nurse and have her clothes searched. She was told to remove her clothes. As she did, the school nurse and a female school assistant examined each article of clothing, which had no pockets, again, finding nothing. When she was down to her bra and underwear, they demanded she pull her bra and underwear away from her body, which exposed her breasts and pelvic area, to search for pills. No pills or any other unlawful item was found on her.

Incidentally, possession of ibuprofen and over-the-counter drugs was not illegal in school; however, without prior approval the possession may have been a school rule violation. Her mother helped her file a lawsuit in Federal Court on the basis that Redding's Fourth Amendment rights were violated.

The Court said this was not a "reasonable" search, especially since it was decided long after the T.L.O. case. The question in this case was more about whether the school administrator would have, or could have, or should have known that this was an illegal search. The majority opinion repeated the words from the T.L.O. case:

> A search will be permissible in its scope when the measures adopted are reasonably related to the objectives of the search and not excessively intrusive in light of the age and sex of the student and the nature of the infraction.[158]

As explained above, sometimes a public employee will be granted "qualified immunity," meaning that they will not be personally liable for mistakes made in the line of duty, unless the public employee violated a clearly established law. In this case, the majority opinion granted the school administrator immunity so that he would not be personally liable for the illegal search. Justice Stevens, along with Justice Ginsburg, found this portion of the majority opinion to be absurd. Justice Stevens wrote, "[i]t does not require a constitutional scholar to conclude that a nude search of a thirteen-year-old child is an invasion of constitutional rights [of privacy] of some magnitude."[159] They disagreed with the majority that the school administrator should be granted immunity.

Consider This:

Ronisha Ferguson v. City of New York (2022)[160]

The US Supreme Court did not decide this case. It does not involve any school. In fact, it is not even a case where a student has been subjected to an illegal search and seizure. But the facts of this case touch the lives of so many students and children that it needs to be discussed. It is a fact that many children's homes are violated under the Fourth Amendment right to be secure against unreasonable searches.

Most states have Child Protective Services (CPS) to intervene when there is suspected child abuse or neglect. But CPS conducts millions of warrantless searches of private family homes. The family lives of roughly 3.5 million children a year (that's about one in twenty) are investigated by CPS, but only about 5 percent are ultimately found to be physically or sexually abused. Only about 0.2 percent of the investigations are made with a search warrant.[161] Most often, it is low-income families who are investigated for neglect, abandonment, or inadequate living conditions. Although CPS is a government entity, the Fourth Amendment right against illegal searches and seizures does not protect families against CPS searches. Oftentimes, it is the children who are the victims of overzealous CPS workers, and the items seized are the children themselves. CPS has been called an antagonistic suspicion based family policing, not child welfare or "child *protection.*"

One of the only cases on record dealing with this violation of privacy rights involves a mother of three who had her two youngest children taken from her in the middle of the night. After the ordeal, she was able to get them back about a month later, and then she sued the City of New York in Federal Court. Here is their story according to the allegations in her complaint for violation of her Fourth Amendment right:

On February 7, 2019, an anonymous reporter from the children's school called the New York State Central Register of Child Abuse and

Maltreatment and reported that "S.J.," who was eight years old at the time, had missed a number of school days, was falling behind in his academic work, had a "visible black and blue bruised eye," and was wearing "dirty clothing" with "body odor." The report was immediately transferred to the New York City Administration for Children's Services, which is New York's Child Protective Services (CPS). The report was not characterized as an emergency, but two CPS investigators showed up at the home of "A.J." and S.J. at approximately 3:15 p.m. that same day.

The two investigators never attempted to contact the informant nor obtain any other information. The two investigators asked to enter Ms. Ferguson's apartment. She denied their request, but stepped outside and answered their questions. She told the investigators that the boys would be arriving soon on the bus and returned to her apartment. They asked again if they could enter the apartment. She again denied their request. They followed her when she came outside to wait at the bus stop for the children. The two boys got off the bus, neatly clothed. They questioned S.J. He told them that he got a scratch below his eye from a cat at his grandmother's house the weekend before. The other boy had a small cut on his forehead. He told them it was from falling during the bus ride home that day, which a school aid on the bus confirmed. They did not attempt to locate or question the grandmother. Instead, the CPS investigators called the police.

A detective from NYPD appeared at the Ferguson home with the two CPS investigators. They demanded that Ms. Ferguson bring the children to a location that investigates child abuse. She refused. The detective told the two investigators that her refusal was her right and that he could not force her to bring the children. There was no evidence of neglect or child abuse other than the noted bruise below S.J.'s eye and the small cut on A.J. Still, simply because Ms. Ferguson refused to admit the investigators into her home, and refused to take her children to a location that investigates child abuse, the two investigators referred the investigation to Emergency Children's Services, a division of CPS that handles after-hours and weekend emergency interventions.

Sometime between 3:45 a.m. and 4:30 a.m. the following morning, new CPS investigators and NYPD officers banged on the door to Ms. Ferguson's home and demanded removal of the children. She grabbed her phone and started videotaping. She opened the door a crack and told them they had no right to enter. One of the officers lodged his foot inside her door. She warned the "Sargent" to tell the officer that without a search warrant he was not allowed in the apartment. They falsely claimed that there was a court order for the children's removal, but when Ms. Ferguson demanded to see it, one of the officers grabbed her phone. They later returned it and she again demanded to see a court order. They could not produce it.[162] They threatened her with arrest if she would not allow the children to be removed. She asked, "arrest me for what?" The officer answered, "for not letting us take your kids."

Not wanting to make matters worse, she then released the children to CPS. The following day, the boys' older sister confirmed to CPS that her brother had a black eye because he was roughhousing with cousins and a cat scratched him at his grandmother's house the previous weekend. No other investigation occurred, except a physical examination of the boys days later. The two boys were placed in a foster home where they *were* physically abused. (This was later substantiated.) They were reunited with their mother approximately one month later.

The children were "temporarily released to the care of Ms. Ferguson under ACS's supervision with a number of terms and conditions, including that Ms. Ferguson engage in counseling, attend anger management, refrain from using corporal punishment on the children, *make the children, the home, and herself available for announced and unannounced visits from the agency, and that the agency shall be permitted to speak privately to the children.*" Ms. Ferguson had to agree to these conditions in order to get her children back.

Ms. Ferguson then sued under the Fourth Amendment right against unreasonable searches and seizures. The lawsuit settled before trial. Each child received $50,000 in a trust to be accessed only when they reached adulthood. Ms. Ferguson received $75,000 and all of her attorney's fees were paid. Needless to say, the settlement does not wipe away the memories or the trauma. As Ms. Ferguson experienced, people who are suspected of crimes, even murder, have more rights against illegal searches and seizures then she had.

The lack of Fourth Amendment protections against invasive CPS investigations is reviewed at length in a law review article by Tarek Z. Ismail, Associate Professor, CUNY School of Law. [163] In it he explains the traumatic effects on homes and families. Children's most important relationship and trust in a parent is fundamentally altered. He found that the impact is especially true in Black communities, where 53 percent of Black children in the United States will endure a CPS investigation in their lifetime. That is nearly two times as often as Whites. While the US Supreme Court has repeatedly affirmed the right of parents to the "care and custody of their children" and affirmed the rights of children to be raised by their parents, the Supreme Court has never addressed constitutional rights during a CPS home search, "notwithstanding its profound impacts."

Ismail suggests a simple solution: require CPS agents to uphold the Fourth Amendment, wherein CPS agencies could enter a home only with *knowing* and *voluntary* consent of the parent or with a properly issued individualized search warrant.

Why hasn't this been the requirement all along? It is Ismail's opinion that Child Protective Services was set up with the best of intentions beginning in the 1960s to benefit the children, not harm the parents intentionally or unintentionally by illegal searches. To receive certain child welfare benefits, these administrative agencies were required to conduct in-home inspections to ensure that the benefits were being used appropriately to assist the children. But caseworkers acknowledge that their investigations have become adversarial and they were never told that parents had rights to deny them access. In other words, it was a good idea that had gone wrong.

"Rights?—No, we never did that. I didn't even know that was a thing," said Natasha Walden, a child protective specialist in Queens, New York, when asked if she ever had to obtain a search warrant to gain entrance to a home being investigated by CPS. She added that her goal was just to get inside any way she could.

Some caseworkers admitted to using coercive and misleading tactics to gain access. Once inside, they search rooms, children's rooms, bedrooms, bathrooms, and kitchens, opening up cupboards, closets and drawers, and even searching a child's body. Perhaps a future US Supreme Court case will decide the question: how can we reconcile the need for the protection of children and the Fourth Amendment right against unreasonable searches and seizures?

Consider This:

In practice, CPS agencies often forget about the rights, the safety, and the protection of the parent-child bond, as well as plain simple human kindness. Childcare centers and parents who are under investigation for whatever reason are often treated as if they are guilty until proven innocent, instead of innocent until proven guilty. Posted all around children's centers and public schools are things like, "kindness is our priority," or "practice random acts of kindness." Child Protective Services could use one of these slogans.

ADDITIONAL RESOURCES

Chapter 10—Rights to Privacy

- Remember that when you are on a public school campus, you are on government grounds. School officials may search a student, the student's property, or district property *when there is reasonable suspicion that the search will uncover evidence that the student is violating the law, OR school board policies, administrative regulations, or rules of the school district!*
- Reasonable suspicion is based on all of the facts known by the school official. Any search of a student must be limited to producing evidence related to the alleged violation. The school official can consider the danger (or suspected danger) to the health or safety of students or staff. They *must* search if there is a reasonable suspicion of weapons, drugs, or other dangerous items. The school official *must* take into consideration the intrusiveness of the search in light of the student's age, gender, ability to comprehend, and the nature of the alleged violation.
- The types of student property that may be searched by school officials include, but are not limited to, lockers, desks (those belong to the school–not you), purses, backpacks, cell phones, electronics, and student vehicles parked on school property.
- Before you report to CPS: of course child abuse does exist, and by all means report it if you are certain that conditions warrant it, but do be aware of the ramifications of an unwarranted search of someone's home and the potential removal of their children.
- Research abuses of power. Check out ProPublica.org. ProPublica is an independent, nonprofit newsroom that

produces investigative journalism with moral force. ProPublica digs deep into important issues, shining a light on abuses of power and betrayals of public trust by governments, businesses, and other institutions.

"Human kindness has never weakened the stamina or softened the fiber of a free people. A nation does not have to be cruel to be tough." FRANKLIN D. ROOSEVELT

CHAPTER 11

Fifth Amendment: Criminal Trials and Investigations

No person .... *shall be subject for the same offence to be twice put in jeopardy of life or limb; nor* **shall be compelled in any criminal case to be a witness against himself,** *nor be deprived of life, liberty, or property, without due process of law; nor shall private property be taken for public use, without just compensation. (Ratified, December 1791)*

Besides the First Amendment right to free speech, one of the best known personal freedoms is the freedom *not* to speak under the Fifth Amendment's right against self-incrimination, or to be "compelled in any criminal case to be a witness against himself." The right seems pretty clear. In fact, most of us are familiar with the *Miranda* warnings: "You have the right to remain silent. Anything you say can and will be used against you in a court of law. You have the right to an attorney . . . ." (*Miranda vs. Arizona*[164]) But where it gets murky is just when the Miranda warning should be given, by whom, and under what circumstances? The simple answer is that the Miranda warning must be given whenever a person is "in custody." But whether a person is "in custody" depends on objective circumstances of the interrogation.

The Fifth Amendment right against self-incrimination is especially murky in the swampy area of public schools. Clearly, the rights in the criminal context are not the same as the individual rights of free people not accused of criminal activity. But this doesn't mean that the wrongly accused are not entitled to certain rights that could impact their freedom. It just means that a public employee (like a teacher or school official) might ask a student who is not suspected of any crime an innocent question without having to provide the student a *Miranda* warning. What would classrooms look like otherwise?

Teacher: "Can anyone tell me how to calculate the density of water?"

Johnny raises his hand to answer. The teacher calls on him but then states: "You have the right to remain silent . . . ."

That would be weird, right? What if the situation was just as innocent, but Johnny's answer might be evidence of a broken school rule? The teacher, seeing Johnny down the hall during classroom time: "Where are you going, Johnny?"

Does the teacher need to provide the student a *Miranda* warning then? How about when it might implicate Johnny in a crime? Teacher: "Johnny, where did you get that phone?" (The teacher recognizes the phone stolen from him last week).

Murky, indeed. And it gets murkier still with the presence of an on-site school police officer during questioning. The US Supreme Court attempted to provide some clarity in these murky waters in the case of *J.D.B. v. North Carolina*.

J.D.B. v. North Carolina (2011)[165]

The town of Chapel Hill in North Carolina is a quiet small town. The most exciting thing that happens there is a close basketball game at University of North Carolina. So the neighborhood was shocked when two break-ins occurred in September of 2005. Jewelry was stolen, along with a digital camera. A few days after the break-ins, police noticed J.D.B. outside of one of the homes. They questioned him and he told them that he was in the neighborhood looking to find work mowing lawns. They also spoke to his legal guardian—his grandmother—and his aunt.

A couple of days after that, the digital camera showed up at Smith Middle School. A student was given the camera by J.D.B., who was a thirteen-year-old seventh grade student at the time. The police were notified. A police investigator was sent to the school to question J.D.B. A uniformed policeman, who was assigned to the school, went to J.D.B.'s classroom, and escorted him to a conference room. The assistant principal, another administrator, and the police investigator were waiting. The door was closed while the two school employees and the two police officers interrogated J.D.B. for at least thirty minutes. The investigator did most of the questioning. J.D.B. was not told that he could leave the room. He was not given his *Miranda* rights and his grandmother was not contacted.

During the questioning, the assistant principal urged J.D.B. to "do the right thing," saying, "the truth always comes out in the end."

J.D.B. then asked if he would still be in trouble if he returned the "stuff." The assistant principal continued to encourage J.D.B. to talk by saying, "What's done is done. Now you need to help yourself by making it right."

The investigator also implied to J.D.B. that he would be sent to juvenile detention before appearing in court if he did not provide information about the break-ins. It was then that J.D.B. confessed that he and a friend were responsible for the break-ins. It was only then that the investigator informed J.D.B. that he could refuse to answer and was free to leave. J.D.B. nodded that he understood, but continued to tell where the stolen items were located in his home. At the investigator's request, J.D.B. put the confession in writing. At the end of the day, J.D.B. was allowed to get on the bus to go home.

When he arrived, the two police officers were there but his grandmother was not. J.D.B. then showed the officers the stolen jewelry that was kept there.

J.D.B. was charged with larceny and breaking and entering. His appointed public defender moved to suppress the confession and all of the evidence of the stolen goods, because it was "fruit from the poisonous tree." In other words, the defense argued that the confession and evidence were obtained illegally because J.D.B. was not given his *Miranda* warnings before being questioned while "in custody."

The *Miranda* warning's primary purpose is to ensure that voluntary confessions are *voluntary* and not the result of coercion. The right to remain silent is so essential to fair prosecution of crimes that, in order to use any confession as evidence, the government has the burden of first proving that the defendant "voluntarily, knowingly, and intelligently" waived his rights before confessing.

The *Miranda* warning does not need to be given before questioning when a suspect reasonably understands that they are free to leave. But any confession obtained while the suspect is "in custody," or objectively reasonably believed they were *not* free to leave, cannot be used at a trial against them without the *Miranda* warning being given prior to the confession. The key issue in most Fifth Amendment rights cases is whether or not questioning resulting in a confession occurred when the suspect was "in custody," or on the other hand, the suspect had a reasonable understanding that they were free to leave. This was the question posed to the US Supreme Court in this case. Did J.D.B., given his age and the circumstances, reasonably believe that he was free to go and not answer the questions at the urging of school officials and police? The Supreme Court majority opinion says, of course not. Given J.D.B.'s age, the closed door to the conference room, the uniformed cop in the room, and the school authorities urging him to tell the truth, there's no way he reasonably believed that he was free to leave without giving them the confession they wanted.

Whether J.D.B. *himself* felt free to leave is not really the legal question. The legal question to be answered is whether a child's age is a factor that police should be concerned with in deciding whether or not to give the *Miranda* warning. What the court is tasked with is setting a standard that can be applied to everyone. In other words, police do not need to decide if a particular suspect understands his freedom. They are not required to make educated guesses about the mental state of a particular suspect. But a child's age is a factor that police can easily take notice of.

The Court reasoned, "a reasonable child subjected to police questioning will sometimes feel pressured to submit when a reasonable adult would feel free to go."

The Court found it common sense that a child's age is a relevant factor to be considered. The *Miranda* warning should be given when the child's age is evident and the circumstance would lead that child to believe they were not free to leave questioning before giving a confession.

J.D.B.'s case was remanded, meaning handed back down to the lower court to decide whether, given his age and the circumstances, J.D.B. was in custody when questioned. With the Supreme Court's instruction, it is likely that the evidence of his confession and the stolen goods would not be considered against him.

In Re Tateana R. (2009 New York)[166]

An iPod belonging to a middle school student went missing. Remember those? Kinda like a phone, but not a phone. Old school. Anyway, you were cool if you had one in 2008. It was not cool to take one and not give it back, though. The "irate" mother of the student missing an iPod appeared at New Day Academy, a public middle school in the Bronx. She claimed that Tateana R. borrowed her daughter's iPod and refused

FIFTH AMENDMENT: CRIMINAL TRIALS AND INVESTIGATIONS   161

to give it back. Tateana, thirteen years old at the time, was called into the dean's office. Two police officers happened to be on campus that morning. The dean asked the police officers to stick around, but told them that the mother only wanted the property returned, she did not want to press charges. One officer sat in on the interview of Tateana in the dean's office, and the other waited in the hallway.

> The interview lasted approximately forty-five minutes, during which time the dean asked [Tateana] what she knew of the whereabouts of the iPod. He confronted [Tateana] with conflicting statements made by other students and pointed out inconsistencies in her own statements. As the meeting progressed, the dean told [Tateana] that her explanations were getting ridiculous, and he pleaded with her to give the iPod back. [Tateana] then stated, 'I am not giving back the iPod.' Until this point, the police officer was mainly observing the interaction. However, upon hearing this inculpatory statement [meaning an admission] he advised [Tateana] that she could be arrested. [Tateana]'s aunt, who was present at the school, also came in to the dean's office and asked [Tateana] to give back the property. [Tateana] denied that she had the iPod, refused to return it, and was placed under arrest.[167]

Just like J.D.B., Tateana argued at her delinquency hearing that her admission should be suppressed because she was not given any *Miranda* warning and her parent had not been called before the questioning. This Court disagreed, and she was found guilty of criminal possession of stolen property and given twelve months of probation. So, what's different here from the J.D.B. case? She was the same age—thirteen! The crime was somewhat the same—possession of stolen property and possible theft. One could argue that the value and seriousness of her alleged crimes were considerably less than what J.D.B. had been questioned about. So why was the evidence against Tateana not suppressed? Why was she found guilty and J.D.B.'s case sent back to court? The J.D.B. case had not been decided at this point, and this was not a US Supreme Court case. However, the different courts were not the determining difference in the two outcomes.

The difference in outcomes is *who* did the questioning. J.D.B. was being investigated by the police for a crime he was already suspected of committing. They came to his school looking for him specifically. The majority of the questioning of J.D.B. was conducted by the police investigator assigned to the case. On the other hand, a school official (the dean) conducted the questioning of Tateana. In her case, the court reasoned she was free to leave or not respond to the questions *of school personnel*. She was therefore not "in custody" when she said she would not give back the iPod. The Court reasoned that the mere presence of the police during the questioning would not indicate to a reasonable thirteen-year-old that they were "in custody" and therefore require the *Miranda* warning.

The reasoning of these two cases is generally followed by most jurisdictions. School officials are generally not required to give a *Miranda* warning to a student being questioned, whether or not police are present during the questioning. However, some legal counsel for school officials have said that it might be a good idea for school officials to give some similar warning to any student who is being investigated for a crime. Students should also know that they are entitled to remain silent and have representation in any criminal investigation against them.

ADDITIONAL RESOURCES

Chapter 11—Criminal Trials and Investigations

- If you are implicated in any crime, consult with an attorney!
- When questioned by any authority (school official or police) about any criminal wrongdoing, always ask, "Am I free to leave without answering your questions?" If the answer is "yes," and you are uneasy because what you say might implicate you in a crime, you should leave and speak with an attorney. If the answer is "no, you are not free to leave," then you are "in custody." If you are in custody, you should be given a warning about the right to remain silent.
- Pay attention to whether or not the authority, especially any police officer, has given you any warning about your right to remain silent. You may, or may not, answer any question that might implicate you in a crime. Know that if the warning was given, whatever you say might be used in court against you.
- If a *Miranda* type warning was not given and you were not free to leave when questioned, and you are charged with a crime, be sure to provide that information to defense counsel so they can bring a motion to suppress on your behalf if a warning was not provided.

CHAPTER 12

Due process under the Fifth Amendment.

No person .... shall *be subject for the same offence to be twice put in jeopardy of life or limb; nor shall be compelled in any criminal case to be a witness against himself, nor* **be deprived of life, liberty, or property, without due process of law;** *nor shall private property be taken for public use, without just compensation. (Ratified, December 1791)*

Just like the First Amendment, the Fifth Amendment has several clauses. The next clause of the Fifth Amendment that we will take a closer look at is the clause that prevents the government from depriving a person of their "life, liberty, or property" without "due process of law." Due process of law is a very broad term, but it generally means that we are entitled to all of the rules and principles of justice. "Due process" typically includes having notice of any action being taken against us, and the ability to be heard to defend ourselves.

Depriving someone of life is probably pretty easily understood. The government obviously cannot take away a life under the death penalty without following a very strict judicial process, which would include giving the person knowledge of the crimes they are accused of, notice of what action is being taken against them, and providing the accused the ability to hire counsel to be heard and defend themselves.

But how exactly should "liberty" be defined? Liberty is a word that gets a lot of attention. And it is a word that can have a variety of meanings. The word conjures up visions of a cracked bell high in a tower, or a flag flying high in a smoke-filled sky and a fist held up with the proclamation to "Give me *liberty* or give me death!" It is a word that many cling to in a self-righteous, indignant cry for freedom. But in the context of the Fifth Amendment, it has been defined simply as freedom from arbitrary and unreasonable restraint. In other words, the government cannot hold you or restrain your movement without certain processes.

The word "property" can also have a variety of meanings. It can mean physical tangible land, or money, or personal possessions. And, as we will see in the following case, it can also refer to intangible items such as an education.

This brings us to the ultimate question that the US Supreme Court decided in the case *Goss v. Lopez*.

Goss v. Lopez (1975)[168]

Question: Does a school official deprive a student of their property right to a free public education if the student is suspended without a hearing in violation of the right to "due process?"

Answer: Yes.

Here are the facts of the case: during the first week of February 1971, several schools in Columbus, Ohio, organized assemblies and demonstrations for "Black History Week." The next week, complaints about the speakers and placement of Black Nationalist flags began. Fights broke out in the weeks following. Four White students were suspended after throwing "anti-Black" propaganda out into the crowd during an assembly. Many protests and classroom walkouts were organized. Rudolph Sutton, Tyrone Washington, Susan Cooper, Deborah Fox, Clarence Byars, Bruce Harris, Dwight Lopez, Betty Crome, and Carl Smith were each suspended from their schools in Columbus, Ohio, in connection with the demonstrations during this period.

These nine students brought a class action lawsuit against the Columbus Ohio School District for themselves and other similarly suspended students. They claimed that the State of Ohio, through its school districts, could not withdraw their right to free public education for misconduct without due process to determine whether the misconduct actually occurred. They argued that their legitimate entitlement to public education is a property interest protected by the Fifth Amendment and incorporated to the states by the Fourteenth Amendment.

This little bit of information is nearly all we know about these nine high school and junior high school students in Columbus, Ohio, who were suspended from February through March 1971. This is all we know because, although these students were suspended, no hearing was conducted to ascertain their true stories. And, after the US Supreme Court ruled that their suspension was unconstitutional, any records of the alleged misconduct were expunged (meaning destroyed).

The Court ruled that due process requires fundamentally fair notice and a hearing.

> For a suspension of ten days or less, a student must be given oral or written notice of the charges against him and, if he denies them, an explanation of the evidence the authorities have and an opportunity to present his version. Generally, notice and hearing should precede the student's removal from school, since the hearing may almost immediately follow the misconduct, but if prior notice and hearing are not feasible, as where the student's presence endangers persons or property or threatens disruption

of the academic process, thus justifying immediate removal from school, the necessary notice and hearing should follow as soon as practicable.[169]

So, if you have ever been summoned to a hearing to provide evidence before a school board to determine a suspension, you have these nine students to thank for it. Seriously. Thank them. Although any hearing prior to suspension is uncomfortable, you are there to protect your interests. Because of them, you have a right to your free public education unless misconduct is proven. Because of them, you have the right to provide evidence to prove your innocence. Because of them, you have the right to have any false allegations of misconduct removed from your school file—information that could follow you through public school, to college, and beyond. Because of them, your right to stand up for yourself has been protected. So, thank you Rudolph, Tyrone, Susan, Deborah, Clarence, Bruce, Dwight, Betty, and Carl.

ADDITIONAL REFERENCES

Chapter 12—The Right to Due Process

- If you are facing a hearing for suspension, know your rights. In most states, you can only be suspended for certain offenses that are described in the state's education code. You may talk to an attorney before the hearing. You are entitled to know the offense you are being questioned about. Make sure you know the maximum number of days that the state allows for suspensions.
- You are entitled to a hearing within thirty days of the incident.
- In some states, if you are non-English-speaking, you are entitled to a translator.
- You may have the right to record the proceedings. You have the right to present evidence and to inspect any evidence from the school against you. You may have other rights as well. Look to your school district's website for specific information on your student rights.
- As a result of *Carey v. Piphus*, 435 US 247 (1978), you also have a right to just compensation for proven emotional damages, on sufficient evidence, if your due process rights have been violated.

"Neither the Fourteenth Amendment nor the Bill of Rights is for adults alone."[170] JUSTICE FORTAS

CHAPTER 13

The Sixth, Seventh, and Eighth Amendments: A Right to Be Heard

Sixth Amendment

In all criminal prosecutions, the accused shall enjoy the right *to a speedy and public trial, by an impartial jury of the State and district wherein the crime shall have been committed, which district shall have been previously ascertained by law, and to be informed of the nature and cause of the accusation;* **to be confronted with the witnesses against him;** *to have compulsory process for obtaining witnesses in his favor, and to have the Assistance of Counsel for his defence. (Ratified, December 1791)*

The Sixth Amendment's several clauses describe many of the due process rights and procedural protections for criminal prosecutions. As it says, the accused of any crime is entitled to be informed of the accusation against them, a speedy trial by a jury of peers, and to be confronted by the witnesses against them. Volumes have been written on the rights of persons charged with crimes, including youths and the juvenile justice system. However, since this book is dedicated to the rights of youth *advocates* and not to criminal justice, only the

Sixth Amendment right to be confronted by the *child* witness against an accused is examined here.

As we have seen, it is important to understand the right being protected. In this case, any person accused of a crime is entitled to be confronted directly by the accuser. The right is meant to prevent an accused from being convicted solely on written testimony of an accuser or hearsay. It is an important right so that the accused has an opportunity to cross-examine witnesses against them and a jury can evaluate the demeanor and manner of both the accused and the accuser. Most importantly, it is meant to provide an opportunity for the accused to look the accuser in the eye to bear out a lying accuser. This has traditionally meant live face-to-face testimony without the aid of technology, such as closed-circuit TV or computer-aided viewing.

But besides this essential right given to the accused, the rights of the accuser (often the crime victim) must be balanced. This is never so obvious as when the accuser is a child and victim of an alleged crime.

Coy v. Iowa (1988)[171]

In 1985, two thirteen-year-old girls were having a sleepover in a backyard in Iowa. According to the girls, they were each sexually assaulted during the night after they had gone into their tent to sleep. They alleged that a man entered their tent with a stocking over his head, shined a flashlight in their eyes, and warned them not to look at him. Neither was later able to describe the man's face. The next-door neighbor, John Coy, was charged with the assault.

The trial court allowed the two girls to testify at John Coy's trial behind a screen, which blocked him from their sight, but allowed him to see them dimly and to hear them. The prosecution argued that it was presumed that the two girls were traumatized as victims of sexual assault and the screen would prevent further trauma during testimony.

The defense argued that the screen denied Coy his Sixth Amendment right to face-to-face confrontation by the accusers. He also argued that the jury would assume he was guilty if the witnesses were being protected from viewing him. John Coy was convicted.

The case was appealed and taken up by the US Supreme Court. The majority of the Court sided with Coy. The Court held that there is no presumption that an accuser has suffered trauma, even if the victim of the alleged sexual assault is a child, because the *accused* is still presumed innocent until proven guilty.

> [t]he Confrontation Clause, by its words, provides a criminal defendant the right to 'confront' face-to-face the witnesses giving evidence against him at trial. That core guarantee serves the general perception that confrontation is essential to fairness, and helps to ensure the integrity of the factfinding process by making it more difficult for witnesses to lie.[172]

The case was remanded (meaning handed back down) to the trial court to hear the case and evidence again with the two girls testifying in court before the defendant.

Maryland v. Craig (1990)[173]

In another part of the country, from 1984 to 1986, a six-year-old girl named Brooke suffered child abuse, sexual abuse, assault, and battery at the hands of Sandra Ann Craig, a woman who owned and operated a kindergarten and prekindergarten center. Maryland had just passed a law to protect child-victims as witnesses against their accused when Craig was tried for the crimes. The Maryland statute permits a judge to receive, by one-way closed circuit television, the testimony of a child witness who is alleged to be a victim of child abuse. But the judge must first determine that testifying face-to-face with the defendant would result in "the child suffering serious emotional distress such that the child cannot reasonably communicate."

The prosecution presented evidence from an expert witness regarding Brooke and the other children who also claimed child abuse at the hands of Craig. The trial judge ruled that each of the children would suffer serious emotional distress if forced to do so. The trial court then found Brooke and three other children competent to testify if shielded from Craig, and permitted them to testify via the one-way closed circuit television.

During their testimony, each of the children and the attorneys left the courtroom and went to a separate room. The judge, jury, and defendant remained in the courtroom. The child witness was then asked questions on direct examination and cross-examined while a video monitor displayed the testimony in the courtroom. During the testimony, the witnesses could not see the defendant.

Craig was convicted on all counts and appealed, arguing that she was denied her Sixth Amendment right to face-to-face confrontation. The US Supreme Court took the case, which was decided in 1990—just two years after the *Coy v. Iowa* decision.

In reconsidering its decision from *Coy v. Iowa,* the Court said that although there is a *preference* to a face-to-face witness at trial, a defendant does not have an *absolute* right to a face-to-face meeting with their accuser at trial. The US Supreme Court drew distinctions because, according to the Maryland statute, "the child witness must [still] be competent to testify and must testify under oath; the defendant retains full opportunity for contemporaneous cross-examination; and the judge, jury, and defendant are able to view (albeit by video monitor) the demeanor (and body) of the witness as he or she testifies."

Seventh Amendment

In Suits at common law, where the value in controversy shall exceed twenty dollars, the right of trial by jury shall be preserved, and no fact tried by a jury, shall be otherwise re-examined in any Court of the United States, than according to the rules of the common law. *(Ratified, December 1791)*

In this context, "common law" means civil cases—those not involving a criminal defendant. The amount of controversy must be over twenty dollars to have a right to a jury trial. You must also have legal capacity to file a lawsuit, which includes being at least eighteen years of age. But you can appoint a guardian to bring a lawsuit if under the age limit.

Once a matter is decided in a court of law, you cannot start the same matter again. If you lose, you can appeal a decision of the court. But if you take a settlement and then decide later that you are unhappy with what you settled for, you cannot start the lawsuit over again or then ask for a jury trial.

There are a number of other rules and nuances to making a civil claim under the law. If you have a claim, consult with an attorney. Some resources for free or low cost legal consultation are provided elsewhere in this book. By all means, where your rights are at issue, do not stop until you find the help you need.

Eighth Amendment

Excessive bail shall not be required, nor excessive fines imposed, nor cruel and unusual punishments inflicted. *(Ratified, December 1791)*

Say you are sitting in class with your feet up on the chair across the aisle from you and your teacher comes along and knocks your feet off the chair. Is that okay? Say you were sleeping in your chair and your teacher comes along and bops you on the head to wake you up. Is that okay? Say this goes on and your teacher hits you so severely that you get a concussion. Okay? Or beats you with a stick to make you write and you end up with a broken arm. Okay? Say you then get hauled off to the assistant principal's office, and he makes you bend over a chair while he hits your backside with a paddle, which has holes in it to make the paddling sting with welts. Is that okay?

NOT OKAY says certain state laws, but the US Supreme Court in 1977 said "that's okay."

Ingraham v. Wright (1977)[174]

The Cruel and Unusual Punishments Clause of the Eighth Amendment does not apply to disciplinary corporal punishment in public schools. Furthermore, paddling of students' buttocks to maintain discipline does not require "due process" notice or hearing.

Two students, Andrews and Ingraham, were enrolled in Drew Junior High School in Dade County, Florida. Ingraham said that when he was slow to respond to a question from a teacher, he was taken to the principal's office, where he was held over a table and given twenty "licks" or hits with a paddle. His injury was so severe that his mother took him to the hospital for medical attention. He suffered an extensive hematoma (a bruise) that kept him out of school for several days. "Andrews was paddled several times for minor infractions. On two occasions, he was struck on his arms, once depriving him of the full use of his arm for a week."

The two sought relief from the courts and filed a lawsuit in District Court claiming their Eighth Amendment right against cruel and unusual punishment and their Fifth Amendment right to due process had been violated. The District Court concluded that the punishment authorized and practiced generally in the county schools violated no constitutional right.

The District Court's opinion and stated:

> [p]addling of recalcitrant children has long been an accepted method of promoting good behavior and instilling notions of responsibility and decorum into the mischievous heads of school children.

The court refused to examine instances of punishment individually:

> We think it a misuse of our judicial power to determine, for example, whether a teacher has acted arbitrarily in paddling a particular child for certain behavior or whether, in a particular instance of misconduct, five licks would have been a more appropriate punishment than ten licks . . . .

The case was appealed to the US Supreme Court. The majority opinion, written by Justice Powell, although long and tedious, amounts to: yeah, it's okay to discipline students by corporal punishment. The 5-4 opinion concluded that the Eighth Amendment only protects *criminals*, not school children.

The dissent, written by Justice White and joined by Justice Brennan, Justice Marshall and Justice Stevens, points out how flawed the majority opinion is with an analogy:

> [I]f it is constitutionally impermissible to cut off someone's ear for the commission of murder, it must be unconstitutional to cut off a child's ear for being late to class. Although there were no ears cut off in this case, the record reveals beatings so severe that, if

they were inflicted on a hardened criminal for the commission of a serious crime, they might not pass constitutional muster.[175]

Just as Ms. Furguson in *Furguson v. City of New York* (reviewed above) discovered, criminals sometimes have more rights and protections under the Constitution than others. Fortunately, states have the ability to provide more protection for individuals than the US Constitution, just not less protections. Many states have since passed laws against corporal punishment of students by teachers and school officials. Although most states have banned corporal punishment in public school settings, the practice is still legal in seventeen states as of August 2023, and only three states—Iowa, New Jersey, and Maryland—have banned physical discipline in private schools.

Consider This:

According to the American Academy of Pediatrics,[176] "when schools use physical pain as a way of controlling kids, research shows they are *less* likely to cooperate, not more. Corporal punishment has also been linked with stress, depression, and low self-esteem, harming a child's chances for success in school and life."

Evidence shows that spanking, slapping, and similar punishments actually lead to an increase in problem behaviors over time. Schools are much more likely to use physical punishments to control Black children and children with special needs than their peers. Physical punishment is closely linked with struggles in mental health, cognitive development, school achievement, and many other negative outcomes for kids.

The seventeen states with the highest populations of Black children are the same states that still allow corporal punishment. Statistics show that those children who are disciplined through pain are more often disciplined at later stages in life because the discipline fosters aggression and anger. It is a vicious circle. Anger and aggression begets anger and aggression. Racial tension and violence is the result.

According to the American Academy of Pediatrics, the latest estimate from the National Center for Education Statistics suggests that more than 70,000 public school kids face physical punishment at least once during the school year. Racism and discrimination are serious threats to the health and academic success of children. US Department of Education figures on public school students in grades K-12 show that Black males are nearly twice as likely to be hit or spanked as their White peers. Black females are more than three times as likely as their White peers to face physical punishments.

Children with disabilities also face higher rates of physical punishment at school than their peers. An estimated 16.5 percent of all kids who are hit or spanked during the school year are eligible for services under the Individuals with Disabilities Education Act (IDEA). Many of these students, especially those with intellectual disabilities, may not fully understand why they are being punished. Their confusion can intensify the negative impact of the physical pain they feel.

ADDITIONAL RESOURCES

Chapter 13—No Cruel or Unusual Punishment

- Congress can act to protect children from physical injury and mental harm at the hands of school personnel by passing the "Protecting Our Students in Schools Act of 2023."
- Know your state and school district's policy on corporal punishment. Many parents in most states can opt out of allowing their child to be punished by corporal punishment.
- Discuss with your parents, school teachers, and administrators what alternatives to student discipline are available.

"Returning violence for violence multiplies violence, adding deeper darkness to a night already devoid of stars."
DR. MARTIN LUTHER KING, JR.

CHAPTER 14

The Ninth and Tenth Amendments: The Vague "Liberty" Rights

Ninth Amendment

The enumeration in the Constitution, of certain rights, shall not be construed to deny or disparage others retained by the people. *(Ratified, December 1791)*

What rights are provided in the Ninth Amendment? It seems to say that even if our Founding Fathers didn't think of a right and put it in the Bill of Rights—the first ten amendments—we cannot be denied of a right that we think of. Right? At least that is one of the arguments used to support a federal legalization of abortion in *Roe v. Wade*[177] (reviewed in Chapter 17).

Griswold v. Connecticut (1965)[178]

It also appeared in the concurring opinion of Justice Goldberg in the case *Griswold v. Connecticut*, which legalized birth control in 1965, and held that there is an implicit right to marital privacy. Both of those cases sought to expand the rights of individuals against government intrusion. However, whether the Ninth Amendment can be used again to expand individual rights beyond the enumerated rights set forth in the Bill of Rights remains to be seen. Below is an argument *for* its use to expand individual rights, and an argument limiting the amendment's use. Both arguments appear in the *Griswold v. Connecticut*[179] case.

Justice Goldberg's concurrence states, in part:

> The language and history of the Ninth Amendment reveal that the Framers of the Constitution believed that there are additional fundamental rights, protected from governmental infringement, which exist alongside those fundamental rights specifically mentioned in the first eight constitutional amendments . . . It was proffered to quiet expressed fears that a bill of specifically enumerated rights could not be sufficiently broad to cover all essential rights, and that the specific mention of certain rights would be interpreted as a denial that others were protected . . .[180]

In his dissent, Justice Stewart disagreed:

> . . . to say that the Ninth Amendment has anything to do with this case is to turn somersaults with history. The Ninth Amendment, like its companion, the Tenth . . . was framed by James Madison and adopted by the States simply to make clear that the adoption of the Bill of Rights did not alter the plan that the federal government was to be a government of express and limited powers, and that all rights and powers not delegated to it were retained by the people and the individual States. Until today, no member of this Court has ever suggested that the Ninth Amendment meant anything else, and the idea that a federal court could ever use the Ninth Amendment to annul a law passed by the elected representatives of the people of the State of Connecticut would have caused James Madison no little wonder.[181]

If Justice Stewart's dissent is right, the Ninth Amendment seems duplicative of the Tenth Amendment, which says basically the same thing only in fewer words. If the Ninth Amendment was instead meant to allow the federal government to expand the rights of citizens, as Justice Goldberg suggests, it has not accomplished that. Although other Supreme Court cases have mentioned the Ninth Amendment, it has not been the backbone to any individual rights other than marital rights of privacy in *Griswold v. Connecticut*. As of now, *Griswold* still stands as precedent for marital privacy, but recently, when *Roe v. Wade* was overturned in *Dobbs v. Jackson Women's Health Organization*[182] (reviewed below), Justice Clarence Thomas wrote in his concurrence that *Griswold* would be another precedent to be "reconsidered" and possibly "correct[ed]."

Tenth Amendment

The powers not delegated to the United States by the Constitution, nor prohibited by it to the States, are reserved to the States respectively, or to the people. *(Ratified, December 1791)*

There are many powers delegated to the Federal government by the Constitution. The most powerful of these is the "Supremacy Clause" of Article VI. But under the Tenth Amendment, powers that are not delegated to the federal government by the Constitution are reserved to the states. Stated another way, through the Tenth Amendment, the states have retained powers to enact laws to regulate in any matter where the Federal government is not authorized to act. The Tenth Amendment allows states to act with autonomy in matters such as state commerce, state police, and regulating schools. Yet, the Supremacy Clause clarifies that the federal government is the supreme law of the land. Where any federal law and state law conflict, the federal government's power supersedes the State. The Supremacy Clause also prohibits the states from preventing the federal government from exercising any of its Constitutional powers.

In addition, the Tenth Amendment is said to "incorporate" the individual rights guaranteed by the Bill of Rights to the states. Whereas the first nine amendments protect the individual's rights against the *federal* government, the Tenth Amendment was written to protect individuals against any *state* government obstructing individual rights.

The next case tests the autonomy of a State that refused to abide by a decision of the US Supreme Court granting certain individual rights under the authority of the ratified Fourteenth Amendment of the US Constitution.

Cooper v. Aaron (1958)[183]

The decision in *Cooper v. Aaron* has the distinction of being signed and authored by the entire Court. It was a signal that it is the opinion of the institution itself—the judicial branch of the federal government—not just the individual justices of the Court. If it was not clear before, it became abundantly clear after the decision of *Cooper v. Aaron* that the supreme law of the land lies in the US Constitution—over any state law. The decision, in no uncertain terms, sent a message to states with segregated school districts nationwide that the federal government would not tolerate attempts to evade or obstruct the Fourteenth Amendment and desegregation after the US Supreme Court decision in *Brown vs. Board of Education* in 1954 (reviewed below).

To understand *Cooper v. Aaron*, one must understand the American culture of segregation in the South in the 1950s. And . . . who can understand it but those who lived it? This case takes place in Arkansas. Nearly one hundred years earlier, Arkansas and the other Confederate states sought to secede from the union in order to keep a class of persons enslaved. Although the Civil War brought an end to slavery, race-based hate continued. This case is about the courage of nine high school students who took a stand against that hate for themselves and others.

The case represents one of the most important, and often overlooked, moments in American history. Not just the US Supreme Court, but also the entire federal government stood up for the rights of minority individuals in this disagreement with a hate-based segregated Southern state government. The federal government, through the judicial branch and its Supreme Court, would no longer tolerate it.

Brown v. Board of Education, decided in 1954, held that segregation was a Constitutional violation, overturning *Plessy v. Ferguson* (reviewed below). In 1955, the school board in Little Rock, Arkansas, formed a plan to desegregate schools with gradual integration, starting with Central High School in 1957, and then lower grades during the next six years. By 1957, frustrated by the lack of progress of the states to desegregate, the US Supreme Court issued a second ruling (*Brown v. Board of Education II*) that required states to desegregate "with all deliberate speed." But neither ruling gave any instruction on how that was to be accomplished.

According to Little Rock's desegregation plan, any student was allowed to transfer from any school if they belonged to a minority race. Parents of minority children attempted to transfer and register their children in all White-schools beginning in 1956. All were denied entrance. Thirty-three of these children (Aaron being the first), represented by the NAACP, filed suit in the federal court in Arkansas, alleging that school officials (including Little Rock School Board member, Cooper) were conspiring to deny Black students their constitutional rights by maintaining segregated schools and fashioning such a gradual plan for integration. In August of 1956, the matter was tried in the lower court. The judge found the plan to be prompt and reasonable. The court's order instructed integration to begin in September 1957 at Little Rock Central High School—with a population at the time of approximately 1,800 all White students.

While the school board was going forward with its preparation for desegregating the Little Rock schools, other Arkansas State authorities, in contrast, were actively pursuing a program designed to perpetuate racial segregation in Arkansas. In November 1956, an amendment to the Arkansas State Constitution was proposed, flatly commanding the Arkansas General Assembly to disobey the *Brown v. Board of Ed.* decisions. The proposed state amendment referred to the *Brown v. Board of Ed.* decisions specifically as the "unconstitutional desegregation decisions of May 17, 1954, and May 31, 1955, of the United States Supreme Court."

Despite this, the "Little Rock Nine," as they became known nationwide, were the nine senior high school students who were allowed to transfer to Little Rock Central High School to end segregation in 1957. They were Thelma Mothershed, Minnijean Brown, Elizabeth Eckford, Gloria Ray, Jefferson Thomas, Melba Pattillo, Terrence Roberts, Carlotta Walls, and Ernest Green. These students were chosen because of their good citizenship and scholastic achievements.

Although allowed to transfer, they were not allowed to join in any of the school extracurricular activities, including dances, band, cheerleading, football, basketball, chess club, glee club, etc. Nevertheless, the nine were excited to attend Little Rock Central High because they knew that an all-White school would have more resources—more books, more lab equipment, advanced methods of teaching, and some of the best teachers in the state.

The day before the 1957-1958 school year began, Orval Faubus, the Governor of Arkansas, broadcasted a speech over the local Little Rock radio station. He said, "Blood will run in the streets if Negro people attempt to enter Central High School."

He called the Arkansas National Guard to be on hand at the school because of the threats of unrest. The thing is, none of the nine students, or the NAACP, or the local or state police, or anyone else for that matter heard any hints of threats of unrest until that point. The nine students knew that it would be a difficult year for many reasons, but they did not believe that they would have to endure the kind of hatred shown to them that year by the governor of the State of Arkansas.

On what was to be their first day of class, on September 3, 1957, a large crowd of about 200 people gathered around the school before they arrived. As promised by Governor Faubus, the Arkansas National Guard was present. The nine believed that the National Guard was there to assist their entrance, only to find that the Guard was instructed to block their entrance while allowing the White students access. When later accused of encouraging segregation rather than integration, Governor Faubus claimed that he was only trying to "preserve the peace."*

The NAACP Regional President, Daisy Bates, advised the students to arrive without their parents, fearing that the sight of the parents might alienate the students further. The night before their first day, Bates arranged to take the students to the school herself. But Bates was not able to reach Elizabeth Eckford because Elizabeth's family did not have a phone. When Elizabeth arrived at school alone without any support, she was met by an angry mob of White students and their parents who shouted at her, spat at her, and threatened to lynch her. The National Guard blocked her entrance to the school. She thought the guards were there to protect her. She said later that she saw White students pass by a guard and tried to do the same, but the guard said nothing and raised his bayonet, pushing her back into the crowd. She returned to the bus stop to escape the crowd, but the crowd followed her. One kind woman assisted her, helping her to get away from the tormenting crowd and then got her on a bus home. The photographs below of Elizabeth alone with the angry mob behind her on her first day at Little Rock Central High School are some of the most iconic photographs of the Civil Rights movement. She was only fifteen at the time.

---

* There are mixed accounts of Orval Faubus's motives for calling in the Arkansas National Guard that day, but the accounts generally agree that he bent to pressures from segregationists, whether his personal beliefs were in alignment or not, because he would seek re-election in the next term.

186 CULTIVATING JUSTICE

Fifteen-year-old Elizabeth Eckford on her first day of school, and her most recognizable tormentor, Hazel Bryan September 3, 1957 Little Rock Central High School, photo credit—twenty-six-year-old journalist Will Counts

Grace Lorch protects Elizabeth Eckford from further harassment. Ms. Lorch stayed with Elizabeth and even boarded the bus with her to make sure she rejoined her mother without further incident.

Fig. 6 Photo by Raymond Preddy, courtesy of University of Arkansas Little Rock. See Permissions and Licensing information.

The Little Rock Nine were kept from attending school until September 25, 1957. The Arkansas National Guard, sent by Governor Faubus, blocked the entrance of all nine on what was supposed to be their first day, September 3, 1957. The next day, the school board and superintendent of schools sought a court order to stall the desegregation plan until 1961. That request was denied. At this point, the federal government got involved and investigated. The federal court judge and the US Attorney General kept Governor Faubus and officers of the Arkansas National Guard from further attempts to prevent the nine students from attending Central High School. The federal court ordered Governor Faubus "not to obstruct or prevent, by threat or other interference, the nine from their constitutional right to attend Little Rock Central High School."

In the meantime, through a series of exchanges, President Eisenhower arranged to meet with Governor Faubus over the issue. The two met on September 14, 1957. According to notes made by President Eisenhower, he recommended that Governor Faubus return home and change the orders of the Arkansas National Guard to continue to preserve order but allow the nine students to enter the school. His personal notes read, "I further said that I did not believe it was beneficial to anybody to have a trial of strength between the president and a governor, because in any area where the federal government has assumed jurisdiction, and this was upheld by the Supreme Court, there could only be one outcome–that is, the state would lose, and I did not want to see any governor humiliated."[184]

The nine students again attempted to attend class at Central High the following Monday. Although a few city and state police now escorted the nine students, entry was still impossible because of the angry mob that had gathered and grown to approximately 1,000 people.

Upon hearing the news of the continuing unrest at Little Rock Central High following his meeting with Governor Faubus, President Eisenhower issued an Executive Order federalizing the entire

10,000-member Arkansas National Guard, taking it out of Faubus's control, and sent approximately 1,000 federal troops from the 101st Airborne Division of the United States Army to Little Rock Central High School to protect the nine students. The Little Rock Nine were finally allowed to attend Central High School on September 25, 1957.

Although the federal National Guard continued to attend Central High School every day for the remainder of the school year, the harassment did not end. The National Guard protected the students at the perimeter of the school, but the students no longer had the protection of the army inside the school. One of the students, Melba Pattillo, wrote a book about her experience called *Warriors Don't Cry*. In her book, she describes incidents of bullying. Acid was thrown in her eyes. In the girls' restroom she was trapped in a stall while pieces of flaming paper were dropped down on her.

Minnijean Brown was also bullied by members of a group of White male students in the school cafeteria during lunch. She fought back and dropped her lunch onto the boys and was suspended for six days. Two months later, after another confrontation, Brown was suspended for the rest of the school year. The others were harassed, as well. They were knocked down, books were knocked out of their hands, and they were jeered at, heckled, mocked, taunted, and abused. The students began to doubt themselves and doubt their choices, but they endured throughout the 1957-1958 school year.

While the hate inside the school continued, the hate at the state government level continued, as well. At the urging of Governor Faubus, Arkansas voters adopted additional state laws which claimed to relieve any obligation to attend integrated public schools. The laws supposedly empowered school boards to spend district funds to pay for legal representation in lawsuits to oppose desegregation. One of the bills proposed the closure of any school threatened with integration. Another bill proposed state money to students who sought private education so they would not have to attend a desegregated school.

In the late summer of 1958, as the 1958-1959 school year drew near, the Little Rock School Board, which had recommended the desegregation plan in 1955, now wanted to delay the plan. The school board blamed the State of Arkansas, and in particular Governor Faubus, for the failed desegregation attempt. The Little Rock School Board argued that their integration plan wasn't working "under the pressure of public opposition." They argued that the next school year would be just as bad, if not worse.

A number of Black students were still waiting for full integration, so the nine students denied that they had a difficult year because they were committed to desegregation, not just for themselves, but also for others. They argued that any difficulties they had were the fault of the school board and the public's general opposition to desegregation. The students argued that the board could have solved the problems the year before, and could still solve the problems, by taking a firmer disciplinary stand against the persons responsible for disorder. They also argued that if the plan to desegregate stalled, the bullies would win and any future integration would be more difficult.

The District Court recognized the student's argument: Whites in the south simply did not want desegregation. It also recognized that White people believed, at their governor's urging, that they did not have to abide by the US Supreme Court's ruling in *Brown v. Board of Ed*.

The District Court's ruling said:

> [T]he source of the trouble was the deep seated popular opposition in Little Rock to the principle of integration, which, as is known, runs counter to the pattern of Southern life which has existed for over three hundred years. The evidence also shows that to this opposition was added the conviction of many of the people of Little Rock, that the Brown decisions do not truly represent the law, and that by virtue of the 1956-57 [state] enactments, . . . integration in the public schools can be lawfully avoided.

...

> [proposed state constitutional amendments and statutes] had their effect at Little Rock and throughout the State in stiffening opposition to the [desegregation] plan and in persuading people that there was no necessity for integration at this time.
>
> The opposition to integration and the feeling that it was not required at this time had been greatly strengthened by numerous newspaper articles and advertisements, and by circulars and cards distributed in Little Rock, copies of which were introduced in evidence ... and many of them emphasize the idea that integration can be avoided by legal, constitutional means.

The federal district judge who wrote the above realized that Governor Faubus created the disharmony in his own state. Gov. Faubus stirred the pot. Perhaps it was already brewing, but it was not necessary to turn up the heat to boil that first day on September 3, 1957. But the district court granted the school board their request to further delay desegregation at Little Rock Central High School, citing an atmosphere of hostility. The NAACP immediately petitioned the US Supreme Court to overturn that ruling in *Cooper v. Aaron*. As noted above, the US Supreme Court, meeting in special session on September 12, 1958, unanimously issued a bold statement of the court:

> Law and order are not here to be preserved by depriving the Negro children of their constitutional rights. The record before us clearly establishes that the growth of the Board's difficulties to a magnitude beyond its unaided power to control is the product of state action. Those difficulties, as counsel for the Board forthrightly conceded on the oral argument in this Court, can also be brought under control by state action.

The controlling legal principles are plain. The command of the Fourteenth Amendment is that no "State" shall deny to any person within its jurisdiction the equal protection of the laws.

Whoever, by virtue of public position under a State government, . . . denies or takes away the equal protection of the laws violates the constitutional inhibition; and, as he acts in the name and for the State, and is clothed with the State's power, his act is that of the State. This must be so, or the constitutional prohibition has no meaning.

Thus, the prohibitions of the Fourteenth Amendment extend to all action of the State denying equal protection of the laws; whatever the agency of the State taking the action.

No state legislator or executive or judicial officer can war against the Constitution without violating his undertaking to support it.[185]

This decision gives us all—every resident of every state—equal protection under the Constitution against any State's limitations of our freedoms. In other words, States have some power, but *the Constitution is the supreme law of the land*! When the US Supreme Court met in special session in September 1958, they ordered the immediate and complete desegregation of Little Rock Central High School on September 12, 1958.

In an outrageous flagrant denial of the constitutional rights of others, and the US Supreme Court's authority, that same day, September 12, 1958, Governor Faubus signed all the bills that the voters passed to bypass desegregation, including the law allowing him to close the schools. He closed all four high schools in Little Rock beginning Monday, September 15, 1958. Whites and Blacks (3,665 students in all) were deprived of their public education that year. Teachers and school administrators were required to go to work despite the empty classrooms. Although none of the students were getting an education, Governor Faubus ordered high school football games to continue.

On September 27, 1958, Arkansas voters were asked to vote either for or against "racial integration of all schools within the Little Rock School District." The segregationists won. All four high schools in Little Rock Arkansas remained closed for the 1958-1959 school year rather than allow desegregation. Private schools for Whites, but not Blacks, opened in Little Rock. In an illegal board action, the State fired forty-four teachers who were members of the NAACP. According to *The Encyclopedia of Arkansas*[186] 93 percent of the 2,915 displaced White students found some form of alternative schooling. Some Black students found other public schools or private schools out of state to attend, or entered college early, but 50 percent of the 750 displaced Black students were unable to attend school at all that year. Some of these students took the year over again, delaying their college education for a year. Many of them dropped out and never returned to school again.

The loss of forty-four qualified teachers, and the thought of additional closures, was more than voters could take. They organized a recall of three of the leading segregationists on the Little Rock School Board. Moderates were then elected to the school board. Then, on June 18, 1959, another federal district court ruled that Arkansas's state laws allowing closure of schools and using school funds to encourage lawsuits to block desegregation was unconstitutional.

All four Little Rock high schools reopened in the fall of 1959, fully desegregated.

Ernest Green became the first person of color to graduate from Little Rock Central High in 1958. Martin Luther King, Jr. attended the graduation ceremony. Ernest graduated from Michigan State with a Bachelor of Arts degree in 1962, and a master's degree in sociology in 1964.

Elizabeth Ekford earned enough credits to graduate high school from correspondence school during the 1958-1959 shutout. She then graduated from Central State University in Ohio, where she earned a Bachelor of Arts degree in history. She served in the army for five years. She taught history to middle school students for much of her working career. In 2018, she authored an autobiography titled *The Worst First Day; Bullied While Desegregated Little Rock Central High,* coauthored by Dr. Eurydice Stanley and Grace Stanley. In 2019, Elizabeth and Dr. Stanley taught American civil rights history to more than 4,000 students in New Zealand. She often speaks about the students who harassed her and those who saw but did nothing to stop it. Her talks deliver an important message to speak up if you or someone you know is a victim of bullying.

Carlotta Walls LaNier was the youngest of the nine. Just months before her graduation from Little Rock Central High in 1960, her home was bombed. No one was hurt, but her father was first considered a suspect because he was not home that night. According to *History of Racial Injustice,* police arrested and beat Carlotta's father in unsuccessful efforts to coerce a confession. Police then arrested two young Black men, Herbert Monts, a family friend, and Maceo Binns, Jr. Carlotta never believed either man was responsible, but both were convicted and sentenced to five years in prison. In 2010, Carlota described the bombing and its aftermath the worst part of the integration experience and firmly asserted 'the segregationists were behind all of it—the bombing and the arrests of Herbert and Maceo.' Carlotta returned to Central High the very next day after the bombing. She is the only female of the nine to have attended a graduation ceremony at Central High. She attended Michigan State University and graduated from Colorado State University.

Jefferson Thomas graduated from Central High in 1960. He attended Wayne State University and graduated with a bachelor's degree from Los Angeles State College. In 1964, Jefferson narrated a film titled *Nine* *from Little Rock*. In the film, he said, "If Little Rock taught us nothing more, it taught us that problems can make us better. Much better."

Terrence Roberts transferred in 1958, and completed his senior year at Los Angeles High School. He attended the University of California, Los Angeles and Los Angeles City College before graduating from California State College. He graduated from California State University, Los Angeles with a bachelor of arts degree in sociology in 1967. He received his master's degree in social welfare from UCLA in 1970, and his Ph.D. in psychology from Southern Illinois University in 1976.

Gloria Ray Kolmark transferred to Kansas City Central High School in 1958, where she graduated. Gloria attended Illinois Institute of Technology and received a bachelor of science degree in chemistry and mathematics. In 1970, she joined IBM in Stockholm, Sweden, working as a systems analyst and technical writer. She then earned a law degree in Sweden and worked as a patent attorney for IBM from 1977 until 1981. From 1976 to 1994, she founded and was editor-in-chief for the international journal, *Computers in Industry*.

Minnijean Brown graduated high school in New York after she had been expelled from Little Rock Central High. She then attended Southern Illinois University and majored in journalism. She studied in Canada and completed a master of social work degree. From 1999 through 2001, she served as the deputy assistant secretary for workforce diversity at the US Department of Interior under the Clinton Administration. She became a public speaker and has spoken extensively in the US and other countries.

Thelma Mothershed took correspondence courses and attended summer school in Saint Louis, Missouri, during the 1958-1959 shutout. She received her diploma from Central High by mail. In 1964, she earned her master's degree in guidance and counseling.

Melba Patilla Beals relocated to Santa Rosa, California, to complete her senior year at Montgomery High School in 1958. She earned a bachelor's degree from San Francisco State University. Melba earned a master's degree in journalism from Columbia University. In 2009, she received a doctoral degree in education from the University of San Francisco.

More to Consider:

Many of the decisions coming out of the US Supreme Court in recent years leave it up to the States' legislators to make laws concerning personal freedoms. This means that particular states are being given the power to decide questions such as what books are banned, what regulations should apply to abortion rights, gun control regulations, voter registration regulations, border crossing regulations, and many issues concerning public schools. The states are becoming more and more divided on these issues. Do you agree or disagree with the US Supreme Court handing these issues back to the states?

Do you think the current US Supreme Court is allowing states to "re-segregate" in violation of the Equal Protection Clause of the Fourteenth Amendment because of its decision to leave many of these issues up to states' legislation?

How can America collectively protect against re-segregation?

"If democracy is to live, segregation must die."
DR. MARTIN LUTHER KING, JR.

CHAPTER 15

The Thirteenth and Fourteenth Amendments; Equality for All

Thirteenth Amendment

Section 1

Neither slavery nor involuntary servitude, except as a punishment for crime whereof the party shall have been duly convicted, shall exist within the United States, or any place subject to their jurisdiction.

Section 2

Congress shall have power to enforce this article by appropriate legislation. *(Ratified, December 1865)*

Fourteenth Amendment

Section 1

All persons born or naturalized in the United States, and subject to the jurisdiction thereof, are citizens of the United States and of the State wherein they reside.

No State shall make or enforce any law which shall abridge the privileges or immunities of citizens of the United States; nor shall any State deprive any person of life, liberty, or property, without due process of law; nor deny to any person within its jurisdiction the equal protection of the laws. *(Ratified, July 1868)*

The Fourteenth Amendment was one of three amendments adopted after the Civil War to protect the liberties of recently freed slaves. Before the Civil War ended, President Abraham Lincoln issued an executive order on January 1, 1863, known as the "Emancipation Proclamation," proclaiming that, "all persons held as slaves . . . are, and henceforward shall be free."

The Confederates surrendered, and the Civil War was over on April 9, 1865. But a plan for reconstruction of the Union was yet to be decided. President Lincoln wanted at least 10 percent of White men from each state to pledge freedom to the slaves. A prior plan demanded 50 percent, so by the time the war was over, no agreement for reconstruction had been reached. Then, less than a week after the war's end, President Lincoln was assassinated. He died on April 15, 1865, and Andrew Johnson, a slaveholder himself, was sworn in as President of the United States.

President Johnson clashed with Congress, which wanted to preserve President Lincoln's vision of citizenship, with the right to vote, to all Black men. For the first time in US history, Congress voted to investigate a president under the Constitutional provision of impeachment. Impeachment of a president requires a two-thirds majority vote. Just one vote kept President Johnson in office. A bill was then introduced in Congress to include the Thirteenth, Fourteenth, and Fifteenth Amendments. The Thirteenth Amendment abolished slavery, the Fourteenth granted citizenship to people once enslaved, and the

Fifteenth guaranteed Black men the right to vote. (All women would not gain the right to vote for another fifty years.) These three amendments were ratified by the Union (meaning the Northern States) in December of 1865.

Yet, with the exception of Tennessee, the Southern Confederate states initially refused to ratify the Fourteenth Amendment. However, the Reconstruction Act of 1867 set forth the conditions that the Southern states *had* to accept before they were admitted back into the Union, which included ratification of the Fourteenth Amendment. The Fourteenth Amendment was fully ratified by all the states in 1868. Its passage meant that every previously enslaved person was now a "citizen" of the United States, and that, no matter what state a person lived in, they were all entitled to all of the privileges set forth in the Constitution.

Nevertheless, mindsets, especially in the previous Confederate states of the South, have been slow to change throughout the following 150-plus years.

Plessy v. Ferguson (1896)[187]

Homar Plessy, who was, according to his own testimony, "seven-eighths Caucasian and one-eighth African blood," bought a first-class ticket for the train in New Orleans, Louisiana. He boarded the train and took a seat in the White section of the train. Although he appeared to be White, the conductor asked if he was Black. He admitted he was. He planned to challenge the segregation laws after being involved in a group called the Social Club. At that time, the Louisiana state constitution prohibited separate schools based on race, but the reality was that the wealthier White families' children went to private schools, while the public schools taught mostly Black students and were underfunded. The Social Club wanted to establish a library for all and ensure a good public education for Black students. The conductor asked Plessy to move to the "colored section" of the train. When he refused, he was thrown off the train and immediately arrested. He was convicted of violating the "Separate Car Act" of Louisiana.

The case was appealed, and the US Supreme Court affirmed the conviction. It held that Louisiana's Separate Car Act was constitutional. The majority opinion said:

> The object of the [Fourteenth] amendment was undoubtedly to enforce the absolute equality of the two races before the law, but, in the nature of things, it could not have been intended to abolish distinctions based upon color, or to enforce social, as distinguished from political, equality, or a commingling of the two races upon terms unsatisfactory to either. Laws permitting, and even requiring, their separation in places where they are liable to be brought into contact, do not necessarily imply the inferiority of either race to the other, and have been generally, if not universally, recognized as within the competency of the state legislatures in the exercise of their police power. The most common instance of this is connected with the establishment of separate schools for White and colored children, which have been held to be a valid exercise of the legislative power even by courts of states where the political rights of the colored race have been longest and most earnestly enforced.[188]

On the other hand, Justice Harlan, the sole dissenting voice at that time, wrote:

> In respect of civil rights common to all citizens, the Constitution of the United States does not, I think, permit any public authority to know the race of those entitled to be protected in the enjoyment of such rights.

I am of the opinion that the statute of Louisiana is inconsistent with the personal liberty of citizens, White and black, in that State, and hostile to both the spirit and letter of the Constitution of the United States.

If laws of like character should be enacted in the several States of the Union, the effect would be in the highest degree mischievous. Slavery, as an institution tolerated by law would, it is true, have disappeared from our country, but there would remain a power in the States, by sinister legislation, to interfere with the full enjoyment of the blessings of freedom to regulate civil rights, common to all citizens, upon the basis of race, and to place in a condition of legal inferiority on a large body of American citizens now constituting a part of the political community called the People of the United States, for whom and by whom, through representatives, our government is administered.

Such a system is inconsistent with the guarantee given by the Constitution to each State of a republican form of government, and may be stricken down by Congressional action, or by the courts in the discharge of their solemn duty to maintain the supreme law of the land, anything in the constitution or laws of any State to the contrary notwithstanding.[189]

The legacy of segregation under the "separate but equal" doctrine announced in *Plessy v. Ferguson* lived on for fifty-eight years without Constitutional review by the US Supreme Court. Many states passed laws to legally segregate theaters, passenger trains, eating establishments, water fountains, restrooms, building entrances, elevators, cemeteries, public pools, phone booths, hospitals, asylums, jails, and schools. Laws forbade Blacks from living in White neighborhoods. These were known as "Jim Crow" laws. Violence erupted at the hands of the Ku Klux Klan, which started as a private club of Confederate men in Tennessee and spread across the Southern states. During those fifty-eight years, Justice Harlan's words spoke a terrible truth in America. "There remained a power in the States, by sinister legislation, to interfere with the full enjoyment of the blessings of freedom to regulate civil rights, common to all citizens, upon the basis of race, and to place a condition of legal inferiority on a large body of American citizens . . . ."

Plessy v. Ferguson was finally overturned in the case *Brown v. Board of Education of Topeka* in 1954.

Brown v. Board of Education of Topeka (1954)[190]

This famous US Supreme Court case overturned *Plessy v. Ferguson* and the resulting Jim Crow laws. The high Court held that "separate but equal is inherently *unequal.*" A series of cases prior to 1954 announced new thoughts on the Fourteenth Amendment and segregation. By 1948, the US Supreme Court unanimously agreed that a law school in Oklahoma could not deny entrance to law school solely on race. (*Sipuel v. Regents of University of Oklahoma*[191]) A similar result occurred in Texas in 1950. (*Sweatt v. Painter*[192]) That same year, the Supreme Court held that a graduate student in Oklahoma could not be required to sit in a separate space because of his race because it interfered with his "ability to study, to engage in discussions, and exchange views with other students, and, in general, to learn his profession." (*McLaurin v. Oklahoma State Regents*[193]) Meanwhile, in South Carolina and in Washington D.C., cases were filed arguing that segregation in all public schools in those states was unconstitutional under the Fourteenth Amendment. Then, in 1951, a similar lawsuit was filed in Kansas against the Board of Education of Topeka, Kansas. (*Brown v. Board of Education of Topeka*[194])

The lawsuit in Kansas was brought by Oliver Brown on behalf of his daughter, Linda Brown, who had to travel several miles by bus to reach the segregated school for Black students although she lived close enough to walk to the all-White school in Topeka, Kansas. Although Brown is the named plaintiff, just days before oral arguments, the Court consolidated five cases concerning segregation in all public schools in Kansas, Delaware, South Carolina, Virginia, and Washington D.C. The consolidation joined hundreds of children in the lawsuit. This move was significant because it demonstrated a national problem, not a state problem.

At the time, Thurgood Marshall was lead counsel for the NAACP. He later became the first Black man to serve as a Justice of the US Supreme Court. Marshall successfully argued that social sciences proved that Justice Harlan's dissent in *Plessy v. Ferguson* was the reality in segregated states. Statistics on the psychological effect of segregated schools showed that Black students felt inferior to Whites.

Oral arguments first took place in the consolidated cases before the US Supreme Court from December 9-11, 1952, under the supervision of Chief Justice Vinson. The Court was absolutely aware that Southern states would balk against desegregation in public schools and therefore stalled in coming to its decision. Then, in September 1953, before a decision could be reached in the case, Chief Justice Vinson died suddenly. Dwight D. Eisenhower appointed the former Governor of California, Earl Warren, to replace Justice Vinson. The "Warren Court," as it is now known, arguably brought about the most significant social changes in the US Supreme Court's long history. The consolidated *Brown v. Board of Education* cases had to be reargued before the "Warren Court" from December 7-9, 1953. The decision was announced on May 17, 1954. The Court's opinion reads, in part:

> Segregation of white and colored children in public schools has a detrimental effect upon the colored children. The impact is greater when it has the sanction of the law, for the policy of separating

the races is usually interpreted as denoting the inferiority of the negro group. A sense of inferiority affects the motivation of a child to learn. Segregation with the sanction of law, therefore, has a tendency to retard the educational and mental development of negro children and to deprive them of some of the benefits they would receive in a racially integrated school system.

...

Today, education is perhaps the most important function of state and local governments. Compulsory school attendance laws and the great expenditures for education both demonstrate our recognition of the importance of education to our democratic society. It is required in the performance of our most basic public responsibilities, even service in the armed forces. It is the very foundation of good citizenship. Today it is a principal instrument in awakening the child to cultural values, in preparing him for later professional training, and in helping him to adjust normally to his environment. In these days, it is doubtful that any child may reasonably be expected to succeed in life if he is denied the opportunity of an education. Such an opportunity, where the state has undertaken to provide it, is a right which must be made available to all on equal terms.

...

We conclude that, in the field of public education, the doctrine of 'separate but equal' has no place. Separate educational facilities are inherently unequal. Therefore, we hold that the plaintiffs and others similarly situated for whom the actions have been brought are, by reason of the segregation complained of, deprived of the equal protection of the laws guaranteed by the Fourteenth Amendment.[195]

As discussed above in *Aaron v. Cooper*, the *Brown v. Board of Education* decision was not immediately accepted as the law in several states.

The first critics observed that it provided no timeline for implementation for schools across the country, which had practiced segregation for many years. The court addressed that criticism in *Brown v. Board of Education II*[196] the next year, stating only that desegregation should occur "with all deliberate speed." The next critics saw that *Brown II* still did not provide concrete direction on how best to accomplish desegregation "with all deliberate speed."

Nevertheless, desegregation began, albeit slowly. Criticism of the decision still exists today. Even some legal scholars claim the decision binds states in deciding matters that would be better left to the states rather than the federal government. Challenges to the decision persist, yet it provided a foundation for the Civil Rights movement and other decisions that brought about social reform in the United States, not just for Blacks, but also for other minorities.

Plyler v. Doe (1982)[197]

In 1975, Texas enacted a law that barred funds for the education of undocumented students. According to the state law, school districts in Texas were allowed to deny education to any child who could not establish that they were legally admitted into the United States. As a result, in 1977, the school district in Tyler, Texas, began charging $1,000 tuition annually to any student in public school who could not demonstrate legal entry into the country.

The Mexican American Legal Defense and Education Fund (MALDEF) organized children of illegal immigrants and filed a class action lawsuit. The class action consisted of all undocumented school-age children of Mexican origin residing within the school district. The lawsuit claimed that the Texas law violated the equal protection of the Fourteenth Amendment. They claimed that a free public education was free to all persons, despite state law regarding citizenship, under the last two clauses of the Fourteenth Amendment, which reads, "... *nor shall any State deprive any* person *of life, liberty, or property, without due process of law; nor deny to any* person *within its jurisdiction the equal protection of the laws.*"

The lower Federal District Court found that, without an education, the undocumented children, "[a]lready disadvantaged as a result of poverty, lack of English-speaking ability, and undeniable racial prejudices ... will become permanently locked into the lowest socio-economic class," and therefore ruled the law was unconstitutional. The State of Texas appealed and argued that undocumented aliens, because of their immigration status, are not "persons within the jurisdiction" of the State of Texas because they are not citizens. In response, the US Supreme Court said:

> We reject this argument. Whatever his status under the immigration laws, an alien is surely a 'person' in any ordinary sense of that term. Aliens, even aliens whose presence in this country is unlawful, have long been recognized as 'persons' guaranteed due process of law by the Fifth and Fourteenth Amendments.

Texas also argued that the presence of illegal aliens in the state was a financial hardship, to which the US Supreme Court said:

> While a State might have an interest in mitigating the potentially harsh economic effects of sudden shifts in population, [the Texas law] hardly offers an effective method of dealing with an urgent demographic or economic problem. There is no evidence in the record suggesting that illegal entrants impose any significant burden on the State's economy. To the contrary, the available evidence suggests that illegal aliens underutilize public services, while contributing their labor to the local economy and tax money to the State. The dominant incentive for illegal entry into the

> State of Texas is the availability of employment; few if any illegal immigrants come to this country, or presumably to the State of Texas, in order to avail themselves of a free education. Thus, even making the doubtful assumption that the net impact of illegal aliens on the economy of the State is negative, we think it clear that 'charging tuition to undocumented children constitutes a ludicrously ineffectual attempt to stem the tide of illegal immigration . . . .'
>
> Next, the State of Texas, suggests that undocumented children are appropriately singled out for exclusion because of the special burdens they impose on the State's ability to provide high-quality public education. But the record in no way supports the claim that exclusion of undocumented children is likely to improve the overall quality of education in the State.[198]

In coming to its decision, the US Supreme Court emphasized that the matter of immigration is a federal issue, not a state issue. Under the US Constitution, states do not have the power or control with respect to foreign relations. In dealing with immigration laws, the states must act harmoniously with the federal government.

> The Constitution grants Congress the power to 'establish an uniform Rule of Naturalization.' [US Constitution] Drawing upon this power, upon its plenary authority with respect to foreign relations and international commerce, and upon the inherent power of a sovereign to close its borders, Congress has developed a complex scheme governing admission to our Nation and status within our borders.
>
> The States enjoy no power with respect to the classification of aliens. This power is committed to the political branches of the

federal government. Although it is a routine and normally legitimate part of the business of the federal government to classify on the basis of alien status, and to take into account the character of the relationship between the alien and this country, only rarely are such matters relevant to legislation by a State. As we recognized, the States do have some authority to act with respect to illegal aliens, at least where such action mirrors federal objectives and furthers a legitimate state goal.

Consider This:

The *Plyler v. Doe* decision is still under attack. Proponents of states' powers versus the federal government's Constitutional powers would like to see *Plyler v. Doe* reversed. For example, in 1996, California voters voted for a measure to deny admission to any student who was unable to show legal immigration status and to report any such student to federal immigration authorities. The measure was held unconstitutional. In Illinois, a student was denied admission due to overstaying on a tourist visa. Same result. In 2010, Arizona created a state law making it a state crime to be unlawfully present in the US and a state crime for working or seeking work without a work visa and authorized warrantless arrests of aliens. In the resulting US Supreme Court case, *Arizona vs. United States*[199] (2012), the Court held once again that Federal immigration laws preempted state-created laws. State law enforcement could only inquire about a resident's legal status during lawful encounters, but the State cannot enforce immigration laws, which are preempted by Federal law. As a result, any state, any public school or school district that denies an education to any undocumented child has violated the US Constitution.

ADDITIONAL RESOURCES

Chapters 14 and 15—Liberty and Equality

- If any of your rights of equality are being denied, start with an attorney who is knowledgeable in that field. The American Civil Liberties Union (ACLU) can assist in retaining an experienced attorney to protect your constitutional rights.
- Any undocumented immigrant has the same rights as any person under the Constitution and is entitled to free speech, due process, fair trials, public education, and has a right to legal counsel, etc. In most elections, however, non-citizens cannot vote, but may be able to vote in local elections. An attorney specializing in immigration may assist you.

"Equality is the soul of liberty; there is, in fact, no liberty without it." FRANCES WRIGHT

CHAPTER 16

The Right to Vote!

The Fifteenth, Nineteenth, and Twenty-sixth Amendments

Fifteenth Amendment

Section 1

The right of citizens of the United States to vote shall not be denied or abridged by the United States or by any State on account of race, color, or previous condition of servitude.

Section 2

The Congress shall have power to enforce this article by appropriate legislation. *(Ratified, February 1870)*

United States v. Reese (1876)[200]

It is commonly believed that the Fifteenth Amendment granted Black slaves the right to vote in 1870. While technically correct, in reality, racial discrimination at the polls continues. The US Supreme Court decision of *United States v. Reese* (1876) is partially to blame. During the Reconstruction era, Congress passed a number of federal laws to end violence against African Americans, allowing them access to polling places. These laws were known as the Enforcement Acts of 1870 and 1871. The Enforcement Act of 1870 prohibited groups banding together to intimidate, threaten, and harass with the intention of violating citizens' Constitutional rights. The Enforcements Acts of 1871, also known as the Ku Klux Klan Acts, placed national elections under the control of the federal government instead of the states. Federal judges and US marshals were allowed to supervise local polling places under the Enforcement Acts.

Shortly after the enactment of the Enforcement Acts, an election official in Kentucky refused to register an African American to vote. He was denied because of a failure to pay the $1.50 voting tax. Nevertheless, it was obvious that the denial was race-based because most Blacks, previously enslaved, did not have cash. If they held jobs at all, they worked for credit, not cash. The election official was indicted under the federal Enforcement Acts. The election official appealed the case in *United States v. Reese,* which was eventually heard by the US Supreme Court in 1875.

The *United States v. Reese* opinion eviscerated the Enforcement Acts. The opinion said that the Fifteenth Amendment did not give the federal government the power to penalize an election official for anything but denial of the right to vote based on race, or color, or previous servitude. According to the Supreme Court, the Fifteenth Amendment did not say anything about who has the "right to vote;" but only on what basis a person *cannot be denied the right to vote.* The Court said that before the Fifteenth Amendment, states were allowed to discriminate for a variety of reasons. "It was as much within the power of a state to exclude citizens of the United States from voting on account of race and color, as it was on account of age, property, or education. Now it is not."

The Court then reasoned that the states could continue to bar citizens from voting on account of age, property, or education—just not race, color, or previous servitude. The 1876 US Supreme Court said that the Enforcement Acts exceeded the scope of the Fifteenth Amendment and were unconstitutional.

The case set forth precedent so that states were free to enact voter laws that were inequitable, preventing Blacks from voting, but appeared valid for purposes of the Fifteenth Amendment. States that had not previously done so adopted poll taxes that Blacks, who had previously been supported as slaves, could not pay unless now employed for cash. (Poll taxes are now prohibited under the Twenty-Fourth Amendment, adopted in 1964.) States adopted literacy tests, which without previous formal schooling, many Blacks could not pass. States also adopted grandfather clauses allowing White citizens to be "grandfathered in" without passing the literacy tests if they or their family members had voted prior to the ratification of the Fifteenth Amendment. This meant that virtually all illiterate Whites could vote, while Blacks could not. (This practice was struck down later in *Guinn v. US* (1915)).[201] States also adopted strict residency requirements, meaning homeless people could not vote. States adopted "moral character" assessments to deny Blacks the ability to vote. Through 1910, all former Confederate states revised their state constitutions to adopt some creative form of voting law for the effect of preventing Blacks from exercising their right to vote.

Then in *Smith v. Allwright* (1944),[202] the US Supreme Court began to provide some Constitutional review of states' practices preventing citizens from voting. The State of Texas attempted to prohibit Blacks from voting in the primary elections, arguing that the primaries were not "federal elections" because a primary election only identified the leading candidate for a party. Thus, Texas argued, the private Republican and Democratic parties, which are private entities, controlled the primary elections, and the Fifteenth Amendment should not apply.

But the US Supreme Court determined that because Texas (and other states) delegated the authority to the private parties, these were in fact "state actors." These delegated state actors could not violate the US Constitution any more in the primary elections than the states could in the general elections.

Then, in 1965, Congress enacted the Voting Rights Act (the Act). The Act sought to eliminate State race-based voting practices. Prior to 1965, individuals who were subjected to race-based voter suppression had to litigate against the state or county responsible. Litigation is a long, costly, and risky process, often not resolving the underlying issue. The Act eliminated the need for costly litigation. The hammer protecting voting rights was found in Section 5 (§5) of the Act. Under §5, counties and states with histories of voter suppression were required to get federal pre-clearance to enact new election laws. Pre-clearance deterred States from creating new race-based voting requirement laws.

The Act was unprecedented because only certain states had to comply with the pre-clearance process. The Act initially required federal pre-clearance of new voting laws in Alabama, Georgia, Louisiana, Mississippi, South Carolina, and Virginia, as well as thirty-nine counties in North Carolina and one in Arizona (it was later expanded to include Alaska, Texas, and certain townships in California, Florida, Michigan, New York, North Carolina, and South Dakota); anywhere where data showed that voter discrimination was at its worst.

The Voters Rights Act of 1965's placement of control of national elections with the federal government was successful in eliminating discrimination at the polls. The Voting Rights Act of 1965 was upheld in the US Supreme Court case *South Carolina v. Katzenbach* (1966).[203] The Court said there that the Act rectified "an insidious and pervasive evil which had been perpetuated in certain parts of our country through unremitting and ingenious defiance of the Constitution."

The US Supreme Court continued to uphold the pre-clearance requirement of the Voting Rights Act of 1965 until 2013. A state could "bail out" of the system upon a showing that racial suppression of voter registration was no longer an issue. Although it was intended to only be a temporary solution to force states to adopt equal voter rights, Congress extended the Act several times. In 1975, it was extended to expire in 2031. But in 2013, the US Supreme Court took the teeth out of the Voting Rights Act of 1965 in the case *Shelby County v. Holder*.

Shelby County v. Holder (2013)[204]

Shelby County, Alabama, did not elect to "bail out" of the §5 requirements under the guidelines of the Act, but instead took the matter up in federal court. Shelby County, Alabama, home to many of the violent acts that precipitated the Voters Rights Act of 1965, argued that the Act was "facially unconstitutional." That means that the county did not argue that the Act was objectionable only as applied to Shelby County. The county argued that on its face, for nearly fifty years, Congress and the US Court's prior decisions upholding the Act were just plain wrong.

Much like the Enforcement Acts of 1870 and 1871, the US Supreme Court eventually rendered much of the Voters Rights Act unenforceable. The majority 5-4 opinion by Chief Justice Roberts in *Shelby County v. Holder* doubted the existence of further need for the Voter Rights Act.

> . . . the conditions that originally justified these measures no longer characterize voting in the covered jurisdictions. By 2009, the racial gap in voter registration and turnout was lower in the States originally covered by §5 [of the Act] than it was nationwide. Since that time, Census Bureau data indicate that African-American voter turnout has come to exceed white voter turnout in five of the six States originally covered by §5 [of the Act], with a gap in the sixth State of less than one-half of one percent.

> At the same time, voting discrimination still exists; no one doubts that. The question is whether the Act's extraordinary measures, including its disparate treatment of the States, continue to satisfy constitutional requirements.[205]

The majority decided that the Voting Rights Act of 1965's unequal requirements of some states, although necessary at the time, did not "continue to satisfy constitutional requirements." The majority held that the formula for determining which states should be covered by §5 needed to be updated. Justice Ginsberg pointed out in her dissent that Congress, not the Supreme Court, was in the best position to determine whether the Act should be reviewed or revised due to current conditions. Justice Ginsberg said, "The Constitution vests broad power in Congress to protect the right to vote, and in particular to combat racial discrimination in voting." And, under the Act, Congress regularly reviewed data to determine whether race-based voter discrimination continued in the designated areas.

And both the majority and the dissent on the US Supreme Court agreed that the federal pre-clearance requirement of the Act is responsible for shrinking the racial gap in voting in those states. In other words, it worked! Justice Ginsberg's dissent basically says, if it works, why fix it?

> Just as buildings in California have a greater need to be earthquake-proofed, places where there is greater racial polarization in voting have a greater need for prophylactic measures to prevent purposeful race discrimination.
>
> ...
>
> The sad irony of today's decision lies in [the Court's] utter failure to grasp why the VRA [Voting Rights Act] has proven effective. The Court appears to believe that the VRA's success in eliminating the specific devices extant in 1965 means that pre-clearance is

no longer needed. With that belief, and the argument derived from it, history repeats itself. The same assumption—that the problem could be solved when particular methods of voting discrimination are identified and eliminated—was indulged and proved wrong repeatedly prior to the VRA's enactment. Unlike prior statutes, which singled out particular tests or devices, the VRA is grounded in Congress' recognition of the "variety and persistence" of measures designed to impair minority voting rights. In truth, the evolution of voting discrimination into more subtle second-generation barriers is powerful evidence that a remedy as effective as pre-clearance remains vital to protect minority voting rights and prevent backsliding.[206]

Justice Ginsberg's dissent goes on,

> Throwing out preclearance [under §5] when it has worked and is continuing to work to stop discriminatory changes is like throwing away your umbrella in a rainstorm because you are not getting wet.

Just as Justice Ginsberg predicted, "backsliding" on voter suppression laws occurred almost immediately after the *Shelby County* decision. States began to redraw their districts to reduce the number of districts where minorities outnumbered Whites. Many of those states were the very same that were required to seek pre-approval to change voter registration laws under the Act. One of those states was Alabama. Although the majority decision in *Shelby County v. Holder* gutted the formula to determine which states required the pre-clearance mandate in §5 of the Voter Rights Act, the remainder of the Act still protects minority voting rights. And voter discriminatory laws were challenged again just ten years later, again in Alabama, in *Allen v. Milligan*.

Allen v. Milligan (2023)[207]

Allen v. Milligan is a recent victory for minority voting rights. In 2021, the governor of Alabama signed a new voting district map for the state. The map provided only one majority-Black district out of seven, even though the state has a population of over 25 percent Black. And that one district was the result of a prior hard fought challenge to the State of Alabama's district laws. Just as Justice Ginsberg predicted in her dissent in *Shelby County v. Holder*, states with large populations of minorities were backsliding into voter discriminating practices. Minorities in Alabama had to challenge the map in litigation because it racially polarized voting. They sued the State of Alabama under the remaining provisions of the Voter Rights Act.

The attorney for the plaintiffs, Abha Khanna of the Elias Law Group, who works exclusively in voter rights, argued that the state had illegally packed Black voters into a single district while dividing other clusters of Black voters across multiple districts. She explains that racially polarized voting "is when Blacks and Whites are voting so opposite, in such opposing manners, for different parties, different kinds of candidates, that if you do not provide a majority district, or something near a majority district, the White majority will consistently defeat the Black-preferred candidate." She said, "So, what we argued is that, given the geography and the demography and the racial politics and the racial polarized voting of Alabama, Black voters in Alabama are entitled to a second opportunity district, a second district in which they have an opportunity to elect their candidates of choice."

Khanna explained that one aspect of the Act that still stands is that "plaintiffs are not required to prove racial animus or discriminatory intent. You don't have to go in and establish that there was racism behind the map, in the heart and mind of the map drawer . . ." it is sufficient to show that the result of the voter law has an adverse effect on the voting rights of a minority population.

Perhaps as a means of correcting the error of *Shelby County v. Holder*, just ten years later, Chief Justice Roberts wrote for the majority, granting relief to the plaintiffs in *Allen v. Milligan*. According to the Supreme Court ruling, Alabama is now required under the Act to draw a map providing minorities a second district.

Elk v. Wilkins (1884)[208]

Black minorities are not the only minorities to benefit from the Civil Rights movement and the Voter Rights Act of 1964. Although Native Americans were here first, their children were born here, their heritage is here, and this land was theirs before you can say "Christopher Columbus," Native Americans were the last minority group to be fully granted US citizenship under the law. The Snyder Act of 1924 finally gave full US Citizenship to Native Americans born in the US

Early America attempted to "assimilate" Native Americans into the culture and customs of White Americans, which only alienated many Native Americans from their tribes. As a result, many tribes disbanded and Native American heritage was lost.

In 1880, John Elk, a Native American who had previously severed all ties with his tribe, tried to register to vote in his home of Omaha, Nebraska. The voter registrar, Charles Wilkins, denied him. Although Elk had renounced his former tribal allegiance and claimed US citizenship under the Fourteenth Amendment, the US Supreme Court held that he did not have rights as a US citizen. In this 1884 decision, the majority said that under the Constitution, Native Americans were dependents of the State, much like "a ward to his guardian," insinuating that Native Americans were not civilized enough to become citizens.

But Justice Harlan's dissent expresses outrage in the treatment of Native Americans:

> If [Elk] did not acquire national citizenship on abandoning his tribe and becoming, by residence in one of the states, subject to the complete jurisdiction of the United States, then the Fourteenth Amendment has wholly failed to accomplish, in respect of the Indian race, what, we think was intended by it, and there is still in this country a despised and rejected class of persons with no nationality whatever, who, born in our territory, owing no allegiance to any foreign power, and subject, as residents of the states, to all the burdens of government, are yet not members of any political community, nor entitled to any of the rights, privileges, or immunities of citizens of the United States.[209]

Even after the passage of the Snyder Act of 1924, giving citizenship to Native Americans, they too have had to fight for the right to vote. The same issues that prevented Black slaves from voting kept Native Americans from voting. Racially motivated tests appeared after the Fourteenth Amendment's passage in Arizona, Alaska, and New Mexico—all states with high Native American populations. The Civil Rights Act of 1965 assisted Native Americans too, and the *Shelby County v. Holder* decision hurt them too. Currently, voter registration sites and polling locations are far from tribal lands. Many tribal lands are vast and postal delivery is scarce. Access to internet services is even more rare on tribal lands. Furthermore, where states like Arizona mandate "government" identification to vote, tribal ID cards are often insufficient.

The American Bar Association reports that voter turnout is lower in the Native American group than any other group in the country. The Native American Voting Rights Coalition did a study and found that there are a number of contributing issues. Trust in the American government is low among Native Americans, and there is a lack of information on how and where to register and vote. There are long distances to travel and register and low levels of access to the internet among Native American groups. Hostility toward Native Americans, economic disparities, lack of transportation, and lack of residential addresses on tribal lands all contribute to low voter turnout among Native Americans.

The American Bar Association concludes, "[l]egislation suppressing the right to vote purports to be neutral; however, in many instances it undermines the most basic right to participate in our democracy. The loss of the right to vote is the loss of a voice in the democratic process. We should do more to ensure that all Americans, including Native Americans, can exercise this right easily and with undue hardship."[210]

Consider This:

Help from Congress was reintroduced in September 2023. The John R. Lewis Voting Rights Advancement Act hopes to restore the protections of the Voting Rights Act of 1965 by: (1) modernizing the Voting Rights Act's formula for determining which states and localities have a pattern of discrimination; (2) ensuring that last-minute voting changes do not adversely affect voters by requiring officials to publicly announce all voting changes at least 180 days before an election; and (3) expanding the government's authority to send federal observers to any jurisdiction where there may be a substantial risk of discrimination at the polls on Election Day or during an early voting period.

Nineteenth Amendment

The right of citizens of the United States to vote shall not be denied or abridged by the United States or by any State on account of sex.

Congress shall have power to enforce this article by appropriate legislation. *(Ratified, August 1920)*

Susan B. Anthony and Elizabeth Stanton were largely responsible for the passage of the Nineteenth Amendment, although both died before its passage. The two met and became friends as they fought for justice. Their fight for equal rights for women was born in the 1830s, along with the fight for abolition. By 1848, the first Women's Rights Convention was held in the United States and the suffrage movement was born. Although both opposed slavery, Stanton and Anthony opposed the passage of the Fourteenth and Fifteenth Amendments in 1870, because the proposed amendments did not include a right for *women* to vote. Anthony, a gifted public speaker, spoke often on women's suffrage. In November 1872, Anthony and thirteen other women were arrested for voting at the presidential election in Rochester, New York. Only Anthony was tried and found guilty, and was given a fine of $100. Women could be citizens, but were still not allowed to vote.

In *Minor v. Happersett* (1875),[211] the US Supreme Court held that citizenship does not confer a right to vote, and therefore state laws barring women from voting were constitutionally valid. The Nineteenth Amendment, granting women the right to vote, was not ratified until August of 1920—fifty years after enslaved *men* were granted the right to vote.

Leser v. Garnett (1922)[212]

After passage and ratification of the Nineteenth Amendment, in October of 1920, Cecilia Streett Waters and Mary D. Randolph registered to vote in their home of Baltimore, Maryland. Oscar Leser and other male voters brought a lawsuit to disqualify them on the sole grounds that they were women. The state constitution of Maryland at that time granted the right to vote only to men. Although the Nineteenth Amendment had passed, the men argued that "because of its character," the amendment was not validly a part of the US Constitution.

The legislature of Maryland had refused to ratify the Nineteenth Amendment, as well as the Fifteenth Amendment on similar grounds. To this argument, in 1922, the US Supreme Court responded:

> This amendment is in character and phraseology precisely similar to the Fifteenth. For each, the same method of adoption was pursued. One cannot be valid and the other invalid. That the Fifteenth is valid, although rejected by six states, including Maryland, has been recognized and acted on for half a century.[213]

The US Supreme Court held, of course, that both the Fifteenth and the Nineteenth Amendments are valid, granting the right to vote to previously enslaved men *and* to all women.

Consider This:

There remain several myths regarding women's right to vote. Here are some myths and truths according to the *Smithsonian Magazine*[214]:

- Myth: Since 1920, all women have had equal access to voting rights.
- Truth: Minority women, as well as men, were often denied their right to vote with the same disparaging treatment until the Civil Rights movement and the Voter Rights Act of 1965.
- Myth: Women don't exercise their right to vote as often as men.
- Truth: Women have registered and voted at higher rates than men in every presidential election since 1980, with the turnout gap between women and men growing slightly larger with each successive presidential election.
- Myth: Women vote the same as their male counterparts, making their vote invalid.

- Truth: Statistics do not support this myth. It is difficult to calculate the "women's vote," since women cannot be viewed as one group. Women, just like men, may vote differently depending on their race, community values, education, age, profession, and other factors. However, generally speaking, women vote for women. Today, more women are registered Democrats than Republicans.[215] During the Regan years, however, when Republicans were raising "women's issues," such as abortion and childcare, more women voted Republican. Regan returned the favor and appointed Sandra Day O'Connor as the first woman US Supreme Court Justice at his first opportunity in 1981.

Twenty-Sixth Amendment

Section 1

The right of citizens of the United States, who are eighteen years of age or older, to vote shall not be denied or abridged by the United States or by any State on account of age.

Section 2

The Congress shall have power to enforce this article by appropriate legislation. *(Ratified, July 1971)*

The Twenty-Sixth Amendment was passed in record time—only four months after it was introduced. But perhaps no other group in America fought harder for their right to vote. Starting with World War II, when eighteen year olds became eligible for the draft in 1940, it seemed unfair that they were not able to vote for the representatives of our government who put them under fire. "Old enough to fight, old enough to vote" became a widespread slogan. Beginning in 1942, many bills were introduced to Congress to lower the voting age. All were denied.

In the late 1960s and early 1970s, eighteen year olds were demonstrating in the streets, bringing more attention to the fact that, while some were financially able to go to college, others were unable to avoid the draft and were sent to Vietnam—many to die. More than ever, young people wanted a chance to be heard in *their* government. By 1965, the US was heavily involved in the Vietnam War. By 1970, casualties of eighteen to twenty-one-year-olds mounted. Youths—Whites, Blacks, and Native Americans—fought side by side in a war that they did not understand, in a land that was not their own. And they fought side by side in their homeland for their rights and the rights of others. The slogan, which started as a low rumbling protest in 1940, became an outright battle cry for rights in the early 1970s. The movement to lower the voting age to eighteen was thus swept up and made a part of the greater Civil Rights movement.

The Voter Rights Act of 1965 was to be reviewed by Congress in 1970. Congress debated at length about the provisions of the act, including the formula to select states that would need federal pre-clearance to change voter requirements. Senator Edward Kennedy proposed lowering the voter age along with the renewal of the act. After much debate, when the act was renewed, Congress included the provision to lower the voting age to eighteen. This met with great controversy. Most youths were opposed to the US involvement in the war, and wanted the right to vote for candidates who promised to end it. President Nixon, who would run for a second term in 1972, believed he was that candidate, and he signed the act lowering the voting age to eighteen. Nevertheless, many States felt that the States, and not federal law should determine election laws.

Oregon v. Mitchell (1970)[216]

Oregon, Texas, Arizona, and Idaho all challenged the constitutionality of the provisions added in 1970 to the Voter Rights Act. The States argued that three provisions in particular were under the domain of the individual states, and that Congress did not have the power to overtake the States' rights in setting voting laws in the states. First, the States objected to the ban on literacy tests. Second, the States objected to a provision that would not allow States to disqualify voters for not meeting the states' residency requirements. And third, the States objected to the provision lowering the eligible voting age to eighteen. Youths, they said, "lacked good judgment." They claimed that youths did not have the experience, responsibilities, and intelligence to vote. William G. Carlton, a professor of social sciences at the University of Florida and an outspoken challenger of lowering the voting age, said that in his view, youths lack "common sense and the capacity to understand the political system."

The US Supreme Court heard the case, and the Court split into factions on the three issues. First, all justices agreed and voted unanimously that the ban on literacy tests was necessary because literacy tests were discriminatory. Next, in an 8-1, vote the majority determined that all the citizens of the US can move about the country without losing their rights, including their right to vote, without being discriminated against. Finally, the Court grappled with the voting age requirements. In a 5-4 ruling, the Court held that Congress could lower the voting age in federal elections (presidential elections), but did not have the power to change the voting age in state elections.

With the 1972 presidential elections looming, mass confusion erupted in the eighteen to twenty-one-year-old voting age group. Were they allowed to vote or not? Would states turn them away? When and where could an eighteen-year-old register to vote? Would the states be required to have two separate rolls for elections—one for federal elections including eighteen to twenty-one-year-olds, and one for state elections without the lower age group? Congress got busy immediately, and although the *Oregon v. Mitchell* case was decided in December of 1970, by March 1971, the Twenty-Sixth Amendment was introduced. By July 1971, the amendment passed. Eighteen-year-olds were now eligible to vote in any state or federal election as a Constitutional right, and did so in large numbers in the 1972 election!

Consider This:

Voter discrimination still exists. Since the expiration of the pre-clearance requirement of §5 of the Voter Rights Act, we are back to having States, and not the Federal Constitutional guarantees, decide voter rights and courts deciding where discrimination exists. Litigation is long and expensive, and it seems that we have gone two steps forward and three steps back.

There is currently an undecided case before the US Supreme Court that deals with this issue: *Alexander v. South Carolina NAACP*[217] (pending 2023-2024). This case will decide whether courts must presume that a State acts in good faith when it draws election districts. It will also decide if a court must separate race from politics when considering race challenges in drawn districts. The second question would definitely be a difficult task for any federal court judge to determine, which places a tremendous burden on the courts and on the litigants hoping to reform voter districts to make voting rights equal for all.

ADDITIONAL REFERENCES

Chapter 16—The Right to Vote

- Read more about what you can do to provide equal access to voting. Visit the Brennan Center for Justice article on voting reforms. The Brennan Center for Justice was inspired by Justice William J. Brennan, Jr. The Center works to strengthen democracy and liberty, and to protect fundamental freedoms for all Americans. www.brennancenter.org/issues/ensure-every-american-can-vote/voting-reform/strengthening-voting-rights-act
- Get involved. To help assist the John R. Lewis Voting Rights Advancement Act, visit the Brennan Center for Justice: www.brennancenter.org/get-involved.
- Recognize that others fought hard to give you the opportunity to vote. Do not take it for granted. Study the proposed laws and candidates and exercise your right to vote!
- Find credible sources of information on the issues and candidates. Your state may supply a voter information guide containing summaries of the measures you will vote on with pro and con arguments. It will most likely also include information about the state of the law now and how it will change with a yes or no vote. Finally, it may provide you with information on groups who are for or against the measure, which might give you some insight as to whether the measure is in alignment with your views.
- Vote, vote, vote! Recognize that this is an honor, a privilege, and a duty. Also, recognize that after reading this far you do *NOT* lack "common sense and the capacity to

understand the political system," as Professor Carlton described. Hopefully, you are now motivated to be a part of our great democracy.

"Someone struggled for your right to vote. Use it!"
SUSAN B. ANTHONY

CHAPTER 17

The Non-Existent Amendment– The Equal Rights Amendment

Section 1

Equality of rights under the law shall not be denied or abridged by the United States or by any state on account of sex.

Section 2

The Congress shall have the power to enforce, by appropriate legislation, the provisions of this article.

Section 3

This Amendment shall take effect two years after the date of ratification *[Proposed, 1923; Passed, 1972; Ratified 2020?]*

Virginia was the last state to ratify the Twenty-Eighth Amendment guaranteeing legal gender equality in 2020. With the inclusion of Nevada and Illinois in 2017 and 2018 respectively, the Equal Rights

Amendment (ERA) has now been ratified by the threshold thirty-eight states. But, to say that the Equal Rights Amendment is now law and cannot be challenged is like saying the Titanic was unsinkable. To say this amendment has enjoyed a smooth sail to ratification would be like saying that the North Atlantic Ocean does not have icebergs.

The ERA was first drafted in 1923, two years after women were finally granted the right to vote. It was a logical next step. Introduced by two women, Alice Paul and Crystal Eastman, the amendment was introduced to every Congress without passage from 1923 to 1970. Proponents believed that passage of the ERA would help overcome the obstacles that kept women as second-class citizens. There was only one problem—Congress was comprised almost entirely of men. Only ten women had *ever* served in Congress by 1970. Then, in 1972, after renewed interest in civil rights for all, the amendment passed by two-thirds in both the House and the Senate with the help of two new Representatives, Martha Griffiths and Shirley Chisholm. But the ERA still also needed to pass in thirty-eight *states* to be ratified. A deadline was set for ratification. To become the Twenty-Eighth Amendment, the ERA had to be ratified within seven years of its passage in Congress. Just one year later, thirty of the required thirty-eight states had voted to ratify the ERA. But, in 1971, Phyllis Schlafly organized the "STOP ERA" (an acronym for Stop Taking Our Privileges) campaign. It effectively stopped the passage of the ERA. Only thirty-five of the thirty-eight states needed ratified the ERA before the first deadline in 1979.

Schlafly preached to America that the ERA would take away "gender-specific privileges" enjoyed by women, like dependent wife benefits, separate restrooms for men and women, and exemption from the military draft. She claimed women would lose alimony and custody of their children. Although Schlafly was opposed by groups like National Organization for Women, the ERAmerica coalition, and the Homemaker's ERA, she gained a following that froze ratification.

Joan C. Williams, a distinguished professor of law at the University of California, Hastings Law School, wrote that the "ERA was defeated when Schlafly turned it into a war among women over gender roles."

Historian Judith Glazer-Raymo said, "As moderates, we thought we represented the forces of reason and goodwill but failed to take seriously the power of the 'family values' argument and the single-mindedness of Schlafly and her followers."[218]

As a result, interest in the passage of the ERA in many conservative states was lost by the mid-1970s. Congress extended the deadline for ratification by the states many times. But has time run out? In 2020, the House of Representatives removed the previous 1982 deadline. Removal of that deadline passed the House, but still needed passage in the Senate. In April 2023, Senate supporters were nine votes shy of the sixty votes needed to pass the Amendment.[219]

The block of the ERA has a negative impact on Americans in almost every area of their lives—personally, financially, politically, in career, family, parenthood, home-life balance, health care, education, our economy, and socially. Either blatantly or latently, historically or currently, America still suffers from the effects of gender discrimination.

But let's step back for a moment and see how far women have come, baby.* Let's start with financial freedom. New York was the first state to adopt the "Married Woman's Property Act" in 1848, which allowed women to own real estate. Prior to that, only single women could own real property (likely inherited). Property inherited by a married woman went to her husband, who had full control of all property. By 1900, many other states followed suit. Yay! Both married women and single women could now *own* real estate in many states. But, for more than the next century, it was difficult, if not impossible,

---

* Pun very much intended. In 1968, Phillip Morris began an ad campaign to sell a cigarette brand to women. The *Virginia Slims* ad used the phrase, "You've come a long way, baby." With a name that would suit a tampon, insinuating we now have it all because we have our own cancer-causing cigarette, and on top of that, call us "baby"—surely, women did not design this ad campaign.

for both married and single women to *purchase* real estate, largely due to gender discrimination in lending.

Beginning in 1960, women could technically open a checking account or get a credit card, but nearly all banking institutions required a male counterpart to co-sign. And the gender pay gap prevented most women from achieving financial success. It's no secret that if a woman and a man were equally qualified for the same job, the man would get it. Why? Men would not take maternity leave and would not miss work for sick children. At least that has been the social perception in America until recently.

Then, in 1963, Congress passed the Equal Pay Act. Under the act, employers cannot legally pay a woman less than a man doing comparable work. But according to Bankrate.com, "The gender pay gap was and still is a significant barrier for women in building wealth and participating in the financial market. While the Equal Pay Act improved payment practices among employers, gender differences in wages still exist today," [220] because of the types of jobs typically offered to women as compared to men.

There was a trend in the 1970s through the 1980s when the Court expanded women's rights by holding a series of state and federal laws unconstitutional that differentiated explicitly on the basis of gender. In the case of *Frontiero v. Richardson*[221] in 1973, the Court ruled that married women in the military were entitled to housing and family medical benefits that previously were only available to married men; In 1975, in *Stanton v. Stanton*,[222] the Court held it was unconstitutional for a State to allow a parent to stop supporting a daughter once she was eighteen years of age, while requiring support to a son to age twenty-one. Also, in 1975, in *Taylor v. Louisiana*[223] the Court held that state jury selections could no longer exclude women as a class. And, in *Kirchberg v. Feenstra*[224] in 1981, the Court held that state law cannot designate the husband "head and master" of the household.

With the fate of the ERA being uncertain, Congress passed the Equal Credit Opportunity Act in 1974. This law prohibits lending institutions from discriminatory practices such as requiring larger down payments from females, requiring higher interest rates from females, and requiring male co-signers on loans to females. The law now prohibits treating females differently in obtaining credit and loans.**

According to Bankrate.com, gender discrimination has been allowed to continue without legal scrutiny because the ERA is not a valid amendment. And gender discrimination still exists in lending. Bankrate.com reports that, although credit given to men and women is now generally equal, the way females and males spend is different. Women tend to use loan funds for emergencies, necessities, and education, while men are granted loans for "luxury expenses," including boats, new cars, and luxury vacations. A larger number of women borrow for college and take longer to repay the debt. This irregularity may be because women-dominated occupations tend to come with lower wages and gender discrimination in the workforce. And one study found that parents still tend to save more for a son's college education than for a daughter's.

Gender *inequality* is about the perception of power one gender has over the other. Having an Equal Rights Amendment would help eliminate gender biases, human trafficking, and domestic violence, and possibly aid in obtaining reproductive rights. Front and center of the arguments for and against the ERA's passage is the ideology of women's biology. Two cases expand women's freedom of choice and one case overturns both.

** Tired of unequal treatment by men leading the financial service industry, eight women opened their own Women's Bank in Denver, Colorado in 1978. The Women's Bank opened with only $8,000, invested by the women founders. By the end of the first day, the deposits were over $1 million.

Roe v. Wade (1973)[225]

The woman at the heart of the most controversial issue in America of this century was not your typical freedom fighter. Her name was Norma Leah Nelson McCorvey, but to the rest of the nation she is known as "Jane Roe." She was allowed to use this pseudonym in the litigation to keep her anonymity, since there was sure to be controversy surrounding her. And the controversy that bears the title *Roe v. Wade* still exists fifty years later. Norma-Jane, as I like to think of her, was as conflicted, controversial, and complex as the issue she represented. She had at least two sides to her that appeared to clash. She appeared tough and confrontational to some, malleable and impressionable to others. Perhaps she struggled with her demon opposites internally as well as externally. But just like Schlafly, Norma-Jane's internal opposites started what would become a moral war between women.

In 1994, when Norma-Jane was forty-six years old, she looked back and wrote her life's story with Andy Meisler in the book *I Am Roe: My Life, Roe v. Wade and Freedom of Choice*. Then, in 1998, she wrote a different version of her life in the book titled *Won by Love*. And, when journalist Joshua Prager realized that birthing a case in the US Supreme Court takes far longer than birthing a child, he recognized that Norma-Jane had given birth to a child before the US Supreme Court decided her case. As he put it, Norma-Jane had become a symbol for the right to a procedure that she herself never underwent. So Prager searched for and found the child that the entire nation realized had been unwanted from birth. He told the bizarre story of Norma-Jane, her family, and her daughters in his book *The Family Roe; An American Story*, putting together yet another version of the truth from retrieving hundreds of documents found in a Texas home abandoned by Norma-Jane and her lover. He obtained interviews with persons once close to her. And in the 2020 documentary *AKA Jane*

Roe, the camera caught a dying declaration from the woman herself. We cobble together what can be understood about this complex woman from these various sources.

Norma-Jane was born in Louisiana, but she moved with her family to Texas when she was very young. She described her grandmother as a sort of carnival-fortuneteller-prostitute. From all accounts, her mother was hopelessly alcoholic. Her father was a television repairman. From Norma-Jane's first book, we learn that she was part Cajun, part Cherokee, and raised a Jehovah's Witness. Both she and her mother report that she was trouble in the making. In Prager's interview with Norma-Jane's mother, she admitted that her own behavior was less than perfect. She admitted to beating Norma-Jane, claiming that she was nervy and "*Wild.*"

On the other hand, Norma-Jane said her mother "was a bitch and a drunk." She claimed her mother never wanted another child—her. And her father left.

Norma-Jane stole money from a cash register at ten and ran away to Oklahoma. One story reports that it was then that her homosexuality was first confronted. As the story goes, she was found in a hotel room kissing a female friend. The hotel reported them to the police. Norma-Jane later said, "Anytime you do anything out of the main frame of society, it's considered dirty."[226] Norma-Jane was sent to a girl's reform school, where she stayed until she dropped out of school entirely after the ninth grade.

Norma-Jane described being sexually molested by a nun and a male relative by the time she was fifteen. By the time she was sixteen, Norma-Jane had married a steel worker, McCorvey, and was pregnant with her first child—Melissa. But McCorvey beat Norma-Jane, and they divorced before Melissa was born. She moved back to Dallas and lived with her mother until she gave birth to her first child. According to Norma-Jane, her mother took her daughter from her, tricking her into signing adoption papers. According to her mother, however,

Norma-Jane was incapable of raising the child. Mary disapproved of Norma-Jane's sexual orientation and her wild nature. By her own admission, Norma-Jane was sleeping with both men and women and abusing drugs and alcohol. At age nineteen, Norma-Jane worked at a bar and at the carnival, where she had an affair with a co-worker, resulting in her second pregnancy. Abortion was illegal in Texas, and she could not afford to go out of state. She made the decision to give her second child up for adoption.

At the age of twenty-one, Norma-Jane had another affair, this time with a married man, which resulted in her third pregnancy—the "Roe baby." At that point, Norma-Jane sought an abortion, which was illegal in Texas in 1969. In Texas, an abortion was only legal on medical advice to save the mother's life, regardless of the conditions of the fetus, the mental health of the woman, or financial means to support a child. In 1969, abortion was banned in most states. So Norma-Jane did what many women did—she sought an illegal abortion. Up to that point, doctors performing illegal abortions faced criminal charges, but the women involved did not. The pregnant women were therefore left out of the legal discussion completely regarding when they would and when they would not bear children.

In Norma-Jane's attempt to get an abortion, she sought the assistance of two young women attorneys, Sarah Weddington and Linda Coffee. Sarah graduated from law school in 1967. Linda graduated from law school in 1968. Sarah was only twenty-two, and Linda was twenty-six. Both had only earned their license to practice law two years before the case was filed. Sarah later revealed that she went to Mexico to have an abortion herself while in her third year of law school.

Sarah was one of only five females in her law school class of one hundred. She finished in the top quarter of her class in 1968, but jobs for young women lawyers were not easy to come by in Texas at that time. She and a group of students organized to help provide Texas women information on contraceptives and help pregnant women get to California where abortions were legal. It was at this clinic that Linda and Sarah first met Norma-Jane.

Norma-Jane found herself pregnant and alone with her third child in the fall of 1969. By then, Sarah and Linda helped women arrange for out of state abortions, taught about contraceptives, and arranged for adoptions. They also developed an approach to challenge Texas's anti-abortion laws and were actively looking for pregnant women willing to participate in a lawsuit. They needed to represent a pregnant woman so that the case would be *justiciable*—ripe for redress and not moot. In many ways, Norma-Jane was a perfect candidate. She was desperate to have an abortion and could not afford to leave the state. Linda and Sarah believed that they could help Norma-Jane and women like her best by changing the law so that there would no longer be a need to undergo risky illegal abortions. Yet, they likely knew that the birth of new laws would come too late to enable Norma-Jane to get an abortion to end her pregnancy, a fact they may have omitted in their counsel to Norma-Jane until it was too late for an abortion.

Norma-Jane later criticized the two attorneys involved in her case. She said she only wanted an abortion. She claimed she never wanted to be the poster-child for the cause. In an interview in 1994, before her first book came out, she said,

> Sarah sat right across the table from me at Columbo's pizza parlor, and I didn't know until two years ago that she had had an abortion herself. When I told her then how desperately I needed one, she could have told me where to go for it. But she wouldn't because she needed me to be pregnant for her case. I set Sarah Weddington up on a pedestal like a rose petal. But when it came to my turn, well. Sarah saw these cuts on my wrists, my swollen eyes from crying, the miserable person sitting across from her, and she knew she had a patsy. She knew I wouldn't go outside of the realm of her and Linda. I was too scared. It was one of the most hideous times of my life.

During Norma-Jane's first trimester of pregnancy in early 1970, Sarah and Linda filed a lawsuit in the US Federal District Court in Dallas, Texas, on behalf of Norma-"Jane Roe." Norma-Jane was not the only plaintiff in the case, however. The lawsuit was also filed as a class action for all similarly-situated women in Texas. Sarah and Linda also represented a married couple. Any pregnancy would be medically risky to the woman, and they were unable to find a suitable contraceptive solution. Since she was not pregnant at the time the lawsuit was filed, the Court later dismissed the couple from the lawsuit because their claim was not "ripe for redress."

In a 2018 interview, Sarah said Norma-Jane was "a changeable person," adding, "the problem I had was trying to tell when she was telling the truth and when she wasn't.... I was very careful in drafting the materials that were filed with the court to be sure I only put in things I was sure were accurate."[227]

Perhaps the biggest of Norma-Jane's lies was about the identity of the father of "Roe-baby." Norma-Jane first claimed that she had been impregnated by rape, thinking an abortion would be more palatable in the case of rape. She later admitted in a televised interview that was "a lie."[228]

By June 1970, the District Court found in Norma-Jane's favor. The State of Texas immediately appealed the decision to the US Supreme Court. "Roe-Baby" was born that same month, and adopted at birth in Dallas, Texas.[229] Norma-Jane went on with her life, not paying much attention to the life of the case. Later that year, she met her life-long companion, Connie Gonzalez. Norma-Jane moved in with Connie and the two spent their lives together for over a quarter of a century.

In December 1971, Sarah Weddington argued the case before the US Supreme Court. She was only twenty-six years old and had never tried a case before. She was the youngest person to ever win a case in the US Supreme Court. One of the most convincing portions of

Sarah's argument was her explanation of the need for changes in the laws concerning abortion. She said:

> I think it's without question that pregnancy to a woman can completely disrupt her life. Whether she's unmarried; whether she's pursuing an education; whether she's pursuing a career; whether she has family problems; all of the problems of personal and family life, for a woman, are bound up in the problem of abortion.
>
> For example, in our state there are many schools where a woman is forced to quit if she becomes pregnant. In the City of Austin that is true.
>
> A woman, if she becomes pregnant, and is in high school, must drop out of the regular education process. And that's true of some colleges in our state.
>
> In the matter of employment, she often is forced to quit at an early point in her pregnancy. She has no provision for maternity leave. She cannot get unemployment compensation under our laws, because the laws hold that she is not eligible for employment, being pregnant, and therefore is eligible for no unemployment compensation. At the same time, she can get no welfare to help her at a time when she has no unemployment compensation and she's not eligible for any help in getting a job to provide for herself. There is no duty for employers to rehire women if they must drop out to carry a pregnancy to term.
>
> And, of course, this is especially hard on the many women in Texas who are heads of their own households and must provide for their already existing children. And, obviously, the responsibility of raising a child is a most serious one, and at times an emotional investment that must be made, cannot be denied. So, a pregnancy to a woman is perhaps one of the most determinative aspects of her life. It disrupts her body. It disrupts her education. It disrupts her employment. And it often disrupts her entire family life.

> And we feel that, because of the impact on the woman, this certainly and as far as there are any rights which are fundamental is a matter which is of such fundamental and basic concern to the woman involved that she should be allowed to make the choice as to whether to continue or to terminate her pregnancy. . . .
>
> We do not ask this court to rule that an abortion is 'good' or 'desirable.' We are here to advocate that the decision as to whether or not a particular woman will continue to carry or to terminate a pregnancy is a decision that should be made by that individual.

As Justice Stewart put it, she made "a very eloquent policy argument," but she needed to ground her argument on some constitutional basis. Sarah argued that women had liberty and privacy rights under the Ninth Amendment—the catchall vague "liberty" rights. Remembering Justice Stewart's harsh comments in his dissent in *Griswold v. Connecticut* (reviewed above) about the ability of the Ninth Amendment to change the nation's laws, this was not Sarah's strongest argument. She also argued that the State of Texas had deprived women of their Fourteenth Amendment right to life and liberty. Of course, if the ERA had been ratified by the necessary thirty-eight states in 1970, Sarah could have relied on it to provide a more solid basis for her argument that women have a right protected by the Constitution to decide for themselves when to bear a child.

The attorney for the State of Texas, Jay Floyd, made a less eloquent argument. In fact, he made probably the worst joke in the history of the Court. Since it is the plaintiff in most civil rights cases that seeks change, the plaintiff has an uphill battle. As such, the plaintiff is allowed to give their argument first, then the opposing side gives their response, and then the plaintiff may give a "rebuttal." This is true in every case. But at the outset of Jay Floyd's opposition to Sarah Weddington and

Linda Coffee's presentation of the plaintiffs' argument, he said, "It's an old joke, but when a man argues against two beautiful ladies like these, they are going to have the last word."

Not a sound, not even a snicker, was heard from the crowded courtroom. To the credit of the all-male Court at that time, the Justices were visibly annoyed by the flagrant sexist comment. Jay Floyd might have made a better impression as a standup comedian than he did during oral argument before the US Supreme Court.

Mr. Floyd argued that the case of Jane Roe was not justiciable. It was moot because Norma-Jane had already given birth to "Roe-Baby" and given her up for adoption. In this portion of her argument, Sarah Weddington explained why the case was not moot. These women had no other means of objecting to laws that harmed their mental well-being, not just their physical life. And the Court could not decide her "innocence" because she was not charged with any offense. Under Texas law, the woman having an abortion was the "victim" who would not need court clemency. Justice Byron White considered the argument made by Sarah that women in the State of Texas have no means to bring the matter to the attention of the Court precisely because of those facts. The litigation process takes longer than pregnancy and the women receiving an abortion are considered "victims" of the abortion, even if they seek the procedure and give full consent.

So Justice White, being mindful of the plaintiff's argument, asked the attorney for Texas then, "[w]hat procedure would you suggest for any pregnant female in the State of Texas ever to get any judicial consideration of this constitutional claim?"

> Your Honor, let me answer your question with a statement, if I may.
>
> I do not believe it can be done. There are situations in which, of course as the Court knows, no remedy is provided.

Now I think she makes her choice prior to the time she becomes pregnant.

That is the time of the choice.

To this, Justice White responded, "Maybe she makes her choice when she decides to live in Texas."

Then the crowded courtroom erupted with laughter. But perhaps his comment was more insightful than it was comic. As we shall see, abortion laws are now state dependent once again.

Justices Black and Harlan both retired from the Court that year. They were replaced with Justices William Rehnquist and Lewis Powell, Jr. Because of the internal changes in the Court, and the difficulty in finding a Constitutional basis and a balance for women's right of choice, it is no wonder that a decision could not be reached in *Roe v. Wade* for another year. A rehearing was ordered for the following session.

In December 1972, almost three years after the initial action was filed, oral argument before the US Supreme Court continued. Sarah Weddington re-argued for Norma-Jane and other women's right to choose. The State of Texas, now represented by Robert C. Flowers, argued against it. In that oral argument, Sarah made one of the most compelling arguments for personal freedom over State rule ever made. She said, "No decision of the Supreme Court has ever permitted anyone's constitutional right to be directly abridged to protect a state interest which is subject to such a variety of personal judgments."

The justices then asked Sarah when she thinks a fetus becomes a person. She responded that other precedents do not provide a fetus with individual rights as a "person" under the Fourteenth Amendment to the Constitution, but "here, we have a *person*, the *woman*, entitled to fundamental constitutional rights as opposed to the fetus prior to birth where there is no establishment of any kind of federal constitutional rights."

Robert C. Flowers, for the State of Texas, argued that a fetus is a "person" under the Constitution and that there was a "compelling state interest in saving the life of an unborn fetus," which outweighs the rights of a woman's private choice. Perhaps Mr. Flowers was a bit uncomfortable in his advocacy role in this case. He said numerous times that he "did not envy" the Court's position of having to determine when life begins.

The Court finally handed down its 7-2 decision in January 1973. Justice Blackmun wrote the decision. It is perhaps his legacy, or perhaps the unluckiest card drawn in his career depending on your own views. In the introduction he states:

> We forthwith acknowledge our awareness of the sensitive and emotional nature of the abortion controversy, of the vigorous opposing views, even among physicians, and of the deep and seemingly absolute convictions that the subject inspires. One's philosophy, one's experiences, one's exposure to the raw edges of human existence, one's religious training, one's attitudes toward life and family and their values, and the moral standards one establishes and seeks to observe, are all likely to influence and to color one's thinking and conclusions about abortion. In addition, population growth, pollution, poverty, and racial overtones tend to complicate and not to simplify the problem.
>
> Our task, of course, is to resolve the issue by constitutional measurement, free of emotion and of predilection. We seek earnestly to do this, and, because we do, we have inquired into, and in this opinion place some emphasis upon, medical and medical-legal history and what that history reveals about man's attitudes toward the abortion procedure over the centuries.
>
> We bear in mind, too, Mr. Justice Holmes's admonition in his now-vindicated dissent in *Lochner v. New York*, 198 U. S. 45, 76 (1905):

> "[The Constitution] is made for people of fundamentally differing views, and the accident of our finding certain opinions natural and familiar or novel and even shocking ought not to conclude our judgment upon the question whether statutes embodying them conflict with the Constitution of the United States."[230]

After the fact, in a 1983 interview, Justice Blackmun predicted that abortion would not be as great a legal issue in fifty years, depending on the fate of the Equal Rights Amendment. He did think, however, that it would continue to be a moral issue. Justice Blackmun died in 1999. He was a Methodist. He said, "People misunderstand. I am not for abortion. I hope my family never has to face such a decision. I still think it was a correct decision. We were deciding a constitutional issue, not a moral one."

The opinion first deals with the challenge as to "mootness." As to Norma-"Jane Roe," the Court accepted that she was pregnant at the time of filing and the birth of "Baby Roe" did not render her case moot. Next, the Court grappled with an extensive review of abortion throughout history. Abortion only became illegal in the State of Texas and a few other states in the mid-1800s. Those laws condemned abortion after "quickening," or when the fetus first moved, but made provisions to allow abortions when necessary to save the mother's life. This seems to have been the Court's focus. At what point in a woman's pregnancy does a State have the right to keep a woman from getting an abortion? In other words, at what point in pregnancy does a woman lose her right to make a personal medical decision and the State's decision is imposed upon her? The opinion reads as follows:

> This right of privacy, whether it be founded in the Fourteenth Amendment's concept of personal liberty and restrictions upon state action, as we feel it is, or, as the District Court determined,

in the Ninth Amendment's reservation of rights to the people, is broad enough to encompass a woman's decision whether or not to terminate her pregnancy. The detriment that the State would impose upon the pregnant woman by denying this choice altogether is apparent. Specific and direct harm medically diagnosable even in early pregnancy may be involved. Maternity, or additional offspring, may force upon the woman a distressful life and future. Psychological harm may be imminent. Mental and physical health may be taxed by child care. There is also the distress, for all concerned, associated with the unwanted child, and there is the problem of bringing a child into a family already unable, psychologically and otherwise, to care for it. In other cases, as in this one, the additional difficulties and continuing stigma of unwed motherhood may be involved. All these are factors the woman and her responsible physician necessarily will consider in consultation.[231]

The Court held, however, that the right is not absolute and that States may impose restrictions on abortions.

> [A] State may properly assert important interests in safeguarding health, in maintaining medical standards, and in protecting potential life. At some point in pregnancy, these respective interests become sufficiently compelling to sustain regulation of the factors that govern the abortion decision. The privacy right involved, therefore, cannot be said to be absolute.[232]

So at what point in a pregnancy does a State's interest in saving the fetus outweigh the privacy rights of the pregnant woman, which are "sufficiently compelling enough to sustain regulations?" The line was drawn at the end of the first trimester of pregnancy. Some evidence supports the notion that pinning abortions to that strict timeline was both "arbitrary" and erroneous. Nevertheless, the decision is summarized in Justice Blackmun's opinion as follows:

> To summarize and to repeat:
> 1. A state criminal abortion statute of the current Texas type, that excepts from criminality only a lifesaving procedure on behalf of the mother, without regard to pregnancy stage and without recognition of the other interests involved, is violative of the Due Process Clause of the Fourteenth Amendment.
> (a) For the stage prior to approximately the end of the first trimester, the abortion decision and its effectuation must be left to the medical judgment of the pregnant woman's attending physician.
> (b) For the stage subsequent to approximately the end of the first trimester, the State, in promoting its interest in the health of the mother, may, if it chooses, regulate the abortion procedure in ways that are reasonably related to maternal health.
> (c) For the stage subsequent to viability, the State in promoting its interest in the potentiality of human life may, if it chooses, regulate, and even proscribe, abortion except where it is necessary, in appropriate medical judgment, for the preservation of the life or health of the mother.[233]

Since that time, the decision has been dissected and rejected by many. One notable critic is Justice Ginsberg. Perhaps most known for her liberal views and support of women's causes, you might not suspect she would be a critic of the opinion written by Justice Blackmun. But prior to her appointment to the Supreme Court in 1973, she criticized the decision not for its holding, but for the Court's reasoning. She would have liked the opinion to be more focused on gender equality, rather than an "abortion right." Including the need to consult with a physician, the decision is not really about a woman's right to choose, she observed, "It's about a doctor's freedom to practice his profession as he thinks best," Ginsburg said. "It wasn't woman-centered. It was physician-centered."

She believed that the opinion "seemed to stop momentum on the side of change." She said that the decision gave "opponents a target to aim at relentlessly." As the controversy unfolds, we see how right she was.

Ginsburg's way of combating inequality as a civil rights lawyer was often to fight for the other side of the coin to show the injustice. Her primary concern was *gender equality* for both men and women. Justice Ginsburg believed that a more step-by-step approach focused on gender equality would have been longer lasting to loosen abortion laws in the states. To make her point, Ginsburg would have liked *Struck v. Secretary of Defense*[234] to be the deciding abortion case instead of *Roe v. Wade*. In 1970, Ginsburg represented US Air Force Captain Susan Struck, who was twenty-five years old and the only female service member on base. She was a career officer and became pregnant while serving in Vietnam. At that time, the US Air Force required a pregnant woman to be immediately discharged or terminate the pregnancy. Captain Struck wanted neither. Ginsburg argued that this woman should not be required to have an abortion to keep her job. Ginsburg believed she could have brought the Court to realize that the regulation made the female parent responsible for a child, but not a male parent, while at the same time disabling her from her career. She believed that, given that case, the Court might have comprehended, or at least had a glimpse of, the reality it later resisted, "that disadvantageous treatment of woman because of her pregnancy and reproductive choice is a paradigm case of discrimination on the basis of sex." The issue is the woman's choice, and as Ginsburg put it, "Government, stay out of this!"[235]

Justice Ginsburg also predicted that if *Roe v. Wade* were overturned, many states would still allow safe legal abortions. Yet, she predicted, probably more so for women who have the financial means, "It would be the poor who wouldn't have a choice, and I don't think that makes much sense as a matter of policy."[236]

What Ever Happened to Norma-Jane?

After the *Roe v. Wade* decision came out in 1973, people assumed they knew "Jane Roe." To Catholics, she was a threat to the Pope. To Protestants, she was not a savior, nor a demon. To most, she was likely just a young, unmarried woman seeking higher education, and, desiring to postpone her first pregnancy, sought her abortion in Texas. But that description fit Sarah Weddington, not Norma McCorvey, although that was probably the image feminists of that era wanted Jane Roe to be. But the real Jane Roe, Norma McCorvey, was just about as far from that as you can imagine. She was tough talking with an edge and an obvious disdain for rules. She said, "I learned straight on that if you're nice and polite and quiet, nobody pays any attention to you. And I like attention."[237]

In 1980, Norma-Jane was interviewed by a TV newscaster in Dallas and revealed her identity as "Jane Roe." In 1989, she was invited to a pro-choice rally in Washington, D.C., where she met many notable feminists, including Gloria Allred. Gloria Allred took Norma-Jane under her wing to Los Angeles, where she began to be center stage. But soon things began to unravel. First, Norma-Jane admitted the story of rape was a lie in a televised interview.*** She was admittedly a lesbian. She was not educated beyond the ninth grade and "Roe-Baby" was her third pregnancy at twenty-one years old—facts that pro-choice advocates were uncomfortable with. At pro-choice rallies, she was propped up for photographs but rarely asked to speak. When she found out that Sarah Weddington had an abortion herself and had not assisted Norma-Jane in getting one, she was angry. She felt she should have been told that getting an abortion was not going

---

*** The rape lie damaged Norma-Jane's credibility but it was never an issue in the court case, thanks to the wisdom of her attorneys Linda Coffee and Sarah Weddington.

to be part of the litigation process. She also thought the pro-choice feminists were a snobby bunch. She felt that she had been denied the opportunity to be recognized and acknowledged for making abortions legal. No one recognized how much it cost her emotionally. But she was recognized! She was a hero among the women who needed abortions. And the pro-life activists began to recognize her as a threat to their cause.

She and her partner, Connie, began working in a Planned Parenthood clinic in Dallas in 1992. In 1994, Norma-Jane's first memoir, *I Am Roe: My Life, Roe v. Wade and Freedom of Choice,* was published. The book recounted her troubled upbringing, her pregnancies, and her attempt to get an abortion. Pro-life demonstrations occurred regularly in front of the clinic where Norma-Jane and Connie worked. Pro-life demonstrators greeted women seeking abortions with hate in the name of religion. Bomb threats and news of clinics burning to the ground were regular occurrences. Norma-Jane and Connie's home became a target. Pro-life demonstrators were cruel. Instead of showing love to these women in need, they fought with them. They burned buildings, blocked access, intimidated them, told them they were killing their babies, and they accused Norma-Jane of killing 35 million babies. In a 1994 interview for the *New York Times*, after her book came out, Norma-Jane was asked what her life would have been like if she hadn't been Jane Roe. She responded:

> I don't know. Once people read 'I Am Roe,' I think they'll understand where I'm coming from. I'm a simple woman with a ninth-grade education who wants women not to be harassed or condemned. It's no glamorous thing to go through an abortion. I never had one, but I've worked in three clinics and I know. The anti-choice people all ask me, 'When do I think life begins?' I don't know. I'm not a rocket scientist. I just wanted the privilege of a clean clinic to get the procedure done. I don't require that

much in my life. With Connie, my cats, and my plants, I'm a pretty happy girl. I just never had the privilege to go into an abortion clinic, lay down, and have an abortion. That's the only thing I never had.[238]

Those were Norma-Jane's words in 1994, but "a changeable person," as Sarah Weddington later described her, is perhaps the best description of Norma-Jane. In 1995, she flipped to the other side. While working at the abortion clinic in Dallas, an extremist anti-abortion group led by Rev. Rob Schneck called "Operation Rescue" opened up next door to the clinic. Flip Benham, the evangelical minister who ran the Operation Rescue center next door, began to ingratiate himself to Norma-Jane. Norma-Jane's longtime partner, Connie, described him as a slick smooth talker.

It is easy to see that Norma-Jane was lost and impressionable. Whatever one might think of abortion, anyone can have compassion for Norma-Jane. She had a terrible upbringing and felt she had no purpose. Then, she came to believe she was a savior of women. In fact, she notably *loved* women. And Norma-Jane loved attention. Although she was not initially seeking that, she wanted to be put on stage with her feminist allies. When she did not get that with the pro-choice crowd, she got that with Operation Rescue. In her role as "Jane Roe" the pro-choice advocate, women only displayed how much they despised her. In her role as an evangelical Christian, she could save babies. That sent her to the other side. Soon, she was seen on TV getting baptized. In 1998, she published a second memoir, *Won by Love*, detailing her change of heart on abortion. She started advocating for pro-life. She appeared at a National Memorial for Preborn, which was a memorial for unborn babies organized by the Operation Rescue leader Rev. Rob Schneck. The event had a lot of media attention. It was held in the US Capitol complex in Washington, D.C., which is just a short walk from the US Supreme Court building where it all began. There, Norma-Jane apologized on stage for all the harm she caused and hoped that *Roe v. Wade* would be overturned. It was a huge upset to her previous feminist allies. But the person most hurt by her change of heart was her lover of so many years, Connie Gonzales.

According to Prager's book, *The Family Roe; An American Story*, "just as Norma didn't feel at home on the pro-choice side, she doesn't feel at home on the pro-life side, because they're exploiting her, too. And one big, big, big problem is that they basically tell her that she can't be gay—she has to renounce her homosexuality. And this causes her untold grief and suffering." According to Rev. Rob Schneck and Flip Benham, she could not be a Christian and a homosexual. She would be kicked out of the Christian faith. It also caused Connie Gonzales visible emotional pain.

McCorvey's life is splayed out in the documentary *AKA Jane Roe*,[239] which came out in 2020. Nick Sweeney directs the film. He began filming in 2016, just one year before Norma's death at age sixty-nine. The documentary is a glimpse into the life of this troubled woman, and into the lives of all women who must choose between family, career, and society's expectations. The documentary is a culmination of prior appearances of Norma-Jane up to her "death bed confession."

At one point in her pro-choice activities, Norma-Jane said, "Jane Roe is every woman who has ever been denied anything in her whole life. Because we've all been denied something at some point, so we're all Jane Roes."

The issue is quite emotional in the abstract. If you add on top of that all of the internal struggles a woman may have—abuses, complex relationships, religious beliefs, insecurities or self-loathing, compassion for all the Jane-Roes could lead the way to equality in this sensitive area.

In the documentary, Norma-Jane confesses that all of her pro-life work was a lie. She admitted to being paid by pro-life advocates to say that she regretted ever seeking an abortion. She said, "I think it was a mutual thing. I took their money, and they'd put me out in front of the cameras and tell me what to say. That's what I'd say."

Rev. Rob Schneck confirmed that Operation Rescue paid her at least $450,000 for what she says was "all an act."

Just a few months before her death, in what she called a deathbed confession and visibly ailing, she told the camera, "If a young woman wants to have an abortion, that's no skin off my ass. You know, that's why they call it choice."

Rev. Rob Schneck also admitted to previously berating women, terrorizing women, telling them they were murderers, and shocking people with fetal remains at Planned Parenthood clinics. He said the pro-life movement felt "morally vindicated." He admitted that once Norma-Jane began speaking out in support of *Roe v. Wade* and women's choice with Gloria Allred, she became a threat that "needed to be dealt with." That's when the pro-life movement decided to exploit her. Norma-Jane became a target. "Her greatest weaknesses could be exploited." He confirmed that they paid her a "benevolent gift" to speak against abortion.

Rev. Rob Schneck later expressed regret for the harm they caused Norma-Jane. He said, "[w]hat we did with Norma was highly unethical." In 2020, on camera, Rev. Schneck said, "What does it profit a man if he should gain the whole world and lose his soul? If you do what we did to Norma, you lose your soul." He said:

> I still identify as Evangelical. But I like to think of myself as lovingly critical of my community. I guess in some ways I'd like to use whatever years I have remaining to undo the damage that I did and that many movement leaders did on the pro-life side. I used to think that Roe v. Wade would never be overturned. I think that Roe v. Wade could be overturned now. And I think the result of that would be chaos and pain. And to impose that kind of crisis on a woman is unthinkable.

At the end of her life, Norma-Jane did not want *Roe v. Wade* tampered with. "*Roe v. Wade* helped save women's lives," she said.

Planned Parenthood of Southeastern Pa. v. Casey (1992)[240]

Ever since *Roe v. Wade* was decided, conservatives on the Court have been chipping away at it. Recently, in *Dobbs v. Jackson Women's Health Organization* (reviewed below), the Court annihilated it. But in 1992, in the 5-4 decision of *Planned Parenthood of Southeastern Pa. v. Casey*, the Court upheld *Roe v. Wade*. It also held that States could put certain restrictions on the availability of abortions so long as the restriction is not an "undue burden" on fundamental rights. The "undue burden" standard means a State cannot impose a regulation that is a "substantial obstacle in the path of a woman seeking an abortion before the fetus attains viability." (Viability is generally understood to mean when a fetus can live on its own.)

Five provisions of the Pennsylvania Abortion Control Act were at issue. They were (1) a woman seeking an abortion must give informed consent; (2) the woman must be given a waiting period of twenty-four hours after receiving information and consent; (3) minors must have informed consent of one parent (but the minor may receive a judicial bypass in certain circumstances); (4) a married woman must have her husband's informed consent; and (5) certain reporting requirements on facilities providing abortion services.

The Court held that each of the restrictions did not place an "undue burden" on fundamental rights, with the exception of the requirement that a married woman receive her husband's consent. In other words, a State could put all but the one reasonable restrictions on abortion. In all other ways, the Supreme Court upheld *Roe v. Wade*.

Dobbs v. Jackson Women's Health Organization (2022)[241]

In 2022, the most conservative majority on the US Supreme Court of the last century overturned both *Roe v. Wade* and *Planned Parenthood v. Casey*. This case came out of Mississippi. In 2018, Mississippi passed a law banning abortions after fifteen weeks of pregnancy with few exceptions. Most states had exceptions for rape, incest, or medical abnormalities evident in the fetus. The ONLY women's health facility that was licensed to conduct abortions in ALL of Mississippi challenged the law in court. Jackson Planned Parenthood argued that under *Roe v. Wade* and *Planned Parenthood v. Casey* the Mississippi law was unconstitutional. They argued that, under the Court's previous direction, the law placed a "substantial obstacle in the path of a woman seeking an abortion" because the law had a strict numerical cut-off, rather than any evidence of the fetus attaining "viability."

The State's primary argument was that there was no guarantee of abortion under the Constitution and the Court should reconsider and overrule *Roe* and *Casey*, allowing each State to regulate abortion as its citizens wish.

The lower District Court found the Mississippi ban unconstitutional, as did the US Court of Appeals for the Fifth Circuit, under the precedent set by the US Supreme Court in *Roe v. Wade* fifty years earlier and in *Planned Parenthood v. Casey* thirty years earlier. The case was appealed to the US Supreme Court, who then overruled *Roe v. Wade* and *Planned Parenthood v. Casey*.

The most frequent criticism of *Roe v. Wade* by legal scholars is that a right to abortion is not found in the language of the Constitution. That was not new criticism of *Roe v. Wade*. In fact, the dissent in *Roe v. Wade*, written by Justice Byron White, was blunt. To him, the opinion was an "exercise of raw judicial power." This is the foundation of the *Dobbs* decision.

Justice Alito wrote the opinion for the conservative majority in *Dobbs*. He said the Court went too far in "creating" a right to an abortion in *Roe v. Wade*, or a law where one did not exist before. *Dobbs* also overruled *Casey*. The major criticism of *Casey* is that it relied on *Roe v. Wade* as precedent. If *Roe v. Wade* was wrong, then, the Court reasons, *Casey* must be wrong too. Legal critics claimed that the *Casey* decision was meant to clarify *Roe*, but it did not accomplish that. It was also meant to solve the national divide on the issue, but it did not accomplish that either.

One legal resource succinctly summarized the five reasons announced in *Dobbs* for overturning *Roe v. Wade* and *Casey v. Planned Parenthood*: (1) The *Roe v. Wade* decision short-circuited the democratic process, (2) both *Roe v. Wade* and *Planned Parenthood v. Casey* lacked grounding in constitutional text, history, or precedent, (3) the tests they established were not 'workable,' (4) they caused distortion of law in other areas, and (5) overruling them would not upend concrete reliance interests. Of these five reasons, the fifth is perhaps the hardest for a free society to swallow.

The majority opinion, written by Justice Alito states:

> We hold that Roe and Casey must be overruled. The Constitution makes no reference to abortion, and no such right is implicitly protected by any constitutional provision, including the one on which the defenders of Roe and Casey now chiefly rely—the Due Process Clause of the Fourteenth Amendment. That provision has been held to guarantee some rights that are not mentioned in the Constitution, but any such right must be "deeply rooted in this Nation's history and tradition" and "implicit in the concept of ordered liberty."
>
> ...
>
> The abortion right is also critically different from any other right that this Court has held to fall within the Fourteenth

Amendment's protection of "liberty." Roe's defenders characterize the abortion right as similar to the rights recognized in past decisions involving matters such as intimate sexual relations, contraception, and marriage, but abortion is fundamentally different, as both Roe and Casey acknowledged, because it destroys what those decisions called "fetal life" and what the law now before us describes as an "unborn human being."

...

Stare decisis, the doctrine on which Casey's controlling opinion was based, does not compel unending adherence to Roe's abuse of judicial authority. Roe was egregiously wrong from the start. Its reasoning was exceptionally weak, and the decision has had damaging consequences. And far from bringing about a national settlement of the abortion issue, Roe and Casey have enflamed debate and deepened division.

...

It is time to heed the Constitution and return the issue of abortion to the people's elected representatives. 'The permissibility of abortion, and the limitations, upon it, are to be resolved like most important questions in our democracy: by citizens trying to persuade one another and then voting.' (citing Justice Scalia's concurring and part dissent in Casey, 505 U. S., at 979). That is what the Constitution and the rule of law demand."

...

Both sides make important policy arguments, but supporters of Roe and Casey must show that this Court has the authority to weigh those arguments and decide how abortion may be regulated in the States. They have failed to make that showing, and we thus return the power to weigh those arguments to the people and their elected representatives.[242]

While it is true that many changes have occurred since *Roe v. Wade*, the majority seems immune to realizing that states would revert back to pre-*Roe* days once it is overruled. Several states have once again banned abortions, or limited access to the point of what amounts to a complete ban. Women, at least pregnant women, are apparently not *persons* in the US Supreme Court's eyes, but simply a uterus owned by the state in which they reside. For or against abortion, make no mistake—the US Supreme Court stripped away women's Constitutional rights of equality in *Dobbs v. Jackson Women's Health Organization*.

The Dissenters

The *Dobbs* case was decided 6-3. Justices Stephen Breyer, Sonia Sotomayor, and Elena Kagan authored a joint dissent. It is worth reading the entire sixty pages, but here are some of the important points of the three Justices dissent:

> For half a century, *Roe v. Wade*, and *Planned Parenthood of Southeastern Pa. v. Casey*, have protected the liberty and equality of women. Roe held, and Casey reaffirmed, that the Constitution safeguards a woman's right to decide for herself whether to bear a child. . . . [I]n the first stages of pregnancy, the government could not make that choice for women. The government could not control a woman's body or the course of a woman's life: It could not determine what the woman's future would be. Respecting a woman as an autonomous being, and granting her full equality, meant giving her substantial choice over this most personal and most consequential of all life decisions.
>
> . . .
>
> In [Roe and Casey] the Court held, a State could not impose a "substantial obstacle" on a woman's "right to elect the procedure"

as she (not the government) thought proper, in light of all the circumstances and complexities of her own life.

Today, the Court discards that balance. It says that from the very moment of fertilization, a woman has no rights to speak of. A State can force her to bring a pregnancy to term, even at the steepest personal and familial costs. . . . Across a vast array of circumstances, a State will be able to impose its moral choice on a woman and coerce her to give birth to a child.

...

Whatever the exact scope of the coming laws, one result of today's decision is certain: the curtailment of women's rights, and of their status as free and equal citizens. Yesterday, the Constitution guaranteed that a woman confronted with an unplanned pregnancy could (within reasonable limits) make her own decision about whether to bear a child, with all the life-transforming consequences that act involves. And in thus safeguarding each woman's reproductive freedom, the Constitution also protected "[t]he ability of women to participate equally in [this Nation's] economic and social life." (Casey) But no longer.

...

Some women, especially women of means, will find ways around the State's assertion of power. Others—those without money or childcare or the ability to take time off from work—will not be so fortunate. Maybe they will try an unsafe method of abortion, and come to physical harm, or even die. Maybe they will undergo pregnancy and have a child, but at significant personal or familial cost. At the least, they will incur the cost of losing control of their lives. The Constitution will, today's majority holds, provide no shield, despite its guarantees of liberty and equality for all.[243]

The question of balancing competing interests

> ... That fact—the presence of countervailing interests—is what made the abortion question hard, and what necessitated balancing. The majority scoffs at that idea, castigating us for "repeatedly prais[ing] the 'balance' the two cases arrived at (with the word balance in scare quotes). To the majority 'balance' is a dirty word, as moderation is a foreign concept. The majority would allow States to ban abortion from conception onward because it does not think forced childbirth at all implicates a woman's rights to equality and freedom. Today's Court, that is, does not think there is anything of constitutional significance attached to a woman's control of her body and the path of her life.
>
> Roe and Casey thought that one-sided view misguided. In some sense, that is the difference in a nutshell between our precedents and the majority opinion. The constitutional regime we have lived in for the last fifty years recognized competing interests, and sought a balance between them. The constitutional regime we enter today erases the woman's interest and recognizes only the State's (or the federal government's).[244]

As to the majority's reliance on history, the dissent answers that the Constitution is meant to adapt to change:

> [I]n the words of the great Chief Justice John Marshall, our Constitution is "intended to endure for ages to come," and must adapt itself to a future "seen dimly," if at all. *McCulloch v. Maryland* (1819). That is indeed why our Constitution is written as it is. The Framers (both in 1788 and 1868) understood that the world changes. So they did not define rights by reference to the specific practices existing at the time. Instead, the Framers defined rights in general terms, to permit future evolution in their scope and meaning. And over the course of our history, this Court has

taken up the Framers' invitation. It has kept true to the Framers' principles by applying them in new ways, responsive to new societal understandings and conditions.

...

"'[P]eople' did not ratify the Fourteenth Amendment. Men did. So it is perhaps not so surprising that the ratifiers were not perfectly attuned to the importance of reproductive rights for women's liberty, or for their capacity to participate as equal members of our Nation. Indeed, the ratifiers—both in 1868 [when the Fourteenth Amendment was ratified] and when the original Constitution was approved in 1788—did not understand women as full members of the community embraced by the phrase "We the People."

...

Because laws in 1868 deprived women of any control over their bodies, the majority approves States doing so today. Because those laws prevented women from charting the course of their own lives, the majority says States can do the same again. Because in 1868, the government could tell a pregnant woman—even in the first days of her pregnancy—that she could do nothing but bear a child, it can once more impose that command. Today's decision strips women of agency over what even the majority agrees is a contested and contestable moral issue. It forces her to carry out the State's will, whatever the circumstances and whatever the harm it will wreak on her and her family. In the Fourteenth Amendment's terms, it takes away her liberty. Even before we get to stare decisis, we dissent.[245]

Stare Decisis

Stare decisis means a court may not overrule a decision, even one made by the US Supreme Court, without special justification or a very good reason for change. The dissent addresses *Stare decisis*, which means literally 'to stand by things decided,'[246] showing that overruling *Roe* and *Casey* will have a long lasting injurious affect, not just to women, but also to the Court's reputation.

> We fear that today's decision, departing from stare decisis for no legitimate reason, is its own loaded weapon. Weakening stare decisis threatens to upend bedrock legal doctrines, far beyond any single decision. Weakening stare decisis creates profound legal instability. And as Casey recognized, weakening stare decisis in a hotly contested case like this one calls into question this Court's commitment to legal principle. It makes the Court appear not restrained but aggressive, not modest but grasping. In all those ways, today's decision takes aim, we fear, at the rule of law.
>
> ...
>
> The Court reverses course today for one reason and one reason only: because the composition of this Court has changed. . . . Casey explained that to do so—to reverse prior law 'upon a ground no firmer than a change in [the Court's] membership'— would invite the view that 'this institution is little different from the two political branches of the Government. No view . . . could do more lasting injury to this Court and to the system of law which it is our abiding mission to serve.'[247]

Dobbs Effect on Women

> For half a century now, in Casey's words, '[t]he ability of women to participate equally in the economic and social life of the Nation has been facilitated by their ability to control their reproductive lives.' Indeed, all women now of childbearing age have grown up expecting that they would be able to avail themselves of Roe's and Casey's protections.
>
> ...

Withdrawing a woman's right to choose whether to continue a pregnancy does not mean that no choice is being made. It means that a majority of today's Court has wrenched this choice from women and given it to the States. To allow a State to exert control over one of 'the most intimate and personal choices' a woman may make is not only to affect the course of her life, monumental as those effects might be. It is to alter her 'views of [herself]' and her understanding of her 'place in society' as someone with the recognized dignity and authority to make these choices. Women have relied on Roe and Casey in this way for fifty years. Many have never known anything else. When Roe and Casey disappear, the loss of power, control, and dignity will be immense.

After today, young women will come of age with fewer rights than their mothers and grandmothers had. The majority accomplishes that result without so much as considering how women have relied on the right to choose or what it means to take that right away. The majority's refusal even to consider the life-altering consequences of reversing Roe and Casey is a stunning indictment of its decision.

With sorrow—for this Court, but more, for the many millions of American women who have today lost a fundamental constitutional protection—we dissent.[248]

Consider this:

Do you think the *Dobbs* decision put an end to the legal discussion on abortion?

Do you think that decisions related to women's reproductive rights should be left to the federal government? The individual States? The counties? The cities? The medical profession? Or the individuals involved?

If you are like most people, you probably already have strong emotions related to this topic. Can you consider the merits of opposing points of view? If you can consider opposing viewpoints, or if you have conflicting feelings on this subject, can you conceivably become comfortable knowing that both sides have merit? If you can see both sides of this issue, are you able to find a middle-ground solution, or is it an all-or-nothing issue?

After you read this chapter, do you think that *Roe v. Wade* would have been overturned in *Dobbs* if the majority of the US Supreme Court saw *Roe v. Wade* as a Fourteenth Amendment right to equality, rather than an "abortion case" as Justice Ginsburg suggested?

Do you think that passage of an Equal Rights Amendment would have any legal impact on reproductive rights of women?

Do you think the words of the majority opinion in *Cooper v. Aaron* that, "the prohibitions of the Fourteenth Amendment extend to all actions of the State denying equal protection of the laws . . ." would help in the fight for gender equality?

Since many of the arguments made by pro-life advocates are made on religious grounds, do you think a First Amendment argument that abortion rights are a "freedom of religion right" would assist pro-choice advocates? Do you think that bans on abortion are a violation of the Establishment Clause?

More to Consider:

In 1994, the Freedom of Access to Clinic Entrances (FACE) (18 US Code § 248) was enacted. This law prohibits the use of physical force, threat of physical force, or physical obstruction to intentionally injure, intimidate, interfere with, or attempt to injure, intimidate, or interfere with any person who is obtaining an abortion. Harassment and violence still occurs at Planned Parenthood clinics throughout the country. The US Justice Department keeps a running list of crimes against reproductive health care providers.[249] There are many, but at least there is a means to bring criminal charges against the harassers. This is just one small example of the hate that continues today:

- In 2023, four defendants were charged with Civil Rights Conspiracy and FACE Act offenses for their 2022 targeted attacks on pregnancy resource centers in Florida. The defendants vandalized the facilities with spray-painted threats, including "If abortions aren't safe then neither are you," and "We're coming for U." The defendants' conduct intimidated reproductive health care providers and damaged the pregnancy resource centers' property.

"Today, in 2024, in America, women are being turned away from emergency rooms and forced to travel hundreds of miles for health care, while doctors fear prosecution for providing an abortion. . . . The disregard for women's ability to make these decisions for themselves and their families is outrageous and unacceptable," PRESIDENT BIDEN.

ADDITIONAL RESOURCES

Chapter 17—The Equal Rights Amendment

- Since the *Dobbs* decision, fourteen states have banned abortions entirely. Review your state's current abortion laws here, from the Center for Reproductive Rights: www.reproductiverights.org/maps/abortion-laws-by-state/
- To assist in the passage of the Equal Rights Amendment, tell your senators to support the ERA. Visit: www.equalrightsamendment.org and the League of Women Voters at www.lwv.org/take-action/tell-your-senators-support-equal-rights-amendment

"Unless you can put yourself in the mind of a woman facing a pregnancy she is not ready for, you cannot pronounce what she must do." REV. ROB SCHNECK

CHAPTER 18

An Additional Amendment to the US Constitution?

The Future Looks Brighter

This next story has not yet reached the US Supreme Court. It is only relevant to our discussion because our future depends on the young people who will be here tomorrow. In the hopes of creating a better future, these youths are taking it upon themselves to use our judicial system and science together to make a difference in their own backyard—and potentially in the world. Science is the evidence proving that they have been harmed by the pollution and practices of their state. The world—the future—is theirs, they argue. And we are destroying it.

Held v. State of Montana (2023)[250]

Montana is known for its beauty and rich history, yet it is surprising that it is one of the worst polluters in the nation, emitting tons of greenhouse gases every year. So, it is not surprising that the young people in this state may lead us in protecting Earth's natural resources. To protect their land, indeed the world, sixteen youth plaintiffs sued in the Montana State Court. Judge Kathy Seeley ruled in their favor after a victory in state court in the summer of 2023. The sixteen plaintiffs now range in age between six and twenty-six years old. They claim that the State violates their *Montana State constitutional rights* to "a clean and healthful environment; to seek safety, health, and happiness; and to individual dignity and equal protection of the law."

The youth plaintiffs proved to the trial court with scientific evidence that it was not disputed that climate change is caused by humans. And they proved to the satisfaction of the court that Montana's legislature has done nothing to address the problem. In fact, they claim, Montana laws support and prioritize fossil fuel extraction.

Under current Montana law, the State does not consider the effects of greenhouse gases when issuing permits for fossil fuel projects unless the federal government declares carbon dioxide a regulated pollutant. This, the plaintiffs argue, is ruining the Big Skies of Montana, along with their health and happiness.

The State made three arguments to oppose the plaintiffs. First, the State claimed that the sixteen plaintiffs do not have standing to bring the lawsuit because they could not show direct injuries to themselves. But the court found that the sixteen youths have suffered injuries to their physical and mental health, homes and property, recreational, spiritual and esthetic interests, tribal and cultural traditions, economic security, and happiness. Thus, they have standing to bring the lawsuit.

The State's second argument against the youths was that the lawsuit was not "ripe for redress," meaning that the court would not be able to fix the problem and only the state legislature could change Montana's environmental policies. The state court held that the Montana State Constitutional right to "a clean and healthful environment" requires "enhancement" of Montana's environment, which places "an affirmative duty upon the government to take active steps to realize" that right.

The State's final argument was that the youths did not have evidence showing a connection between the greenhouse gas emissions and their injuries. But the court concluded that the State's actions to permit fossil fuel activities without environmental review of greenhouse gas emissions causes further harm to Montana's environment and its citizens, especially its youth,* who are uniquely vulnerable due to "their stages of development as youth, and their average longevity on the planet in the future." And that, "Plaintiffs face lifelong hardships resulting from climate change."

What a win for these young citizens! What a win for us all, thanks to these youths. In fact, another group of youths are suing in Federal Court in the case *Juliana v. United States*.[251] That case was initiated by twenty-one youths ranging in ages from eight to nineteen years old at the time the case began in 2015. Nearly all of the plaintiffs are now adults. These youths are represented by litigators for Our Children's Trust, a nonprofit organization providing legal services to youth from all backgrounds to secure their legal rights to a safe climate. One of the senior litigators working for Our Children's Trust said that youth have the most to lose. They will lose their future, yet they are among the most politically powerless people in the country, since young people do not have money to lobby legislatures or pay for attorneys in litigation.

Most litigators who have studied this issue believe that the *Juliana* plaintiffs have a steep uphill battle. After all, there is no specific *US Constitutional* right for a clean environment. The complaint in *Juliana* claims that the US government has known of the dangers of fossil fuels for decades and has allowed and encouraged an economy based on fossil fuels. This may be true, and it may even be a fact that can be proven at trial, but plaintiffs have discovered that they will also need to show that the government acted in a manner that caused harm to them specifically.

---

* According to research conducted by Stockholm Environment Research Institute, Montana's yearly carbon dioxide emissions resulting from the extraction, transportation, and burning of fossil fuels "emits the sixth-highest volume of greenhouse gas emissions per capita among US states—which is also more than the total amount from one hundred countries."

Nevertheless, progress is being made due to these and other youths who are taking action through the judicial process. Despite all of the roadblocks from the US Department of Justice, on June 1, 2023, US District Judge Ann Aiken ruled to allow the youths to amend their complaint and go to trial. She said, "Exercising my 'reasoned judgment,' I have no doubt that the right to a climate system capable of sustaining human life is fundamental to a free and ordered society." Aiken wrote in her decision, "It is a foundational doctrine that when government conduct catastrophically harms American citizens, the judiciary is constitutionally required to perform its independent role and determine whether the challenged conduct, not exclusively committed to any branch by the Constitution, is unconstitutional."

For these and other plaintiffs in similar lawsuits, winning at trial is a distant dream. Yet, they recognize that winning isn't everything. Just bringing attention to their cause is a win. Similar State actions have been filed in Florida, Hawaii, Utah, and Virginia. The world has taken notice. Six youths from Portugal who were motivated by a tragic fire there in June of 2017 have brought a similar lawsuit against thirty-two countries for failing to address the human-caused climate crisis. Their matter will be heard in the European Court of Human Rights. In the meantime, Montana is already showing signs of complying with Judge Seeley's order. The Montana Department of Environmental Quality is now asking for public approval on potential updates to the Montana Environmental Policy Act. The director recently admitted in a statement, "These regulations are showing their age and it's time to hear from Montanans about what [the EPA Policy] should look like today and into the future."

Juliana v. U.S. plaintiffs, courtesy of Our Children's Trust

Fig. 7 Photo by Our Children's Trust, June 11, 2023. Reproduced with permission from Creative Commons.org under Attribution 3.0 Unported License (Additional licensing information located at the back of the book under Permissions and Licenses.)

Consider This:

After reading this chapter, do you think the US Constitution needs an amendment similar to the State of Montana Constitution, which guarantees the right to a clean and healthful environment; to seek safety, health, and happiness; and to individual dignity and equal protection of the law?

ADDITIONAL RESOURCES

Chapter 18: The Future of Climate and the US Constitution

- View the *Juliana v. United States* case and others here: https://climatecasechart.com/case/juliana-v-united-states/
- Research the work of Our Children's Trust, visit www.ourchildrenstrust.org. Our Children's Trust is an American nonprofit public interest law firm based in Oregon that has filed several lawsuits on behalf of youth plaintiffs against state and federal governments, arguing that they are infringing on the youths' rights to a safe climate system.

"The future belongs to those who believe in the beauty of their dreams." ELEANOR ROOSEVELT.

Epilogue

Opinions were issued just prior to publication of this book in a few of the cases previously mentioned as "undecided" or "pending."

Second Amendment

U.S. v. Rahimi 602 U.S. ___ (2024)

Remember this guy? That bad dude that beat his girlfriend, and under a domestic violence restraining order was ordered to give up his guns, and used a gun in the fast food line? Recall also his argument that there was no equivalent "history and tradition" dating back to 1791 regulating "domestic abusers" having their Second Amendment right taken away. To their credit, the U.S. Supreme Court majority opinion, which was delivered by Chief Justice, and nearly unanimous (all but Justice Clarence Thomas) held,

> "[w]hen an individual has been found by a court to pose a credible threat to the physical safety of another, that individual may be temporarily disarmed consistent with the Second Amendment."

The majority opinion said,

> [T]he Second Amendment permits more than just regulations identical to those existing in 1791. Under our precedent, the appropriate analysis involves considering whether the challenged regulation is consistent with the principles that underpin the Nation's regulatory tradition. . . . When firearm regulation is challenged under the Second Amendment, the Government must show that the restriction "is consistent with the Nation's historical tradition of firearm regulation." . . . A court must ascertain whether the new law is "relevantly similar" to laws that our tradition is understood to permit, "apply[ing] faithfully the balance struck by the founding generation to modern circumstances." . . . Why and how the regulation burdens the right are central to this inquiry. As Bruen explained, a challenged regulation that does not precisely match its historical precursors "still may be analogous enough to pass constitutional muster."

Finally! A clue! Some breadcrumbs dropped for some smart legislators to propose some regulation consistent with "the Nation's historical tradition of firearm regulation" while "applying a balance to modern circumstances." But of course! Why didn't we think of that! (Hand to forehead. And if there were an accepted sarcasm font, I would be using it now, because, after all, isn't that what we've been trying to do for the last twenty years?)

But seriously, I do believe that this is a call to legislators to find that balance and provide reasonable regulations to criminalize private ownership of weapons of war. I will be sending a copy of this case to my Senator and Congressperson in the hopes that they put it under their pillow each night for safekeeping and dream of the exact language for a new law regulating firearms that passes constitutional muster. Future legislators might also look to the concurring opinions each written separately by Justice Sotomayor, Justice Gorsuch, Justice Kavanaugh, Justice Barrett and Justice Jackson.

While I am delighted to know that a domestic abuser and "an individual . . . found by a court to pose a credible threat to the physical safety of another, . . . may be temporarily disarmed consistent with the Second Amendment," one could argue that *any* individual with access to *any* automatic or semi-automatic weapon, including those equipped with a bump-stock, poses a credible threat to the physical safety of another. But unfortunately, this is not how the majority ruled in the case of *Garland v. Cargill*, also discussed above.

Second Amendment

Garland v. Cargill 602 U.S. ___ (2024)

The majority opinion in this case, written by Justice Clarence Thomas, holds that a semi-automatic weapon equipped with a bump-stock is not a machinegun, even if capable of firing "at rates of those approaching some machine guns."

The dissent, written by Justice Sotomayor, of course disagrees. The dissent reads in part:

> Congress has sharply restricted civilian ownership of machineguns since 1934. Federal law defines a "machinegun" as a weapon that can shoot "automatically more than one shot, without manual reloading, by a single function of the trigger." 26 U. S. C. §5845(b). Shortly after the Las Vegas massacre, the Trump administration, with widespread bipartisan support, banned bump stocks as machineguns under the statute.
>
> Today, the Court puts bump stocks back in civilian hands. To do so, it casts aside Congress's definition of "machinegun" and

seizes upon one that is inconsistent with the ordinary meaning of the statutory text and unsupported by context or purpose. When I see a bird that walks like a duck, swims like a duck, and quacks like a duck, I call that bird a duck. A bump-stock-equipped semi-automatic rifle fires "automatically more than one shot, without manual reloading, by a single function of the trigger." §5845(b). Because I, like Congress, call that a machinegun, I respectfully dissent.

Second Amendment/First Amendment

National Rifle Association ("NRA") v. Vullo 602 U.S. (2024)

This has turned out to be one of the most interesting cases decided this term. It flips notions of political division of the US Supreme Court on its head. First of all, the NRA hired none other than David D. Cole, of the American Civil Liberties Union ("ACLU") to represent it. He is also known for his *defense* of Brandi Levy, in the first case we reviewed. That's enough of a turn around to bring attention to the fact that this should be decided as a First Amendment Free Speech issue, and not a gun issue. What is not that surprising is that the majority found *for* the NRA. But what is also surprising is that the decision was unanimous! And, perhaps the most surprising of all is that Justice Sotomayor, known for her more liberal opinions, wrote the opinion for the majority—clearly identifying this as a Free Speech case.

Recall that this case was decided on a motion to dismiss. A motion to dismiss is an early end to a court case when the trial court judge believes that the plaintiff (the NRA in this case) has not made sufficient factual allegations. The NRA claimed that Vullo, the lead banking and insurance regulator of the State of New York, made statements urging banks and insurance companies to "discontinue their arrangements with the NRA, and to take prompt actions to manage these risks and promote public health and safety." The majority opinion acknowledges that the rule of law is,

> Government officials cannot attempt to coerce private parties in order to punish or suppress views that the government disfavors.

And that,

> Petitioner National Rifle Association (NRA) plausibly alleges that respondent Maria Vullo did just that.... Those allegations, if true, state a First Amendment claim.

And with that, the case was remanded, meaning handed back to the lower court to hear all the evidence from both parties.

Fifteenth Amendment

Alexander v. South Carolina NAACP 602 U.S. (2024)

The NAACP of South Carolina attempted to show that the voting election map in that state was impermissibly drawn to weaken minority votes. This case considered the question of whether courts must presume that a State acts in good faith when drawing election-voting districts. It also considered what showing must be made to prove unconstitutional racially drawing of those districts. In answering the first question, the majority US Supreme Court said, "Yes." District courts must presume that legislatures acted in good faith in drawing a district map. As to the second question, constitutionally permissible "partisan" maps may tend to look very similar to constitutionally impermissible "racially" drawn maps. To prove that a State election map was unconstitutionally drawn on racial grounds, plaintiffs must not "ignore certain traditional districting criteria" such as geographical constraints and the state legislature's party interests. Plaintiffs must also provide a substitute map that shows how the State "could have achieved its legitimate political objectives" while producing "significantly greater racial balance."

Justice Elena Kagan authored a dissenting opinion, in which Justices Sonia Sotomayor and Ketanji Brown Jackson joined. The three sharply criticized the majority for "pick[ing] and choos[ing] evidence to its liking."

ADDITIONAL EXERCISES

- As was said in the introduction to this book, the world keeps advancing and our laws continue to evolve. I encourage you to participate in any way you can. Above all, continue to have hope and believe in our system of democracy and the judiciary. When the scales of justice lean too far to the left or to the right; have faith, it will eventually balance with equilibrium and stability for all.
- At this point, you have learned quite a bit of US history. You have learned about many of the precedential cases that shape our laws and our freedoms. Develop an argument either for or against an issue you are passionate about. Make sure your argument uses your knowledge and utilizes at least one of the cases mentioned in this book to support your argument.
- After completing the above exercise, CONGRATULATIONS, you are an advocate!
- Now that you are an advocate, learn to write. If you want to be a journalist, learn to write. If you want to be a lawyer, learn to write. But learn to write well. If you want to work in politics or government or with one of the nonprofits working for a better future, learn to write.
- Learn public speaking. Practice debate on a variety of issues. Play the game "I Dissent." The issues in this game are completely absurd and ridiculous, but just by playing, you are learning how to debate any issue. Besides, a portion of the game's proceeds will be donated to charities that Justice Ruth Bader Ginsburg supported, including the ACLU. Your voice matters. Read Justice Ginsburg's lecture on civility, "Speaking in a Judicial Voice."** Explain your position rather

---
** New York University Law Review, Speaking in a Judicial Voice, by Ruth Bader Ginsburg, Dec. 1992

than argue it. "Strive to persuade, not pontificate," said Justice Ginsburg.

- Be proactive. Do not become adversarial to, wary of, or apathetic about government, but remember to take part in it. We are the government. Become a speaking voice for fairness and balance in our government. Our system of justice is good, not evil. Our judiciary offers us hope. We can use our freedoms to create an almost idealistic society if we can only remember to practice patience and kindness to all.
- Above all else, become an advocate for cultivating justice for all!

Acknowledgments

I would like to acknowledge the extraordinary debt I owe to the young people whose stories are told in court documents and in these pages, and to the young people whose stories are not yet told, because everyone has a story for freedom. A special thanks to Jaelyn Cogburn Enriquez, Farah Aziz and Aziz Basit Sheikh in memory of Sabika Aziz, and all others who shared their personal stories with me.

I would not be able to get anything done without the love and support of my valued friends, colleagues, and family members. I cannot express how grateful I am to the fellowship to which I belong and have been privileged to rely on for over forty years. These wonderful people guide me without judgment. They've given me courage, serenity, and most of all, faith and trust in a Greater Spirit of my own choosing.

In addition, I am indebted to all educators, which includes all of the students I have been privileged to instruct. They have all taught me so much about the world and myself. Additionally, the entire Harrison Team from Bradley Communications who cheered me on, and especially Valerie Costa, who helped me immensely with her coaching and who copy-edited this book with enormous skill and heart.

Finally, I owe everything to Riley, who told me when she was seven years old that being an attorney and arguing in court sounded awful to her. I hope that one day she changes her mind because she has more courage, heart and soul than anyone I've ever met, and that is precisely what is needed to cultivate justice.

Permissions and Licenses

Fig. 1, photograph by TapTheForwardAssist. Permission to reprint from Creative Commons.org under the Creative Commons License Attribution 4.0 International (https://creativecommons.org/licenses/by/4.0/) The full text of the license is available at https://creativecommons.org/licenses/by/4.0/legalcode.en Some modifications may have been made to size and color in some printed versions of this book. No other modifications have been made.

Fig. 2, photograph by Tyler Merbler, USA. Permission to reprint from Creative Commons.org under the Creative Commons Attribution 2.0 generic license (https://creativecommons.org/licenses/by/2.0/) The full text of the license is available at https://creativecommons.org/licenses/by/2.0/legalcode.en Some modifications may have been made to size and color in some printed versions of this book. No other modifications have been made.

Fig. 3 and Fig. 4 photographs reprinted with permission from Jaelyn Cogburn and the Aziz family.

Fig. 5, photograph by Phil Roeder, Des Moines, IA. Permission to reprint from Creative Commons.org under the Creative Commons Attribution 2.0 generic license (https://creativecommons.org/licenses/by/2.0/) The full text of the license is available at https://creativecommons.org/licenses/by/2.0/legalcode.en Some modifications may have been made to size and color in some printed versions of this book. No other modifications have been made.

Fig. 6 photograph by Raymond Preddy, September 1957, courtesy of University of Arkansas at Little Rock Center for Arkansas History and Culture https://arstudies.contentdm.oclc.org/digital/collection/p15728coll1/id/11654

Fig. 7 photograph by Our Children's Trust #youthvgov, June 11, 2023. Permission to reprint from Creative Commons.org under the Creative Commons Attribution 3.0 Unported License. https://creativecommons.org/licenses/by/3.0 The full text of the license is found at: https://creativecommons.org/licenses/by/3.0/legalcode.en Original photograph at: https://upload.wikimedia.org/wikipedia/commons/7/73/Juliana_vs_United_States_plaintiffs%2C_Our_Children%27s_Trust.jpg

Some modifications may have been made to size and color in some printed version of this book. No other modifications have been made.

Quotes from Britten Follett appear with permission from FollettLearning.com, via Thompson Drake PR. Quotes from Norma McCorvey and Rev. Rob Schneck are from the documentary *AKA Jane Roe* and appear with permission from Director, Nick Sweeney. All quotes from court documents, including transcript of oral arguments and opinions are available through fair use and/or the public domain.

We believe all other quotes and photographs are available for reprint through fair use and/or the public domain.

Supporting Youth

In the spirit of supporting youth, we will select two youth oriented charities to donate to each year. We have selected the following organizations as our charities of choice for this year and will donate a portion of the proceeds from this year's sales of this book to the following charities:

Student Press Law Center

The Student Press Law Center ("SPLC") is a nonprofit organization that provides free legal services to student journalists and protects their First Amendment rights. Donations allow SPLC to answer inquiries at its free legal hotline, stand up for students facing censorship, provide legal training programs in the classroom and advocate for free press.

You can contact this organization at:

Student Press Law Center
1717 K. Street, NW, Suite 900
Washington D.C., 20006
(202) 785-5450
www.splc.org

March For Our Lives

Guns are the leading cause of death of America's youth. March For Our Lives wants to change that by working to build youth leadership. March For Our Lives is a national non-profit organization and movement. March For Our Lives has local chapters across the nation. The chapters are places for young people to connect with one another and turn their anguish and fear into action. Young people learn the skills necessary to make their voices heard from school boards to the White House, seeking responsible safety gun laws across the country.

You can contact this organization at:

March For Our Lives
c/o director of Operations
P.O. Box 3417
New York, N.Y. 10008
www.marchforourlives.org

For further information on donating for youth causes, or if you would like to request donations for other youth-based non-profit organizations contact chillier1@gmail.com.

References

INTRODUCTION

1   Annenberg Public Policy Center Civics Knowledge Survey (www.annenbergpublicpolicycenter.org/political-communication/civics-knowledge-survey/)

2   The National Center for Education Statistics (NCES) is the primary federal entity for collecting and analyzing data related to education.

3   www.fastdemocracy.com Recommended sources. Research bills and track lobbyists.

HISTORICAL NOTES

4   Search and browse all of the US Code laws here: http.uscode.house.gov/browse.xhtml

5   The Amendments can be found in the US Code, front matter, organic laws, under the Constitution beginning with Page VI, Articles in Addition to and Amendment of… www.uscode.house.gov/view.xhtml?path=/frontmatter/organiclaws/constitution&edition=prelim

6   28 US Code §453

7   See also: on November 13, 2023, the US Supreme Court adopted a Code of Conduct for the US Supreme Court justices. www.supremecourt.gov/about/Code-of-Conduct-for-Justices_November_13_2023.pdf

CHAPTER 1

8   Brandenburg v. Ohio, 395 US 444 (1965)

9   *New York Times v. Sullivan,* 376 US 254 (1964)

10   *Mahanoy Area School Dist. v. B.L. (Brandi Levy, a minor,)* 594 US ___ (2021)

11   *Tinker v. Des Moines,* 393 US 503 (1969)

12   *Mahanoy v. B.L.,* 594 US ___

13   *Ibid.* 594 US ___

14   *Hazelwood School District v. Kuhlmeier,* 484 US 260 (1988)

15   *Bethel School District v. Fraser,* 478 US 675 (1986)

16 *Morse v. Frederick*, 551 US 393 (2007)

17 *Tinker v. Des Moines*, 393 US 503 (1969)

18 *Id.* 393 US, at 513

19 *Id.* 393 US 503

20 *Id.* 393 US 506

21 Current oral arguments from the US Supreme Court can be heard live from the SCOTUS website: www.supremecourt.gov/oral_arguments/live.aspx. Achieves of oral arguments can be found on www.Oyez.org. Oral argument in *Tinker vs. Des Moines* is found at https://www.oyez.org/cases/1968/21

22 *Keyishian v. Board of Regents*, 385 US 589 (1967)

23 *Procunier v. Martinez*, 416 US 396 (1974)

24 *Mahanoy v. B.L.*, 594 US ___

CHAPTER 2

25 *New York Times v. United States ("the Pentagon Papers case")*, 403 US 713 (1971)

26 *Id.* 403 US at 717

27 *Knight Institute v. Donald Trump*, 928 F.3d 226 (2d Cir. 2019)

28 *Cornelius,* 473 US at 800

29 Knight First Amendment Institute at Columbia University; Supreme Court Ends Long-Running Lawsuit Over Trump's Now Defunct Twitter Account Lorraine Kenny, April 5, 2021, www.knightcolumbia.org/content Last retrieved, April 26, 2024

30 *Brandenburg v. Ohio*, 395 US 444 (1969)

31 *Id.* 395 US 444

32 *Hess v. Indiana*, 414 US 105 (1973)

33 *Brandenburg v. Ohio*, 395 US at 446

34 *Hess v. Indiana*, 414 US 105 (1973)

35 Evaluating Information; The Cornerstone of Civic Online Reasoning, Executive Summary, Stanford History Education Group, Produced with the Support of the Robert R. McCormick Foundation, November 22, 2016.

36 *Jacobellis v. Ohio*, 378 US 184, (1964)

37 *Ginsberg v. New York*, 390 U. S. 629 (1968)

38 *Bethel School District v. Fraser*, 478 US 675 (1986)

39   *Ibid.* 478 US 675

40   *New York Times v. Sullivan*, 376 US 254 (1964)

41   *Id.* 376 US 254, 256-258

42   *Whitney v. California*, 274 US 357, 375 (1927)

43   *Ibid.* 274 US at 375

CHAPTER 3

44   *Hazelwood School District v. Kuhlmeier*, 484 US 260 (1988)

45   *Id.* 484 US at 267

46   *Id.* 484 US at 277

47   *Id.* 484 US at 278

48   See the article "No rights; The Life of an Atheist," editorial by Krystal Myers here: www.documentcloud.org/documents/296899-a-copy-of-the-editorial-krystal-myers-tried-to.html.

49   Education Week, *Hazelwood* at 25, by Frank D. Lomonte, February 5, 2013 www.edweek.org/policy-politics/opinion-hazelwood-at-25/2013/02, last reviewed April 26, 2024.

50   *Dean v. Utica Community Schools*, 345 F.Supp.2d 799 (E.D. Mich. 2004)

51   *Ibid.* 345 F. Supp.2d 799

52   *Id.* 345 F. Supp.2d, at 804

53   *Id.* 345 F. Supp.2d, at 811, fn5

54   *Ashcroft v. Free Speech Coalition*, 535 US 234 (2002)

CHAPTER 4

55   "The History of Book Bans—and their changing targets—in the US" by Erin Blakemore, National Geographic April 24, 2023 (www.nationalgeographic.com/culture/article/history-of-book-bans-in-the-united-states)

56   *The Right to Read Defense Committee v. School Committee, City of Chelsea*, 454 F.Supp.703 (D.Mass. 1978)

57   *Ibid.* 454 F.Supp. 703

58   *Island Trees School District v. Steven Pico*, 457 US 853 (1982)

59   *Ibid.* 457 US 853, 871

60   PEN protects free expression in the United States and worldwide. www.PEN.org

61   *Book People, Inc. v. Wong,* 23-50668 (5th Cir. 2024)

62   *Book People, Inc. v. Wong,* Complaint filed July 25, 2023 https://publishers.org/wp-content/uploads/2023/07/2023.07.25-Complaint.pdf

63   *Book People, Inc. v. Wong,* Opinion dated January 17, 2024 www.law.justia.com/cases/federal/appellate-courts/ca5/23-50668/23-50668-2024-01-17.html

64   US Department of Education, Office of Civil Rights: www.2.ed.gov/about/offices/list/ocr/index.html

65   US Department of Education, Office of Civil Rights, responsive letter of investigation: www2.ed.gov/about/offices/list/ocr/docs/investigations/more/04221281-a.pdf

CHAPTER 5

66   *Carson v. Makin,* 596 US 767 (2022), dissent J. Breyer

67   *Everson v. Board of Education of the Township of Ewing,* 330 US 1, 15-16 (1947)

68   *Epperson v. Arkansas,* 393 US 97 (1968)

69   *Ibid.* 393 US 97, 99

70   *Id.* 393 US 97, 100 fn5

71   Epperson v. Arkansas oral argument, www.oyez.org/cases/1968/7. Accessed 17 Jun. 2023

72   Arkansas Democrat-Gazette, 'Monkey' law fight: Where is Susan Smith Epperson now? By Frank E. Lockwood, December 18, 2021. www.arkansasonline.com/news/2021/dec/18/monkey-law-fight/

73   *Barnette v. School Board of West Virginia,* 319 US 624 (1943)

74   *Id.* 319 US at 641

75   *Ibid.*

76   *Id.* 319 US at 642

77   *McCollum v. Board of Education,* 333 US 203 (1948)

78   *Id.* 333 US at 209-210

79   *Engel v. Vitale,* 370 US 421 (1962)

80   *Id.* 370 US at 422

81   *Id.* 370 US at 430-432

82   *Santa Fe School District v. Doe,* 530 US 209 (2000)

83 *Id.* 530 US at 295

84 *Ibid.*

85 *Lee v. Weisman,* 505 US 577 (1992), held prayer at a graduation ceremony in public schools violated the First Amendment.

86 *Santa Fe School District v. Doe,* 530 US 209 (2000)

87 *Id.* 530 US at 311-312

88 *Id.* 530 US at 302

89 *Id.* 530 US at 318, dissent of J. Rehnquist, J. Scalia, J. Thomas

90 See also: Texas Monthly: Faith, Friendship and Tragedy at Santa Fe (Sabika's Story), by Skip Hollandsworth, May 2019, www.texasmonthly.com/being-texan/remembering-sabika-sheikh-pakistani-student-killed-santa-fe-school-shooting/

91 *Kennedy v. Bremerton School District,* 597 US ___ (2022)

92 *Garcetti v. Ceballos,* 547 US 410, 421 (2006)

93 *Kennedy v. Bremerton School District,* 597 US ___ (2022)

94 *Ibid.*

95 See also: Seattle Times, Jesus Chants and Jeers Greet Satanists During Bremerton Football Game, by Christine Clarridge, Originally published October 29, 2015 at 11:03 pm Updated February 4, 2016 at 4:54 pm, last accessed April 27, 2024 www.seattletimes.com/seattle-news/education/jesus-chants-jeers-greet-satanists-during-bremerton-football-game/

96 *Kennedy v. Bremerton School District,* 597 US ___ (2022)

97 *Everson v. Board of Education,* 330 US 1, 8 (1947)

98 *Kennedy v. Bremerton School District,* 597 US ___ (2022)

99 "About Three-in-Ten US Adults Are Now Religiously Unaffiliated". *Measuring Religion in Pew Research Center's American Trends Panel.* Pew Research Center. December 14, 2021. Retrieved August 9, 2022.

100 Gallup, US Church Membership Falls Below Majority for First Time, by Jeffrey M. Jones, March 29, 2021. www.news.gallup.com/poll/341963/church-membership-falls-below-majority-first-time.aspx

CHAPTER 6

101 *Brown v. Board of Education,* 347 US 483 (1954)

102 *Everson v. Board of Education of Ewing,* 330 US 1 (1947)

103 *Id.,* 303 US 1, 8-11

REFERENCES

104 *Id.,* 303 US at 16

105 *Lemon v. Kurtzman,* 403 US 602 (1971)

106 *Id.,* 403 US at 649

107 *Zelman v. Simmons-Harris,* 536 US 639 (2002)

108 *Id.,* 536 US at 644

109 *Id.,* 536 US 639

110 *Id.,* 536 US 685-686

111 *Espinoza v. Montana Department of Revenue,* 591 US ___ (2020)

112 *Ibid.*

113 *Carson v. Makin,* 596 US ___ (2022)

114 *Ibid.,* 596 US ___ J. Beyer dissent

115 *Brown v. Board of Education,* 347 US 483 (1954)

116 The Atlantic: Better Schools, Better Economies; What would happen to the GDP if states started investing more heavily in education? By Gillian B. White, December 9, 2015 www.theatlantic.com/business/archive/2015/12/fixing-public-schools-for-a-better-economy/419526/

CHAPTER 7

117 *DeJong v. Oregon,* 299 US 353 (1937)

118 *Edwards v. South Carolina,* 372 US 229 (1963)

119 *Id.,* 372 US at 234

120 *Id.,* 372 US 237-238

121 *Henry v. City of Rock Hill,* 376 US 776 (1964)

122 *Cox v. Louisiana,* 379 US 536 (1965)

123 *Shuttlesworth v. City of Birmingham,* 394 US 147 (1969)

124 *Gregory v. City of Chicago,* 394 US 111 (1969)

125 *NAACP v. Clairborne Hardware Co.,* 458 US 886 (1982)

CHAPTER 8

126 Penn Today: Whatever Happened to the Right to Petition? By, Greg Johnson, December 1, 2020 www.penntoday.upenn.edu/news/whatever-happened-right-petition

127 A Right of Access to Court under the Petition Clause of the First Amendment: Defining the Right, 60 Ohio St. L.J. 557 (1999). Available at: https://scholarship.law.ua.edu/fac_articles/31

CHAPTER 9

128 *New York State Riffle and Pistol Association, Inc. v. Bruen*, 597 US 1 (2022)

129 *District of Columbia v. Heller*, 554 US 570 (2008)

130 *US v. Cruikshank*, 92 US 542 (1875)

131 *Presser v. Illinois*, 116 US 252 (1886)

132 *United States v. Miller*, 307 US 174 (1939)

133 *Lewis v. United States*, 445 US 55 (1980)

134 *District of Columbia v. Heller*, 554 US 570 (2008)

135 *United States v. Hayes*, 555 US 415 (2009)

136 *McDonald v. City of Chicago*, 561 US 742 (2010)

137 *Caetano v. Massachusetts*, 577 US 411 (2016)

138 *New York State Riffle and Pistol Association, Inc. v. Bruen*, 597 US 1 (2022)

139 Pew Research Center: Gun Deaths Among US Kids Rose 50 percent in Two Years (2019-2021), by John Gramlich. www.pewresearch.org/short-reads/2023/04/06/gun-deaths-among-us-kids-rose-50-percent-in-two-years/

140 New York Times, Op Ed. Contributor, John Paul Stevens, Repeal the Second Amendment, By John Paul Stevens, March 27, 2018 www.nytimes.com/2018/03/27/opinion/john-paul-stevens-repeal-second-amendment.html

141 *McDonald v. City of Chicago*, 561 US 742 (2010) J. Stevens dissent

142 *District of Columbia v. Heller*, 554 US 570 (2008)

143 Kate Shaw, *Ask the Author: Interview with Justice John Paul Stevens*, Scotusblog (June 12, 2009, 10:26 AM), www.scotusblog.com/2019/06/ask-the-author-interview-with-justice-john-paul-stevens/

144 *US v. Rahimi* (pending, 2023-2024)

145 *New York State Riffle and Pistol Association, Inc. v. Bruen*, 597 US 1 (2022)

146 *United States v. Hayes*, 555 US 415 (2009)

147 *New York State Riffle and Pistol Association, Inc. v. Bruen*, 597 US 1 (2022)

148 *Cargill v. Garland, Attorney General* (pending, 2023-2024)

149 *William Akins v. United States* No. 08-15640 (11th Cir. 2009)

150 *National Rifle Association ("NRA") v. Vullo* (pending, 2023-2024)

151 *Nat'l Rifle Ass'n of Am. v. Vullo*, 49 F.4th 700, 706 (2d Cir. 2022)

CHAPTER 10

152 *New Jersey v. T.L.O.*, 469 US 325 (1985)

153 *Wong Sun v. United States*, 371 US 471 (1963)

154 *New Jersey v. T.L.O.*, 469 US 325, 337

155 *Id.*, 469 US at 339

156 *Ibid.*

157 *Stafford Unified School District #1 v. Redding*, 557 US 364 (2009)

158 *Id.* 557 US 364 (quoting *New Jersey v. T.L.O.*, 469 342)

159 *Id.* 557 US at 382, n25

160 *Ferguson v. The City of New York*, 22 Civ. 1000 (KPF) (S.D.N.Y. Aug. 17, 2023)

161 Police Need Warrants to Search Homes. Child Welfare Agents Almost Never Get One, by Eli Hager, special to ProPublica and NBC News, Oct. 13, 2022, last reviewed November 13, 2023.

162 NBC News, CPS Workers Search Millions of Homes a Year. A mom who resisted paid a price. Oct. 13, 2022, 5:00 AM PDT, By Eli Hager, ProPublica, published in partnership with ProPublica, a nonprofit newsroom that investigates abuses of power.www.nbcnews.com/news/us-news/child-abuse-welfare-home-searches-warrant-rcna50716

163 Ismail, Tarek, Family Policing and the Fourth Amendment (August 21, 2022). California Law Review,

Vol. 111, (Forthcoming 2023), Tarek Ismail, CUNY School of Law.

CHAPTER 11

164 *Miranda v. Arizona*, 384 US 436 (1966)

165 *J.D.B. v. North Carolina*, 564 US 261 (2011)

166 *In Re Tateana R.*, 64 A.D.3d 459 (N.Y. App. Div. 2009)

167 *Ibid.*

CHAPTER 12

168   *Goss v. Lopez*, 419 US 565 (1975)

169   *Ibid.*

170   *In Re Gault,* 387 U.S. 1, 13 (1967)

CHAPTER 13

171   *Coy v. Iowa*, 487 US 1012 (1988)

172   *Ibid.*

173   *Maryland v. Craig*, 497 US 836 (1990)

174   *Ingraham v. Wright*, 430 US 651 (1977)

175   *Id.* 430 US 651 (J. White dissent)

176   American Academy of Pediatrics, Ending Corporal Punishment in Schools, AAP Policy Explained, By Nathaniel Beers, MD, FAAP

CHAPTER 14

177   *Roe v. Wade,* 410 US 113 (1973)

178   *Griswold v. Connecticut*, 381 US 479 (1965)

179   *Ibid.*

180   *Griswold v. Connecticut*, 381 US at 488, 491, 492

181   *Griswold v. Connecticut*, 381 US 479 (J. Stewart dissent)

182   *Dobbs v. Jackson Women's Health Organization*, 597 US ___ (2022)

183   *Cooper v. Aaron*, 358 US 1 (1958)

184   Notes of President Eisenhower

www.eisenhowerlibrary.gov/sites/default/files/research/online-documents/civil-rights-little-rock/1957-10-08-diary-notes-faubus-meeting.pdf

185   *Ibid.*

186   https://encyclopediaofarkansas.net/entries/lost-year-737/

CHAPTER 15

187   *Plessy v. Ferguson*, 163 US 537 (1896)

188   *Id.* 163 US at 544

189   *Id.* 163 US 537 (J. Harlan dissent)

190 *Brown v. Board of Education of Topeka*, 347 US 483 (1954)

191 *Sipuel v. Regents of University of Oklahoma*, 332 US 631 (1948)

192 *Sweatt v. Painter*, 339 US 629 (1950)

193 *McLaurin v. Oklahoma State Regents*, 339 US 637 (1950)

194 *Brown v. Board of Education of Topeka*, 347 US 483 (1954)

195 *Ibid.*

196 *Brown v. Board of Education of Topeka II*, 349 US 294 (1955)

197 *Plyler v. Doe*, 4457 US 202 (1982)

198 *Ibid.*

199 *Arizona vs. United States*, 567 US 387 (2012)

CHAPTER 16

200 *United States v. Reese*, 92 US 214 (1876)

201 *Guinn v. US*, 238 US 347 (1915)

202 *Smith v. Allwright*, 321 US 649 (1944)

203 *South Carolina v. Katzenbach*, 383 US 301 (1966)

204 *Shelby County v. Holder*, 570 US 529 (2013)

205 *Ibid.*

206 *Shelby County v. Holder*, 570 US 529 (J. Ginsburg dissent)

207 *Allen v. Milligan*, 599 US ___ (2023)

208 *Elk v. Wilkins*, 112 US 94 (1884)

209 *Id.*, 112 US 94 (J. Harlan dissent)

210 American Bar Association; How the Native American Vote Continues to be Suppressed, by Patty Ferguson Bohnee, February 09, 2020. www.americanbar.org/groups/crsj/publications/human_rights_magazine_home/voting-rights/how-the-native-american-vote-continues-to-be-suppressed/

211 *Minor v. Happersett*, 88 US 12 (1875)

212 *Leser v. Garnett*, 258 US 130 (1922)

213 *Ibid.*

214 Smithsonian Magazine. How Women Vote; Separating Myth from Reality, by Jennifer Piscopo, October 6, 2020. www.smithsonianmag.com/history/how-have-women-voted-suffrage-180975979/

215 Pew Research Center: Report: Trends in Party Affiliation Among Demographic Groups, March 20, 2018. www.pewresearch.org/politics/2018/03/20/1-trends-in-party-affiliation-among-demographic-groups/

216 *Oregon v. Mitchell*, 400 US 112 (1970)

217 *Alexander v. South Carolina NAACP*, docket no. 22-807 (pending 2023-2024)

CHAPTER 17

218 Joan Williams (1999). Unbending Gender: Why Family and Work Conflict and What To Do About It. Oxford UP. p. 147. ISBN 9780199840472. Archived from the original on January 2, 2016. Retrieved February 5, 2024.

219 See also: Roll Call: Senate GOP Blocks Resolution Nixing Equal Rights Amendment Ratification Deadline, by John T. Bennett April 27, 2023.

220 Bankrate.com: The History of Women and Loans, by Raija Haughan, Edited by Rhus Subitch, published Sept. 19, 2023; See also, Bankrate.com—The History of Women and Mortgages, by Zach Wichter, Edited by Troy Segal, published March 5, 2024, last retrieved April 29, 2024.

221 *Frontiero v. Richardson*, 411.US 677 (1973)

222 *Stanton v. Stanton*, 421 US 7 (1975)

223 *Taylor v. Louisiana*, 419 US 522 (1975)

224 *Kirchberg v. Feenstra*, 450 US 455 (1981)

225 *Roe v. Wade*, 410 US 113 (1973)

226 *AKA Jane Roe,* documentary, Directed and Produced by Nick Sweeney, released May 22, 2020.

227 Time, "*Roe v. Wade* Lawyer 'Amazed' Americans Still Fighting Over Abortion," by Olivia Waxman, January 20, 2018, last retrieved March 3, 2024

228 Interview with Carl T. Rowan, June 1987 (The Court filings and ruling never mentioned the father of "Roe Baby," but only that Jane Roe was an "unmarried woman.")

229 *The Atlantic*, "The Roe Baby," by Joshua Prager, September 9, 2021, last retrieved March 3, 2024.

230 *Ibid.*

231 *Ibid.*

232 *Ibid.*

233 *Ibid.*

234   *Struck v. Secretary of Defense,* 460 F.2d 1372 (9th Cir. 1971); vacated for mootness 409 US 1011.

235   New York University Law Review, Speaking in a Judicial Voice, by Ruth Bader Ginsburg, Vol. 67, December 1992.

236   Justice Ginsburg: Roe v. Wade, Not 'Women Centered,' by Johnathan Bullington, jbullington@chicagotribune.com, Chicago Tribune, Published May 11, 2013, Updated May 16, 2019, last reviewed March 3, 2024

237   *AKA Jane Roe,* documentary, Directed and Produced by Nick Sweeney, released May 22, 2020.

238   The New York Times: *AT HOME WITH: Norma McCorvey; of Roe, Dreams and Choices,* by Alex Witchel, first published July 28, 1994.

239   *AKA Jane Roe,* documentary, Directed and Produced by Nick Sweeney, released May 22, 2020.

240   *Planned Parenthood of Southeastern Pa. v. Casey,* 505 US 833 (1992)

241   *Dobbs v. Jackson Women's Health Organization,* 597 US ___ (2022)

242   *Ibid.*

243   *Dobbs v. Jackson Women's Health Organization,* 597 US ___ (dissent, J. Sotomayor)

244   *Ibid.*

245   *Ibid.*

246   *Ibid.*

247   *Ibid.*

248   *Ibid.*

249   Review the Federal Justice Department's log of cases against reproductive health care violence www.justice.gov/crt/recent-cases-violence-against-reproductive-health-care-providers, last reviewed March 3, 2024.

CHAPTER 18

250   *Held v. Montana,* No. CDV-2020-307 (1st Dist. Ct. Mont., Aug. 14, 2023). You can read the decision here: https://climatecasechart.com/wp-content/uploads/case-documents/2023/20230814_docket-CDV-2020-307_order.pdf.

251   *Juliana v. United States,* docket 24-684 (pending in US Dist. of Or.)

About the Author

COLLETTE HILLIER has a BA from Redlands University and a J.D. from Santa Barbara College of Law. She was admitted to the American Bar Association and California Bar Association in 2007. She was an Associate Attorney with Andre, Morris & Buttery and a Veterans Advocate with San Luis Obispo Legal Foundation. Before being admitted to practice, she held an externship at the California Courts of Appeal, Second Division, Department Six, in Ventura, California, under the guidance of Presiding Justice Arthur Gilbert. She also served as an Adjunct Professor at Monterey College of Law, San Luis Obispo campus. She currently lives on the Central Coast of California with her longtime honey, and is dedicated to her children and grandchildren.

Learn more about Collette by following her author page on Amazon or connect with her directly at collette@collette.store. If you are interested in engaging Collette as a guest speaker, or attending an event near you, visit www.collette.store. If you would like to continue to empower youth and encourage justice, please rate and review this book on www.Amazon.com.

www.ingramcontent.com/pod-product-compliance
Lightning Source LLC
Chambersburg PA
CBHW070611030426
42337CB00020B/3752